MW00390645

Of Goats & Governors

OF GOATS & GOVERNORS

Six Decades of Colorful Alabama Political Stories

STEVE FLOWERS

FOREWORD BY EDWIN C. BRIDGES

NEWSOUTH BOOKS
Montgomery

NewSouth Books
105 S. Court Street
Montgomery, AL 36104

Published in the United States by NewSouth Books, a division of NewSouth, Inc.,
Montgomery, Alabama.

Publisher's Cataloging-in-Publication data

Flowers, Steve.
Of goats & governors : six decades of colorful Alabama political stories /
Steve Flowers ; with a foreword by Edwin C. Bridges.
p. cm.
Includes index.

ISBN 978-1-60306-364-7 (hardcover)
ISBN 978-1-60306-365-4 (ebook)

1. Governors—Alabama. 2. Legislators—Alabama. 3. Politicians—Alabama.
4. Judges—Alabama. 5. Alabama—Politics and government. I. Title.

2014949259

Printed in the United States of America

To Dale Robinson

In this modern day most folks write and communicate via the internet and email, their thoughts coming through a keyboard. I am a relic of bygone days. I learned to put my thoughts on paper using a pen. I handwrite my weekly newspaper column on Alabama politics and I wrote this book with a pen and legal pads. Most of the book was written from memory. My assistant in all my business and literary endeavors for thirty years has been my friend Dale Robinson. She is responsible for deciphering my handwriting and typing this book and submitting the transcript to the publisher.

Contents

Foreword / ix
Preface / xi
Brief Introduction to Alabama Political History / xiii

Part I—Governors

1 James E. Folsom Sr. / 3
2 John Patterson / 25
3 George Wallace / 32
4 Lurleen Wallace / 65
5 Albert Brewer / 70
6 Other Governors / 84
  Fob James and the 1978 Governor's Race / 84
  Guy Hunt / 87
  Jim Folsom Jr. / 91
  Don Siegelman / 94
  Bob Riley / 96
  Robert Bentley / 98
7 Two Who Never Made It / 105
  Bill Baxley / 105
  Paul Ray Hubbert / 116
8 And Frank Johnson: The 'Real Governor' of Alabama / 124

Part II—Congressmen and Senators

9 Alabama's Three Greatest Senators / 131
10 Others in Alabama's Congressional Delegation / 139
11 Howell Heflin / 154

Part III—Legislators

12 South Alabama Legislators / 167
13 North Alabama Legislators / 178

Part IV—Other Stories

14 Alabama Political Lore / 195
  Two More Well-Known Chief Justices / 195
  Other Offices and Stories / 197
15 My Favorite Political Jokes / 258

Index / 264

Foreword

EDWIN C. BRIDGES

It takes something special to run for public office. It takes even more to win election and more still to climb to the top of the political pyramid. Alabama's political leaders tend to be among the most interesting, vital, and engaging people in the state.

Once they enter the hothouse atmosphere of Alabama politics, those special qualities open into full, luxuriant bloom. In their daily struggles, politicians labor mightily to push their issues and to defeat those they oppose—and, of course, to advance their careers. Over time, their exertions amply expose their abilities and strengths, as well as their weaknesses and foibles, to the view of their fellows.

In this high-pressure world, politicians quickly learn to take each other's measure. They track their colleagues with the keen eyes of people who know how the game is played. And the best way to capture and communicate to others what they see is in stories. A good story helps reveal the essence and character of its subject, and telling or hearing a good story is one of the pleasures of life in the political arena.

For the politicians, staff, reporters, and lobbyists who inhabit the inner circles of Alabama politics, stories about who did what and why are the currency of conversation. Over morning cups of coffee, during pauses in the action, or when players gather for a drink or a meal, everyone enjoys a good story—either from the previous day or from someone's fond recollections. A gifted storyteller is appreciated as much as a good subject, and the more outrageous the story, the better.

In the last half of the 20th century, Alabama politics was dominated by an extraordinarily rich cast of characters. For many fans of the sport of politics, their daily interplay was far more interesting than lesser sports such as hunting, poker, or football. But now in the second decade of a new century, many of those great players have passed from the scene, and there is a danger their stories will pass with them.

This book is a gift for those of us who want to know more of these stories and who want to see them preserved. In it, Steve Flowers has recorded some of the classics, as well as many terrific lesser-known stories. At the same time, he tells us more about the people themselves who were both the stories' subjects and authors. Veteran fans of Alabama politics will enjoy visiting old friends again, remembering some of their own stories and perhaps adding some new ones. Newcomers will find the book a warm and affectionate introduction to an amazingly interesting, entertaining, and gregarious group of people.

In today's environment of continuous television news, political polls, slick advertisements, and the Internet, there is something almost nostalgic about the old days of cigars, eccentric characters, and good yarns. *Of Goats & Governors* offers a peephole through which readers can look back at three exuberant generations of Alabama politics, into a world that seems to be fading ever more quickly from view.

Preface

We have had a colorful political history in Alabama. It seems our politics have been a large part of our entertainment. This book will take you on a journey through the past seven decades of Alabama political history. You will read about the life and times of Alabama political giants like George Wallace, Big Jim Folsom, Lister Hill, John Sparkman, Howell Heflin, Richard Shelby, and many others. The book is based on my having been a participant in and observer of Alabama politics for more than 50 years.

I grew up in Troy, Alabama, and at age 12 I became a page in the legislature and worked at the Capitol throughout my high school years. My interest in politics continued at the University of Alabama where I served in the student senate and graduated in 1974 with a B.S. in political science and history. In 1982, at age 30, I was elected state representative from Pike County, receiving the largest number of votes for any political candidate in county history. I was reelected four times and maintained a perfect House attendance record for 16 years before choosing not to seek reelection in 1998.

Since then I have written a weekly column about state politics that appears in more than 70 Alabama newspapers. I also serve as a political commentator on television. As you can tell, I have always been immersed in Alabama politics. Those of us who have followed Alabama politics most of our lives have heard these incredible and humorous stories. We have shared them with each other. I wanted to share them with you and preserve this era of Alabama political stories for posterity.

I hope you let the book take you down memory lane with stories from Alabama's rich and colorful past.

Acknowledgment

Ed Bridges personifies the term Southern gentleman. His erudite yet warm persona graced the halls of the State Archives Building for three decades. His knowledge of Alabama history is unparalleled. He is truly a walking encyclopedia of Alabama history. He will go down as the greatest archivist of our state's rich past. It is an honor to have him write the foreword for my book.

Brief Introduction to Alabama Political History

Alabama is a magnificent state. We possess abundant natural resources such as waterways and rivers, flora and fauna, and mineral deposits. Water is one of Alabama's most precious natural resources, and almost 10 percent of the freshwater water resources of the continental U.S. flows through or originates in Alabama during its journey to the sea. A sixth of the state's surface area is covered by lakes, ponds, rivers, and creeks.

We have plentiful rainfall, much higher than the national average. The average annual rainfall in north Alabama is 50 inches. The average is 65 inches in south Alabama and along the coast.

Another thing we have plenty of is history and politics.

Alabama is called the "Heart of Dixie" because of banknotes issued by the Citizens Bank of Louisiana before the Civil War. They bore the French word *dix*, meaning ten, and thus the South became known as Dixieland, and with Alabama serving as the first capital of the Confederacy, it was thus the heart of Dixieland.

The early French influence in Alabama is still felt in Mobile, which is much older than the rest of the state. Mobile was the first permanent European settlement in Alabama, founded by the French even earlier than New Orleans, and more than 100 years before Alabama became a state in 1819.

Mobile was settled by the French, but the rest of our European ancestors came primarily from five states: Virginia, North and South Carolina, Georgia, and Tennessee. Ninety percent of the pre-Civil War white population of the state originated or had close ancestral ties in one of these five states. Of the first 16 governors of Alabama, 15 were born in one of those five states, and of the 100 delegates at the Secession Convention in 1861, only 17 were native-born Alabamians, while 72 were born in one of the above five states.

When Alabama became a state in 1819, it accounted for 1.3 percent of the nation's population. There was rapid growth during the next few decades as cotton and slavery dominated the antebellum economy and culture. By 1840, Alabama's proportion of the nation's population was 3.5 percent.

However, Alabama's proportion of U.S. population—and thus of congressional representation—has been in steady decline since the end of the Civil War. Today we account for about 1.6 percent of the country's people.

GOAT HILL

Some of you may be wondering why my book is entitled *Of Goats & Governors*. Obviously a lot of stories are about and revolve around some of our past governors. The "goats" is a reference to our Capitol Hill which is referred to as Goat Hill. You then may ask why the crest that the Capitol sits on overlooking Dexter Avenue is called Goat Hill. The answer is simple, because goats grazed on the hill prior to its becoming the site of the Capitol. Alabama had four other capitals before Montgomery, but when Andrew Dexter, one of the founders of the city, laid out his town plan in 1819, he was planning ahead and laid out a broad avenue leading up to a hill overlooking downtown. In 1846, the legislature voted to move the capital from Tuscaloosa to Montgomery, and in 1846–47 a new Capitol building was completed on the site Dexter had picked out 30 years earlier. The goats presumably went to graze somewhere else, or maybe they became dinner, because Alabama politicians have always enjoyed a good barbecue.

The new Capitol, incidentally, burned to the ground in 1849 and was rebuilt in 1851 on the same footprint and with a similar design as the original. In 1861, the Confederate States of America was organized in the Capitol, and a few months that spring Montgomery was the capital both of Alabama and of the Confederacy before the latter moved its capital to Richmond, Virginia.

Alabamians in that era were Whigs, Democrats, and Republicans, and after the Civil War, Democrats and Republicans. When ex-Confederate Democrats (Redeemers) regained political control of the state after Reconstruction ended in 1876–77, Alabama became essentially a one-party state until Goldwater's Southern landslide of 1964. For those 90 years we were such a Democratic state that during the entire span no Republican served as governor, lieutenant governor, attorney general, treasurer, or secretary of state. We never had a single Republican U.S. senator or congressman. All of our political races were decided in the Democratic primary.

This dogmatic Democratic loyalty was caused by the resentment instilled in white Southerners toward what they viewed as vengeful, vindictive, radical Republicans who were claimed to have invaded, pilfered, and occupied the South during the 10 years of Reconstruction. This loathing was handed down from one generation to the next. Many a dying grandfather told their children and grandchildren, "one, don't ever sell the family farm, and secondly, don't ever vote for any damn Republican." That's why you would hear old people saying, "My granddaddy would roll over in his grave if I voted for a Republican." It didn't matter how good a national Republican candidate was, the Southern white voters voted Democratic. That's how the term "Yellow Dog Democrat" began. It was said that if a yellow dog was the Democratic candidate, he would get the white vote. This Democratic solidarity really made us a no-party state since all the activity was in one party and primary.

We developed a system of choosing governors totally on personality and individual popularity. Other Southern states developed the same way. This bred colorful political characters like Huey Long, Gene Talmadge, Theodore Bilbo, and our own Big Jim Folsom.

'Friends and Neighbors' Politics

This "friends and neighbors" tradition is common throughout Southern political history. However, it is the most pronounced in our dear state known as the "Heart of Dixie." It is not just a trend, but a prevailing thread that is repeated year after year and decade after decade in Alabama politics. This tradition is so pervasive that any serious student of Alabama politics should be aware of its presence, not only yesterday but also today.

In Alabama we simply vote overwhelmingly along the lines of localism for the candidate from our home county or area. With a runoff system in place, and if you have 6 to 12 candidates running for governor, if one draws heavy support from his county and adjacent counties, he just might make the runoff. This trend can be seen in election after election in Alabama, especially in the early to mid 1900s. This practice of voting for the candidate from your neck of the woods is "friends and neighbors" politics.

This pattern of localism helped Big Jim Folsom in his 1946 race for governor that year. He actually claimed two homes. He was born and raised in Elba in Coffee County in the Wiregrass area of the state. He moved to Cullman as a young man and sold insurance all over the counties surrounding Cullman. In the first primary, Big Jim led the field with 29 percent statewide, but in both Cullman and Coffee counties he garnered more than 70 percent of the vote.

In a race for an open U.S. Senate seat that year, "friends and neighbors" politics played out to the benefit of John Sparkman. He carried his home county of Madison overwhelmingly and his Tennessee Valley congressional district propelled him to victory.

Perhaps the most telling "friends and neighbors" scenario played out in the race for the congressional seat Sparkman was vacating after 10 years. The seat historically and still is today the Tennessee Valley counties stretching along the northern tier of the state. They border Tennessee and go from Georgia on the east to Mississippi on the west. In 1946, each county had their favorite son candidate; Colbert was hurt by having two. Jim Smith, the more popular candidate, got 63 percent of the vote in Colbert. The Limestone County candidate got 65 percent. The Madison County candidate got 70 percent, but the Jackson County candidate, Bob Jones, got an amazing 98 percent of the vote in Jackson County. That put him in the lead with 23 percent ahead of Jim Smith of Colbert's 20 percent. Bob Jones went on to win the seat and was the Tennessee Valley's congressman for three decades. He became one of the most powerful and revered congressmen this state has ever had in Washington.

So that is what is meant when some old codger says he won a race because of "friends and neighbors" politics.

Alabama's trend of "friends and neighbors" localism continues unabated. In the 2010 Governor's race, Dr. Robert Bentley would not have won without overwhelming local support. In the GOP primary, he received upwards of 90 percent of the vote in his home county of Tuscaloosa where he had treated a lot of patients in his dermatology practice. He also must have had a lot of patients in the surrounding counties of Fayette, Lamar, and Pickens, where he reaped a similar popular vote. This Tuscaloosa/northwest Alabama support was how he edged Tim James out of the runoff and ultimately beat Bradley Byrne.

In 2014, the only contested statewide GOP primary contest was the secretary of state's race. John Merrill had served in the House from Tuscaloosa. He was facing two probate judges from south Alabama. It appears that the only criteria in a low-level secondary statewide race is localism. Since there are no issues to speak of, where a candidate hails from becomes the most important factor. In Merrill's victory, he defeated his two south Alabama opponents throughout north Alabama. However, in his true home bailiwicks, Tuscaloosa and Cleburne, he trounced them.

Merrill was born and raised in Cleburne County where his daddy, Horace Merrill, was probate judge. An uncle, Pelham Merrill, was elected three times to the Alabama Supreme Court from Cleburne. John went to the University of Alabama and became student government president and then made Tuscaloosa his home and where he had his professional career and raised his family. In the 2014 GOP primary runoff, John got 75 percent of the vote in Tuscaloosa and over 90 percent of the vote in his native Cleburne County.

As a TV commentator on election night in the 2010 and 2014 elections, when I saw the results in the Bentley and Merrill victories, I smiled fondly and tried to convey the continuous display of "friends and neighbors" localism in Alabama politics.

When I reveal this pattern to the students in my Southern politics class, I tell them that this tendency is so pervasive that Alabamians may know that the candidate from their neck of the woods as a drunk or crook, but by gosh he's our own drunk or crook. This is not to suggest that any of the aforementioned victors were or are drunks or crooks. All I am suggesting is that under Alabama's "friends and neighbors" tradition, it wouldn't matter.

Dr. V. O. Key, the famous Southern political historian, first illuminated this Alabama political truism in the 1940s and '50s. He would be proud to know that his theory still holds.

Alabama Politics Today

As stated earlier, for close to 90 years (1877–1964) Alabama was a totally Democratic state. Not so much in the latter part of those nine decades due to philosophy but because of tradition. Everybody just ran in the Democratic Primary. It was one grand election.

It changed presidentially and congressionally in 1964 in the Southern Goldwater landslide. We started voting Republican for national offices that year and haven't looked back.

The GOP captured the governor's office in Alabama in 1986. It has been that way for 30 years now with one exception.

The last Democratic bastion, the legislature, was toppled in 2010 and further entrenched in 2014.

Folks, when we change, we change. We don't do things halfway.

Fifty years ago, every statewide official was a Democrat. Every state judge was a Democrat. Our entire congressional delegation was Democratic and our legislature was almost unanimously Democratic.

Today we are arguably the most Republican state in America from top to bottom.

Since 1964 there have been 13 presidential elections and Alabama has voted for the GOP nominee in 11 of these contests. Jimmy Carter is the last Democrat to carry Alabama and that was by a slim margin in 1976 almost 40 years ago. George Wallace won the state in 1968 as an Independent. That's 11 out of 13 and the last 9 election cycles for president. We are a very solid red Republican state in national elections.

Our congressional delegation has 6 Republicans and one lone Democrat. Both of our U.S. Senators are Republican.

For the first time in history, every statewide constitutional office is held by a Republican including governor, lieutenant governor, attorney general, agriculture commissioner, treasurer, secretary of state, and auditor.

Every member of our state judiciary is a Republican—all nine members of the Supreme Court, all members of the Courts and Criminal and Civil Appeals.

In short, every statewide elected official is a Republican.

The legislature is now overwhelmingly Republican. The House has a 72–33 GOP majority. The Senate numbers are even more daunting at 25–9.

Republican control of Alabama politics today is so dominating that we could safely be called a one-party state again. The Republican Party nomination today for statewide office is tantamount to election.

The Republican dominance will continue unabated in the Heart of Dixie for the foreseeable future.

Two prevailing themes are ingrained in Alabama politics.

One is the aforementioned "friends and neighbors" political tradition. The second and probably even more pronounced is that Alabamians vote based on race and religion. Most parts of the country vote based on pocketbook issues, but Alabama and the Deep South vote on race and religion.

Our state is divided politically based on race. The whites are Republican and the African Americans are Democrats. It's that simple. As long as there are more whites in the Heart of Dixie, the Republican Party will be in control.

When Lyndon Johnson signed the Civil Rights Bill in 1964, he said prophetically that, "I have just signed the South over to the Republican Party." That was 50 years ago and it will probably remain that way for another 50 years.

You could say that Lyndon Johnson drove a stake through the heart of the Democratic Party in the Deep South and Barack Obama drove the final nail in the coffin of the Alabama Democratic Party.

You add to the race equation the fact that Alabama may very well be the most religious and therefore socially conservative state in the nation and it makes a perfect recipe for Alabama to continue as a totally Republican state for years to come.

The more things change, the more they remain the same in politics.

Part I

Governors

1

James E. Folsom Sr.

James Elisha "Big Jim" Folsom, sometimes known as "Kissin' Jim," was by far Alabama's most colorful governor. He was only the second governor—Bibb Graves was the first—in the state's history to be elected to two four-year terms before George Wallace rewrote the history books on state politics beginning with his first term in 1962. The Alabama Constitution was amended to accommodate Wallace's ambitions in 1968, but prior to that a governor could not succeed himself, though he could sit out four years then run for another term. That is exactly what Bibb Graves and Jim Folsom did. Big Jim first served from 1947–51, then won a second four-year term for 1955–59. After that, he was never elected to public office again. Although he ran for numerous positions, his heyday was over and he died penniless in his adopted home county of Cullman.

Big Jim was born in Elba in Coffee County in 1908, the seventh of eight children. His early years were met with little success. He did poorly at college, joined the U.S. Merchant Marine, and drifted around the world. In 1936, he married Sarah Carnley, the daughter of Coffee County Probate Judge J. A. Carnley. That same year he ran against longtime incumbent Congressman Henry Steagall and lost 38–62, which political observers considered a good showing for a first-time candidate. He ran again two years later and lost 36–64. In 1939, he moved to Cullman to enter the insurance business.

He did well in insurance, making good money for the first time in his life. But the political bug was still eating at him, and in 1942 New Dealer Bibb Graves prepared to seek a third term as governor against the Black Belt "Big Mule" leader, Chauncey Sparks. Graves was so ill that liberals feared he would die before the Democratic primary and that the election would go to the conservative Sparks by default. Shortly before the filing deadline, friends convinced Folsom to run. Graves died soon thereafter, and Folsom joined three other candidates in opposing Sparks in the Democratic primary.

Folsom's striking appearance and humorous speeches, honed by three campaigns and years of insurance sales work, made him effective on the stump. He connected with voters, especially the powerless, in ways that confounded the political pundits. The "common man" believed Folsom was one of them and that he understood their problems better than "professional" politicians.

Sparks won, but Folsom's strong second-place showing with 26 percent of the vote was a surprise, not least to the candidate who ran third, former state highway director Chris Sherlock of Mobile. Sherlock was confident that he would easily make the runoff and felt that if Folsom picked up some votes in north Alabama, it would hurt Sparks and he, Sherlock, could lead the ticket. So, according to Jim Folsom Jr., Sherlock offered Big Jim $500 a week to boost his campaign for the last five weeks before the election. This was a lot of money at that time. Big Jim gladly took it. It helped his campaign. In fact, it helped him so much that he beat Sherlock. Sparks ran first, Big Jim ran second, and made the runoff.

Thus, Big Jim had run a successful get-acquainted race. The traditional way to run for governor in Alabama was to run once to get acquainted with the voters, and if you were the runner-up you were almost sure to be the front runner four years later, because the 1901 Alabama Constitution barred the incumbent governor from succeeding himself. It was one four-year term for governor and then out. Therefore, if you wanted to be governor you would run your first race in hopes you would run second to the winner. You would win the race four years later because you had become acquainted with the voters. You had built name identification. You had built your credibility as a serious or viable candidate. If you ran second you were the frontrunner for the next race. This scenario played out over and over during the six decades before the Constitution was amended in 1967.

Explaining the Get-Acquainted Race to the Big Mules

Young Folsom was not only big and colorful, but also a serious student of Alabama politics. He had run his get-acquainted race.

Big Jim ran in 1946 as the liberal, progressive, pro-union, anti-big business candidate. He railed and ranted and ran against the big business interests that ran Birmingham. He called them the Big Mules. The Big Mules organization was the Associated Industries of Alabama, which was supporting Lieutenant Governor Handy Ellis.

Just out of courtesy, the Associated Industries invited Big Jim to their big endorsement meeting. They already had a big check cut for Ellis. Most of these men knew more about business than they did politics. Big Jim got up to make his speech to the group and he gave them a history lesson on Alabama politics. He detailed every race since 1900 which revealed that every candidate who ran second always won the next time. He ended his speech by telling the business folks, "Y'all can support whoever you want to but they ain't gonna win. I ran second in 1942 and I'm going to win this race for governor in 1946."

The Big Mules caucused in a back room and did not un-endorse Ellis, but they decided to cover their bets. They wisely cut Big Jim a check, too.

Big Jim and the Mule

Tragedy struck Big Jim during the interim, when his wife, Sarah, died in childbirth in 1943. Folsom was left with two small daughters to care for and little income. Despite these personal setbacks, he ran for governor a second time in 1946 and won the governorship at age 38.

Folsom's campaign techniques set the standard that would prevail in Alabama for the next 20 years, although nobody could do it like he could. He had crafted a populist tone that sold well in an Alabama that was still mostly rural. His folksy, progressive speeches were preceded with music by a hillbilly band, the Strawberry Pickers. He campaigned wearing Army-issue boots (though he had not served in the military), which he would sometimes remove to let his bare feet dangle as he sat on the edge of a flatbed truck serving as an impromptu speaking platform. On the stump, Folsom used a variety of clever devices, including his famous cornshuck mop, which he said he would use to clean out the Capitol, and a suds bucket to collect the soap he needed to do it, in the form of campaign contributions. He was almost a traveling comedy or road show and he attracted enormous crowds to courthouse squares all over the state. The Strawberry Pickers would strike up the tune and Big Jim would lead the crowd in singing his campaign song, "Y'all Come." The mop would be brandished and the suds bucket would be passed. The country folk loved Big Jim and his performances.

A retired schoolteacher told me that one day she was listening to Big Jim rant and rave in the town square in Troy. The Strawberry Pickers had been playing and now Big Jim was speaking, and everyone in the crowd was mesmerized by the politicking on the square.

Big Jim was wound up with his speech. The traffic around the square was moving slowly. An old farmer was driving by in his wagon pulled by two mules. About midway of the street, one of the mules let out a loud, continuous bray that went on for several minutes.

The crowd started laughing. Big Jim said, "Guess he agrees with me, too."

BIG JIM'S COMMON MAN APPEAL

I met Big Jim in the mid-1970s when he was about 70 years old and had begun to stoop. The history books say he was around 6'8", but I'm 6'6" and he towered over me—he must have been a good 6'9" in his prime. He said, "Flowers, what size shoe do you wear?" I said, "About a 13, Governor." He said, "That ain't nothing, Flowers, I wear a size 17," and he did.

With Big Jim Folsom, 1975.

No wonder he drew a crowd. At 6'9", he was probably considered a giant for that era, and his antics were better than the Grand Ole Opry. Big Jim was simply the best show in town. He claimed a home in Cullman in north Alabama and also in Elba in south Alabama. He went directly to the people and he beat the Big Mules in 1946 and 1954. The entrenched power interests mostly thwarted his legislative efforts because they controlled the legislature. However, the common Alabamians loved Big Jim.

His major opponents in 1946 were Lieutenant Governor Handy Ellis and Agriculture Commissioner Joe Poole. Most daily newspapers disdained Big Jim's folksy style and gregarious, uninhibited demeanor, but his backers didn't read the "lying daily newspapers," as he called them. He didn't say anything against the local weekly papers because his people did read them, if only to see who had died or who grew the largest watermelons or the ripest tomatoes.

Lieutenant Governor Ellis was considered the favorite in the 1946 campaign, and he and Big Jim ended up in a runoff, which Big Jim won handily. The Democratic primary victory was tantamount to election in those days, as Alabama had been a one-party Democratic state since the end of Reconstruction; the Republicans did not even field a challenger in 1946. Folsom's win in 1946 made him the first non-Bourbon Democrat to be elected governor since the enactment of the 1901 Constitution that had disfranchised almost all African American and many poor white voters.

Every 20th-century governor before Folsom had been a well-heeled, aristocratic businessman who was from either the Black Belt or Birmingham. The Big Mules and Big Planters would get together behind closed doors at a corporate office and pick the candidate that they would unanimously support. Their candidate would always win. He would be an arch-conservative who wanted to maintain low property taxes and low wages which helped create more wealth for the large land owners and the big industrialists of the state.

Big Jim beat them by appealing directly to the common man. The state had also changed. Many of the downtrodden young whites who were born poor to yeoman farmers in rural north Alabama and the Wiregrass of south Alabama had gone off to fight in World War II. They came home to a state that was reaping the benefits of a post-war industrial boom. They were no longer relegated to going back to their fathers' lives of scraping a living off 40 acres and a mule, or, worse, sharecropping. They found jobs in the heavy industry of Birmingham, Huntsville, Muscle Shoals, Gadsden, and Tuscaloosa. The state docks in Mobile were booming, and all these industries in Alabama were becoming unionized. Big labor became powerful in Alabama and all of these veterans and new union members could relate to Big Jim. He was one of them. Though he received few newspaper endorsements, many labor unions supported him.

"I Stole for You"

Big Jim was sworn in early in 1947 and began work on his famous Farm-to-Market road program, the work he is most remembered for today. His administration was troubled by allegations of corruption and cronyism, but Folsom remained popular to the end of his first term.

After sitting out for four years, he entered the gubernatorial race again in 1954. He beat three state senators, the president of the public service commission, and the lieutenant governor without a runoff. He beat them with his legendary suds bucket, mop, by "cussin" the lying big city newspapers, and by challenging the Big Mules. When opponents charged that his first administration had been laced with corruption, he responded by saying, "Shore I stole, I stole to build hospitals, I stole to build schools, I stole to build roads." Pointing to overalls-wearing members of his campaign audiences, he would say, "That crowd I got it from, you had to steal it to get it . . . I stole for you, and you, and you."

They loved him. He was "the little man's big friend." He was larger than life. One can truthfully use about him the cliche that when they made Big Jim they broke the mold. He was the most lighthearted, fun-loving, uninhibited, and colorful governor this state has ever seen.

Big Jim lived life to its fullest. He was so happy-go-lucky that he seemed inebriated even if he wasn't, and he often was. He was governor in an era when there was little television coverage and the media did not portray foibles and weaknesses of politicians the way they do today. Big Jim was almost childlike in his love of people, especially the poorer rural Alabamians whom he fought for diligently. He really didn't hate anyone. He seemed to love everybody but he admired you if you were down and out. He lived by the adage "Everything is made for love," coined by another fun-loving

Alabama political legend, the former farmer and long-serving Congressman Frank Boykin from Mobile. Big Jim and Boykin were buddies. Both liked to party. You might say they were cut from the same cloth, though they were starkly different in size. Boykin was a chubby 5'6" and Big Jim was a giant.

"I Didn't Know That"

Big Jim was the epitome of unbridled candidness.

Late in his second term, he had been on a week-long trip to the Port City with his buddies, including Boykin, but he had to come back to Montgomery to give a speech to the national convention of the American Textile Manufacturers Association. It was a big and distinguished crowd of executives from all over the country and they were meeting in Alabama, so the governor was to give them an official welcoming speech. While Big Jim was vacationing in Mobile, somebody in his office had written him a nice speech. But Big Jim had never seen the speech prior to getting up to address the audience. He started reading the speech and it sounded somewhat dry and full of statistics. Big Jim was dutifully reading, ". . . We want to welcome y'all to Alabama. Alabama is truly a textile state. We've got 200,000 people employed in the textile industry, and it means $40 million to our economy. We produce 4 million articles a week . . ." At which point, Big Jim looked up from his reading and said, "I'll be doggone, I didn't know that."

He threw his speech up in the air and said, "Aw hell, y'all don't want to hear all those statistics, What y'all want to hear is about them trying to impeach ol' Jim. They're always trying to get Big Jim. They's trying to set a trap for old Big Jim. Well, they've got a room in downtown Montgomery and in that room they've got whiskey. They got the best whiskey money can buy. They got scotch, they got bourbon, they got vodka. They want to get Big Jim in that room and get him drunk, In the next room they've got women. They've got blondes, brunettes, and redheads. Best-looking women you've ever seen, and they want to get Big Jim in that room and get him in that trap. You know what, fellas? If they bait a hook with whiskey and women, they'll catch ol' Jim every time. I'm going down there right now. I'll see y'all later."

Just Spell My Name right

My ninth-grade Civics teacher was Miss Mary Lamb. She had taught for many years and in fact had taught both my mama and daddy in high school. Besides our civics lesson she would impart wisdom upon us in the way of old sayings. One she particularly liked was, "Fools' names, fools' faces, always found in public places." This one kind of bothered me since I was a budding politician and was already class president. I had learned that one of the first courses of action was to plaster your name all over school. Later in life, I ran for and won election to the Alabama legislature. Every time we would go out to put up campaign signs, I would cringe when I thought about Miss Lamb's admonition. However, as a student of politics, I knew that name identification was essential. You can't expect a voter to vote for you if they haven't even heard of you.

One of the best stories I know on Big Jim Folsom focused on his belief in the importance of name identification.

Big Jim's first term had broken the moneyed interests' stronghold on the governor's office. But the big city dailies and the legislators were still controlled by the Big Mules of Birmingham and the Big Planters of the Black Belt. They hated Big Jim's folksiness. The big dailies like the *Birmingham News, Montgomery Advertiser,* and *Mobile Press Register* would poke fun at him and try to discover scandal on a daily basis. The legislature constantly tried to impeach him.

One of the papers, after days of digging, felt they had another patented scandal to reveal on Folsom. They called to tell him that they had an exposé on his administration and out of courtesy wanted to get his side of the story. Now Big Jim could care less what the big city press said about him. They had written the harshest things about Folsom that could ever be written. It hadn't affected him one bit with his loyal rural friends and constituents, so it is not surprising that Big Jim treated the big-city press with contempt and disdain. When they called, he said, "Boys, come on down and see Big Jim and tell me what you got on me today. I haven't seen y'all in a week or two. Come on down right now."

When they got down to his office, he greeted them with his shoes off and his bare feet resting on his desk, reared back in his chair, with a grin on his face. He said, "Boys, hit me with your best shot. What y'all got on ol' Jim?"

They said, "Governor, this is no laughing matter. We have a list here of 37 people that you hired over in the Highway Department and circumvented the merit system to put them on the state payroll."

Big Jim laughed and glanced at their list and said, "You lying daily newspapers, you lying about Big Jim again, lying, lying, lying. I got a new list right here and I haven't hired 37 people. I hired 72, and the only merit they got is that they're Big Jim's friends."

The reporters were incredulous. They said, "Governor, we are going to put that in the paper tomorrow."

Big Jim smiled and said, "Boys, I don't care what you write about me, just spell my name right!"

Big Jim knew the cardinal rule of name identification. The saying is now famous among Alabama politicians—just spell my name right! Big Jim coined it.

Just Thump It Off

Big Jim got a lot of negative things said about him on the campaign trail while he was governor.

He had a unique way of disarming and diminishing the effect of the mud being slung at him.

He would rear back and tell his rural audiences, "My mama used to tell me that if someone threw mud at you and it landed on your new white starched shirt, you simply ignore it. Don't try to wipe it off right away while its still wet because if you do it will just smear all over your shirt. But if you ignore it and let it dry for a few days you can just thump it off."

The Show on the Aircraft Carrier

An all-time favorite Big Jim Folsom story happened in the mid-1950s during his second term as governor, at the annual Southern Governors Conference. The assembled governors and other dignitaries were scheduled to be guests at a nearby U.S. naval station and to witness an air show exhibition.

Big Jim had a reputation for enjoying libations. The governors were scheduled to gather at the waterfront at 6 a.m., and many doubted Big Jim would make it at that hour since he would have partied most of the night before. That was indeed the case but nonetheless he arrived at the pier on time. It was obvious that he had not slept, he was still wearing the same suit and tie, he was unshaven, and his hair was askew, but he was raring to go.

The governors, dignitaries, and aides were motored in small boats out to a huge aircraft carrier, which then sailed 15 to 20 miles offshore for a state-of-the-art air show previously seen only by high-ranking naval officers and cabinet members.

The sky was perfect, the sea was calm, it was a beautiful day. The crowd gathered on the flight deck. An admiral gave a glowing speech about the Navy and naval aviation and how important and accident-free it had become. The admiral introduced the pilot and then some enlisted men went through the crowd handing out ear muff devices to protect the observers' hearing from the noise of the jet. Big Jim may have looked a little funnier than the rest of the governors in his ear muffs because of his size and his dishevelment.

The air show began; the jet got louder and louder as it whined down the airstrip and made a perfect takeoff. Then suddenly there was total silence. The jet flamed out; the engine quit running; the plane crashed into the water and was lost to the Atlantic Ocean. There was complete bedlam aboard the carrier. Sirens went off, divers prepared to enter the water, and emergency helicopters prepared to take off. Then miraculously word came that the pilot had bailed out of the plane before it sank and was not injured. He was shaken up and wet but alive.

The crowd gave a rousing cheer of relief that the pilot's life had been spared. By this time everyone had taken off their ear muffs except Big Jim, who was still standing on the deck with his ear muffs on and his mouth open in amazement.

Folsom had been watching the scene in absolute astonishment. He couldn't believe his bloodshot eyes. Finally, he could contain himself no longer. Because he was still wearing his ear muffs, he did not realize how loudly he was talking, and in a voice you could hear for miles, Big Jim boomed, "Admiral, if that wasn't a show, I'll kiss your ass."

A Big Jim Man

In Big Jim's day, prison road camps flourished around the state. These mini-prisons housed state inmates in barracks. These convicts were not the most notorious outlaws but were petty, small-time, short-time servers.

Legislators liked for these road camps to be in their county. They served as a means to put friends and supporters on the state payroll as guards or cooks. The merit system was not what it is today, so the governor could hire just about who he wanted. These local patronage jobs were usually awarded through a legislator supportive of the governor. Probably the most coveted job at these camps was to be named chaplain. Some well-meaning somebody had concluded that these convicted felons, these dregs of society, desperately needed spiritual guidance. Whether they got much of that from the chaplains is debatable. Most often the chaplains were hired not because of their political commitment to whomever happened to be governor at the time. Mostly they were farmers or carpenters or loggers who had done a little preaching along the way. The salary for these chaplains was $400 a month, and considering how little they would have to do, it was a plum position.

One of the first road camps during the Folsom administration was in Marion County, because Marion County was represented by the legendary Rankin Fite, one of Folsom's main men in the legislature. Whatever he wanted from Jim Folsom, he got. It was said not entirely in jest that Fite moved everything in Montgomery to Marion County except the State Capitol.

One day Fite made the long drive from Hamilton to Montgomery with a man he wanted Folsom to name as chaplain of the road camp in Marion County. The man was what is called a "peckerwood sawmiller," so-called because he cut about as much timber as the bird by the same name. On occasion he had filled the pulpit at a few Primitive Baptist churches. Most importantly, however, the preacher/sawmiller had voted right.

As Fite told this story, the two men were ushered into Folsom's office and Fite immediately began to extol the Christian virtues of his friend. He told in detail of how this man had been "called by the Lord to preach," of the many souls he had saved, of the hundreds of baptisms he had performed. Billy Graham would have been impressed.

"And he's really good at funerals, Governor," Fite continued. "I went to one of his funeral services and he even had the undertakers crying."

Big Jim, sprawled back in his chair, his feet on the desk, listened to about all of this that he could stand. Finally he held up his hand, a clear signal for Fite to shut up. He turned toward the preacher man and in a booming voice asked, "All I wanna know is this, Preacher, are you our kind of a sonuvabitch or their kind of a sonuvabitch?"

"Governor, I'm your kind of a sonuvabitch," the preacher responded enthusiastically.

He got the job.

THAT WAS NO BULL

During his third run for governor in 1954, Big Jim was giving a homespun speech to a receptive audience in Geneva County. It was a good place for ol' Jim.

Big Jim and Jamelle had nine children. He told the audience that the prize bull at the State Fair was from south Alabama and that he was a good specimen of a bull. He said he decided to take his family to the State Fair to see that prize bull. At the Fair, he asked the ticket seller for 11 tickets. The ticket seller said, "Governor, why in the world do you need 11 tickets?" Big Jim said, "Boy, because I got me and my wife Jamelle and I've got nine children."

The ticket seller looked at Big Jim and said, "Governor, I'm going to give you your money back. I want the bull to see you!"

BIG JIM AND FULLER KIMBRELL'S 'LIFE SENTENCE'

During Big Jim's second term as governor from 1955 to 1958 his finance director was Fuller Kimbrell. That was and still is the most powerful cabinet position in Alabama politics.

At about the same time Big Jim was settling into office, the first of the sensational Albert Patterson murder trials was taking place in Birmingham, at the conclusion of which the jurors convicted the Phenix City deputy sheriff, Albert Fuller, and sentenced him to life in Kilby Prison.

When the news reached Montgomery, an aide rushed into Big Jim's office and blurted out: "Governor, they just gave Fuller life at Kilby."

"Well, I'll be damned," lamented the governor. "And they didn't even give 'im a trial."

The Governor of Eutaw

Many who know the Black Belt or who attended the University of Alabama know of a legendary restaurant called the Cotton Patch in rural Greene County near Eutaw. This eatery was an Alabama landmark with steaks so good they could stop a fight. The Cotton Patch was a must-eat place as early as the 1940s.

One fall during Big Jim's second term, he was attending the national Governors' Conference held that year on the West Coast. Big Jim was always an attraction at these events. He was by far the tallest governor in the country and undoubtedly also the most colorful.

Big Jim never met a stranger. He usually bellowed out a "Glad to meet you" when someone new was introduced to him. He would hug or kiss a new female acquaintance. He would slap a man on the back. He especially liked little men. It seemed that with his gigantic stature he found them interesting and amusing.

While at the Governor's Conference, he ambled out of his room and spied a very short, bald man leaving his own room on the same floor. It never occurred to Big Jim that since it was a Governors' Conference that they just might put some of the governors in suites on the same floor.

Big Jim, anxious to meet a new friend, wildly slapped the man on the back, nearly knocking him down. Unbeknownst to Big Jim, he was pulverizing the Governor of Utah. Big Jim crunched the little fellow's hand and introduced himself. Big Jim asked the little fellow where he was from. The Governor humbly said, "Utah." Big Jim was astonished and excited. "You don't mean it. Hell, I can't believe you're out here all the way from Eutaw. I go to your town all the time to eat at the Cotton Patch."

The Governor of Utah just nodded in acknowledgment, probably afraid to say too much in fear that Big Jim would slap him on the back again.

Some of My Friends Are for It

Big Jim was a true politician and he wasn't above straddling the fence.

But at least he was honest about it. When asked a tough question about a complex or difficult issue, old Big Jim would simply look at the inquisitive reporter with a pensive thoughtful and serious look and simply say with a straight face, "Well you know some of my friends are for it and some of my friends are against it, and I'm always on the side of my friends."

Even Two-Pocket Lawyers Could Be Jim's Friends

Big Jim had a real disdain for lawyers. He called them every name in the book. He especially criticized lawyers serving in the legislature, believing it was unconstitutional for them, as officers of the court, to serve in the legislative branch. He said lawyers belong in the judicial branch and if they wanted to be in politics they ought to be judges (elected positions in Alabama). He would rail against lawyers in the legislature every chance he got. He said they can't serve two masters. They can't serve the Lord and the Devil. He called them two-pocket lawyers.

In reality, he didn't dislike all lawyers. A good many of his best friends were lawyers. Indeed some of his best political friends and supporters were lawyers.

During Big Jim's second term, 1955–59, John Patterson was attorney general (and succeeded Folsom as governor, but we will get to that later). On the surface, it appeared Folsom and Patterson did not like each other because Patterson was quick to condemn and prosecute some of Big Jim's cronies. However, they did like each other and remained friends throughout their lives. Both were astute politicians.

During their time, the Interstate Highway Act was created by the Eisenhower administration. It was and still is the largest federal project ever undertaken. A good bit of federal money began to flow into the states, including Alabama, for development of the interstate system.

There were a good many Alabamians who didn't want to give up their land for highways. Some had land that had been in their families for generations; their forefathers had admonished them never to sell the land.

In those cases, the state and federal governments had to condemn the land and take it over by right of eminent domain. The legal maneuvering fell upon the state attorney general's office, and the work was so overwhelming that the attorney general's staff had to hire outside lawyers. This is and has always been a lucrative plum. Patterson was delighted to get to put a good many of his legal brothers and political supporters on the state's payroll as assistant attorneys general. These lawyers would make a lot of money on these projects.

One of the most expensive acquisitions was the purchase of the area in Jefferson County that is today known as Malfunction Junction, where Interstates 65, 59, and 20 cross and merge. Forty acres of houses, including some nice homes, were located in the path of the highway in the Norwood section of north Birmingham. The cost and legal fees were substantial.

Patterson hired a good many of his Birmingham legal buddies. He sent the contracts over to the governor's office to be approved. The governor legally had to sign off on the contracts. A good amount of time had elapsed between Patterson sending his list of lawyers over and Big Jim signing off on them. Finally, Patterson went over to see Big Jim about his appointments. He said, "Governor, what's the problem? We need to sign off on this work. It's delaying the highway system from moving on in Alabama."

Big Jim looked at Patterson and said, "John, you know I've got a lot of friends that are lawyers, too." The Governor said, "I've got a deal for you. You name half of the lawyers and I'll name half of the lawyers." What could Patterson say? That's the way it came down!

Big Jim believed in helping his friends.

Laying on the Stars

Big Jim was a widower during his first term. He was a tall, handsome, young, single governor who was without a doubt the only 6'9" tall, dark, and handsome bachelor governor in the nation. He was also one of the most gregarious and uninhibited personalities that many in the press had ever seen.

So Big Jim found himself the subject of tabloid publicity, often depicted as somewhat of a jet-set playboy. His fun-loving antics and drinking made him fodder for the *Saturday Evening Post* and other periodicals. Big Jim was photographed with models in New York, and he made several trips to the West Coast. He had a date with the daughter of California Governor Earl Warren, who later became Chief Justice of the U.S. Supreme Court.

His daughter, "Honey Bear" Warren, was romantically linked with Big Jim.

Upon his arrival back in the state from one of his escapades, the *Birmingham News* asked him about his trip to Hollywood and his meetings with movie stars.

Big Jim replied, "Yes, I have indeed been to the West Coast and I am here to tell y'all that I have thoroughly enjoyed laying on the stars and looking down at the sand."

The Snodgrass Bridge

One of Big Jim's favorite political friends was Representative John Snodgrass of Scottsboro, the seat of Jackson County in the northeast corner of Alabama. It is in the heart of the Tennessee Valley in the foothills of the Appalachians and sits near the borders of both Tennessee and Georgia.

Big Jim loved John Snodgrass. The feeling was mutual. Big Jim decided to build a bridge and name it after his buddy. He didn't just build a little bridge. He built a huge bridge over the Tennessee River. The problem was they built the bridge where there was no road. Folks up there marveled at the fact that the bridge they had long yearned for was built without a road leading to it.

Big Jim and Snodgrass never worried about it for a minute. They told the good folks in the Tennessee Valley, "Don't you know if you build a bridge, they've got to build a road to it."

Sure enough, the road was built and is now the main thoroughfare through Sand Mountain: Highway 117 that runs through Jackson and Dekalb counties. Ol' Jim and Snodgrass were right. If you build a bridge, a road will follow.

Big Jim built the bridge for his friend with the intention of calling it the John Snodgrass Bridge. Then there got to be a lot of opposition to naming the bridge after John Snodgrass because some folks didn't believe you should name something after somebody who was living. But Representative Snodgrass was the heir to a great family name in Jackson County. His granddaddy and daddy had both been prominent judges in the county.

One day Big Jim pulled his friend Snodgrass aside and said, "John, what was yore Daddy's name?" Snodgrass said, "John, just like me." "What about your granddaddy?" "John, just like me." Big Jim said, "Well, hell, they're both dead and they're named John Snodgrass. We'll just name it after them and it'll really be named after you."

Big Jim's Run for Congress

Jim Folsom Jr. shared a story about his father's early political life.

Big Jim always knew that he wanted to go into politics. So he jumped right in. His hometown of Elba in Coffee County was in the sprawling old third congressional district which encompassed the southeastern part of the state. It was referred to as the Wiregrass district.

The venerable and dignified Henry Steagall of Ozark had represented the Wiregrass district for 20 years when Big Jim decided to take him on. Steagall had become a powerful and well-known congressman. He was chairman of the House Banking Committee and had authored the famous Glass-Steagall Act which revised the national banking laws during FDR's New Deal.

As you can imagine, Chairman Steagall enjoyed the fruits of his labors. He hobnobbed with New York bankers. The big banking lobbyists were wining and dining Steagall and taking him to Broadway shows. He was living the high life in Washington. When he came home to the Wiregrass, he wore Brooks Brothers suits even when he went quail hunting. You could say, and many did, that Old Henry had lost touch with the common folks in the Wiregrass.

This aloofness and Washingtonitis had created an opening for political challengers, and Big Jim was only one of four in 1936. All four of his opponents jumped on Steagall's lifestyle. They accused him of living the grand life. They said he was not only eating pheasant under glass with New York bankers, but he was also cavorting with young girls in Washington.

In this era in Alabama, politics was conducted mostly through campaign rallies in the courthouse squares. Even in a small town, it was not unusual for 500 people—including many farmers in their overalls—to gather on the square during campaign season for a political rally. Every candidate for every office would show up to speak. The local candidates would talk and then the gubernatorial candidates and then the Congressional candidates. They would draw straws to set the order in which they would speak. On this particular day, all of the candidates for Steagall's seat were there as well as the congressman.

Every one of the challengers jumped on Steagall's personal life. They lambasted his fine dining and they especially harped on the old man's fooling around with young women. Except for Big Jim, who was 26, all the candidates were middle-aged. When it finally became Big Jim's time to speak, he made it short and sweet.

He said, "Folks, I've been listening to all my opponents talk about Mr. Steagall's lifestyle in Washington, especially his liking and running with young girls. Sounds like to me if that's the way things are in Washington, you ought to bring Old Henry home and send a young man up there to take his place. I believe I could do a better job with fine dining and young women. Y'all vote for me."

Big Jim ran second to Steagall that year, but he carried that town.

In that same campaign, Big Jim was politicking down a dirt road in rural Geneva County. He stopped by a farmhouse at the end of the dirt road. The farmer and his wife visited with the young candidate. They gave young Jim Folsom a large glass of buttermilk to drink while they sat on the porch and visited. Big Jim and the farmer bonded. The old farmer lamented that he wished somebody would pave his road so that he could get his produce to market no matter what the weather. Big Jim lost that race for Congress, but he never forgot that old farmer in Geneva County. When Big Jim became governor a decade later, the first dirt road he paved in his famous Farm-to-Market road-building program was that one in Geneva County. It is called the Buttermilk Road.

The Poker Game

Jim Folsom Jr. shared another story about his father that was told by Bill Hobbie, who was Big Jim's pilot when Big Jim was governor.

In the 1940s, there were no interstate highways. Many roads were not even paved. It took longer to get around the state by car than it does now. During Big Jim's first term, the state bought an airplane for the governor to use. It was a small Cessna-like puddle jumper, by no means a luxurious jet. When the state got the plane, Big Jim went out to inspect it. At about that time a big jet zoomed into the airport and out popped a handsome, dapper pilot, Bill Hobbie, who had been an Army Air Corps (now the Air Force) pilot during the just-ended World War II. Hobbie was getting out of the service and needed a job. Big Jim walked over and hired him on the spot as his pilot. Hobbie, the brother of longtime Montgomery County Probate Judge Walker Hobbie, appreciated Big Jim's patronage and became a loyal Big Jim man for the rest of his life.

Big Jim and Bill Hobbie had a good time with the state plane.

Not many folks know that Big Jim was a hell of a poker player. He had developed this skill during his time in the Merchant Marine. He loved a good poker game about as well as he did a bottle of whiskey.

One day Big Jim and Hobbie were sitting around the governor's office about three o'clock in the afternoon. They knew that there was a big poker game going on at a house up on Lake Guntersville in the northeast part of the state. All of Big Jim's cronies, many of whom were in his cabinet, were up on the beautiful lake in a monumental poker game.

Big Jim looked at Hobbie and said, "Let's go." They got in the state plane and took off. Hobbie observed that all the way up there Big Jim did not take one drink. This was very unusual because anyone who knew Big Jim knew he started drinking about three o'clock in the afternoon if not before.

The airstrip was close to the lake cabin. They arrived fairly quickly. Big Jim had called beforehand and told them to save him a place at the table. They had one waiting. They were looking forward to Big Jim's arrival. They knew he would be in his cups by the time he got there and they would be able to take all his money.

Big Jim was as sober as a Baptist judge when he arrived. However, he played like he was dog drunk. He stumbled into the room, slurred his words, and acted like he could hardly walk, much less play cards. He took his seat at the poker table and quickly took their money at poker.

He and Hobbie got back on the state plane and were back at the Governor's Mansion in Montgomery by 8:30 p.m. Big Jim had taken over $2,000 off his gambling buddies that night. That was a lot of money back then. By 9 o'clock Big Jim and Hobbie were sitting in the Governor's Mansion and having a big laugh and, finally, a drink.

Drunk on TV

Sadly, Big Jim's drinking eventually became a serious liability and helped doom his try for a third term in 1962.

The 1960 presidential race between John Kennedy and Richard Nixon was the first to feature television. In fact, TV was the pivotal factor in that contest. John Kennedy was photogenic. The contrast between Kennedy and Nixon on the first televised debates in the fall of 1960 probably tilted the election to Kennedy. Nixon looked pale, nervous, and had a horrible five o'clock shadow. Kennedy looked warm, relaxed, and tanned. It was quite a contrast. Most people who listened to those debates on the radio said they thought that Nixon had won. However, those who watched on TV overwhelmingly thought Kennedy outperformed Nixon. TV won.

The 1962 Alabama governor's race featured the modern media of television for the first time. Big Jim had won his two previous races campaigning from the back of a flat-bed truck, making 15 to 20 speeches a day at every county seat in the state. He traveled with his country band, the Strawberry Pickers, and passed around his famous suds bucket for cleaning out the Capitol. He was used to old-fashioned one-on-one retail politicking. George C. Wallace was, too. They were both masters of the stump. Wallace had run his get-acquainted race in 1958. This time, he was the front-runner, along with Folsom due to his having won the office twice already. Lots of people believed that Big Jim was destined to win a third term but it was not going to happen. No matter what Folsom did or didn't do, Wallace was going to win the governor's race regardless. He had campaigned nonstop for four years and most of all he had taken full control of the race issue. Big Jim was considered by segregationist whites to be soft on the race issue. George Wallace made it the paramount issue.

Ryan DeGraffenreid was a handsome, articulate state senator from Tuscaloosa. He was making his get-acquainted race a damn good one. He was appealing to most of the business voters in the state with a moderate probusiness message. He was Kennedy-like without being a liberal. He was considered a viable candidate although most prognosticators still predicted that it was a two-man race between Folsom and Wallace leading into the final days.

All three candidates had bought 30 minutes of air time on all of the major state television channels for the night before the election. They were all preparing to do a live 30-minute show that would be aired simultaneously by all the stations.

As a 11-year-old political junkie, I was glued to the TV for the live election television shows featuring the three major candidates for governor. My Daddy was a businessman. He was for Ryan DeGraffenreid. My Mom was for Big Jim Folsom. He had kissed her when she was a high school cheerleader at Troy High School and her uncle was a road builder who had gotten some good contracts under Big Jim. I was for George Wallace. I had Wallace bumper stickers on my bicycle and I campaigned for him on my paper route. Wallace got the short end of the stick in my family since I couldn't vote at 11.

George Wallace came on first at seven o'clock. He did pretty well, not great, but he didn't hurt himself.

Ryan DeGraffenreid came on at 7:30 p.m. He was magnificent, much like Kennedy in 1960. He helped himself immensely. He was telegenic and took to TV like a duck to water. He was a hit and picked up some votes.

Big Jim came on last at eight o'clock. They had him sitting on a sofa in a set that looked like a living room. It was designed to make you feel at home, at ease, and cozy. Big Jim was sitting on the sofa like a giant. The sofa was too small for him. His knees jutted up almost to his chest. TV advisors will tell a first-time interviewee to be sure to look squarely into the camera. Obviously the last thing Big Jim had been told before he went on the air was to look right into the camera. He hunkered down like he was staring a hole in the viewer the way he stared at the camera. Unfortunately, the advisor had forgotten to tell Big Jim to comb his hair. He had a wayward strand of hair hanging right down in his face.

His first words portended what was to come. His speech was slurred and he was clearly drunk. After his opening statement of about four minutes, even though I was only 11, I could tell that Big Jim seemed impaired. I walked back to my Mama's bedroom where she was reading and I said, "Mama, you need to come in the living room and see Big Jim on TV. I believe he is drunk." She walked in and glanced at him and assured me that Big Jim was just like that. He was cutting up for the TV. So I settled back in for the remainder of the show.

Big Jim had a bunch of children, so they were going to have him introduce his children one-by-one. Little Jim came out first and he did pretty well with him—"This is my little boy Jim . . ."—although he did tousle his hair pretty badly. The second son, Jack, came out and, although I hate to tell you, Big Jim forgot his second child's name. The poor little fellow came out and Big Jim said, "This is my boy—" He stammered around trying to think of his name. Finally, he blurted out, "Boy, what is your name?" The TV folks dropped the idea of trying to introduce the rest of Big Jim's family after that.

They let him start talking again. He was weaving back and forth. The long strand of hair was hanging right over his nose. He was now pontificating on the virtues of progressivism and free textbooks and Farm-to-Market roads. I called Mama in again to view the spectacle. She stood there for a full two minutes with her mouth open, and she finally said, "Son, I believe you're right. Big Jim is drunk."

He finished by getting mad at George Wallace and calling him a cuckoo bird for trying to steal his platform. He waved his arms wildly for three solid minutes on statewide TV mimicking a cuckoo bird.

Folks around the state had heard tales and rumors about Big Jim's drinking for years. They had dismissed it as political talk. However, seeing Big Jim live and drunk on statewide TV was an eye-opener. He never recovered. He failed to make the runoff the next day. Wallace led the ticket and DeGraffenreid edged Big Jim out of the runoff. Wallace beat DeGraffenreid in the runoff.

Later Big Jim said Wallace's people drugged him. This story is not likely. Big Jim had pretty much succumbed to alcohol by this time in his life. The night Big Jim came on TV drunk was the end of his political career.

But it was a hell of a show!

2

John Patterson

John Patterson served as governor from 1959 to 1963. He holds the distinction of being the only person to ever beat George Wallace in a governor's race.

Patterson and Wallace were both making their first race for governor in 1958. Patterson beat Wallace soundly. Wallace never stood a chance. It would have been hard for anyone to beat a man in a race for governor of Alabama in 1958 who had both the race issue and a sympathy vote.

John Patterson epitomizes the phrase "a Southern gentleman." He is a fine man. There was never any hint of scandal during his four years as governor nor his four years prior to that as attorney general nor his subsequent decades on the Alabama Court of Criminal Appeals.

He and Wallace became friends. Indeed, Wallace appointed Patterson to the appeals court. Patterson was reelected several times and retired in his 70s.

Patterson had became attorney general of Alabama at a very young age after his father, Albert Patterson, was assassinated just 16 days after winning the Democratic nomination for the office in 1954. The elder Patterson had run with the promise to clean up Phenix City, which had become the most corrupt, sinful city in the South. It was the redneck version of Las Vegas. However, unlike Las Vegas, everything they did in Phenix City was not legal and condoned. The east Alabama town near Fort Benning and Columbus, Georgia, was run by a corrupt rural mafia. This mafia gunned down Patterson, in an alley behind his law office. The younger Patterson was then picked to replace his father as the Democratic attorney general nominee. There was only token Republican opposition, so he easily won, becoming attorney general at age 33. Just days after his election, a movie was made about the Phenix City saga. Between that and his well-publicized anti-civil rights actions, by the time John Patterson got ready to run for governor in 1958 he was a folk hero to Alabama's whites.

He had indeed been a tough anti-crime attorney general. He cleaned up the Phenix City mess and also took on the loan sharks as well as some of Big Jim Folsom's cronies. He had a well-earned reputation as a no-holds-barred crime fighter. There was also no hint of corruption during his four years as attorney general. Therefore, he ran for governor as the law-and-order, straight-arrow candidate. He beat George Wallace.

Governor Patterson's First Lesson

Governor Patterson shared a funny story that occurred during the opening days of his administration.

He entered the governor's office in January 1959 as the clean government, strict law enforcement governor. He followed Big Jim Folsom's second administration which had been less than perfect when it came to favoritism, nepotism, and corruption. Patterson was determined to run a clean ship.

His first day as governor he called his cabinet in for a pep talk and told them to run their departments aboveboard and free of any semblance of favoritism. He dismissed them and told them to get to work running the state. He turned to his new public safety director, Floyd Mann, and asked him to stay behind. Floyd Mann was a much-respected man in Alabama politics. He had been chief of police in Opelika prior to Patterson appointing him head of the highway patrol. Mann and Patterson were lifelong friends. They had grown up and gone to school together in Tallapoosa County.

Patterson looked at his friend and said, "Floyd, under no circumstances are we going to fix any tickets during my administration. Do you understand?" Mann looked at Patterson and said, "Governor, I understand."

Mann went on his way to his first day as public safety director and supervisor of the highway patrol. This was about 11 a.m. About 2:30 in the afternoon the new governor got a message that he had had a call from senior U.S. Senator Lister Hill. Within 30 minutes, he had a message that Senator John Sparkman had called, as well as Congressmen George Andrews and Frank Boykin. He assumed that all of our distinguished congressional delegates were calling to wish him well on his first day as governor.

When he called these four very powerful Washington solons back, he learned that an equally powerful congressman from Missouri had been detained and indeed arrested in south Alabama. The congressman had been vacationing in Florida with his family and had been driving back to Missouri when he was caught speeding in Conecuh County. At that time, an out-of-state driver could not sign his own bond in Alabama, so the good congressman had been detained for more than three hours, with his family, waiting to locate a justice of the peace. The congressman was upset, to say the least. Hill and Sparkman were somewhat tactful with the new governor. They simply suggested that the speeder was a powerful and important member of Congress and that it would be helpful to them if Patterson could help their colleague get back on his way home to Missouri. Frank Boykin was more direct. He informed Patterson that this congressman chaired the committee that oversaw all of the appropriations for waterways. He further explained that he and Senators Hill and Sparkman had been working diligently for years to get funding for the Tennessee-Tombigbee Waterway and the project was pending in this congressman's committee at this time.

Governor Patterson called Colonel Mann and said, "Floyd, can you come over here a minute?" When Mann arrived in the governor's office, Patterson told his buddy, "You know, Floyd, when I told you this morning not to fix any tickets? Well, we've had a change in policy." The no-ticket-fixing policy of the Patterson Administration had lasted four hours.

Mann dispatched a trooper to not only release the congressman but to give him a trooper escort out of the state.

Governor Patterson told me he had learned a lesson from that experience—never say never. He also should be given some credit for obtaining funding for the Tennessee-Tombigbee Waterway.

Drinking Sunday "Tea" at the Elite

Alabama's most famous political restaurant and watering hole for 50 years was Montgomery's Elite Restaurant. Until it closed about 1995, the Elite (pronounced *ee-light*) was the place to eat and be seen. Many a political deal was struck at its back tables. Legislators, politicians, and socialites frequented the famous establishment. The politicians and lobbyists not only met there during the sessions, they would meet there for political discussions and dinners and drinks all year long and any night or day, even on Sundays. The original owner and proprietor was Pete Xides. His son, Ed Xides, a wonderful gentleman with impeccable Southern manners and charm, had taken over by the time I got to the legislature. The Elite staff had been with the Xides family for decades. I loved to eat there. Its "Seafood Mélange of Trout Almondine and Shrimp Athenean combine to give the Elite's most famous dish served with rice and lemon butter caper sauce," quoting from the menu, is still among the best meals I've ever eaten.

Governor Patterson had frequented the Elite since he was in law school at the University of Alabama and was a regular there while he was attorney general.

During the 1940s through the 1960s, drinking alcoholic beverages was not as accepted in Alabama as it is today. Many counties were "dry." It was especially taboo for a public official to be seen out in public drinking whiskey and certainly not martinis and sophisticated scotches. Still, a good many did partake. The Elite was glad to serve their patrons the exquisite and expensive libations. Nine times out of ten, a lobbyist was picking up the bill—in fact, they kept a monthly tab at the Elite.

Beside the politicians, many of the sophisticated, social elite of Montgomery frequented the Elite. A good many of the regular patrons were older ladies of Montgomery. They also liked their cocktails. To cover for its discreet customers, the Elite served its alcoholic concoctions in coffee and tea cups. Therefore, when a little old lady from the Methodist Church asked her gin rummy buddy to go to lunch after church, they winked at each other and knew they would have a delightful Sunday afternoon sipping "tea" or "coffee" at the Elite. They would be sipping along with most of the prominent politicians in the state. Of course, it was then illegal to sell or serve alcohol on Sunday in Alabama (in some places, it still is).

When John Patterson became governor, he named Ed Azar, a straight-laced, teetotaling Montgomery lawyer, as head of the Alabama Alcoholic Beverage Control Board.

One day early in Governor Patterson's administration, he got a call from Mr. Pete Xides. Old Mr. Xides told the governor he had a major problem and that he had to see him. He said the matter was urgent and very important.

Governor Patterson told Mr. Xides to come on up to the governor's office. Mr. Xides wasted no time scurrying up to the Capitol; it only took a minute because the Elite was just eight blocks down the street. He first apologized for having to bother the governor and thanked him for seeing him, especially on such short notice. However, Mr. Azar and the ABC Board had raided his famous restaurant and told Mr. Xides that he would have to cease serving alcohol on Sunday even if he did serve it in coffee or tea cups. Mr. Xides pointed out that the governor had been sipping tea on Sundays at the Elite for decades (including while he was the state's top prosecutor, though Mr. Xides might have been too polite to mention that) and in fact had even been sipping there the previous Sunday. Governor Patterson pondered all that and told Mr. Xides that he "would hate for such a tradition to end in Alabama." He promised the old Greek that he would do what he could to take care of the matter.

The Governor then had a long talk with his ABC Board director. Azar was feisty about it, but he ultimately agreed that his boss, the Governor, had the last say. The Elite continued to serve coffee and tea on Sunday. It was quite a political institution in Alabama and is sorely missed.

Supreme Court Hearing over the Page's Paycheck

Alabama Supreme Court Justice Jim Main has a great story that involves Governor Patterson and ends up at the Elite. It dates back to his experience as a boy when he was a Senate page.

Jim grew up in Union Springs, Alabama. He spent much of his childhood days in his daddy's drugstore on Main Street. Jim followed in his daddy's footsteps and went to Auburn and got his pharmacy degree. However, he later earned a law degree from the University of Alabama.

He has enjoyed a distinguished career as a lawyer in Anniston and Montgomery. He became the State Finance Director in Bob Riley's administration, and then Riley appointed him to the Alabama Court of Criminal Appeals and then to the Alabama Supreme Court.

In the late 1950s during Governor John Patterson's tenure, the executive branch enjoyed a collegial relationship with the members of the other two branches of state government. During these years the chief justice of the Supreme Court, Ed Livingston, and the lieutenant governor, Albert Boutwell, were contemporaries and social friends of Governor Patterson. Also on this roster of friends and colleagues was the influential and colorful State Senator L. K. "Snag" Andrews of Union Springs.

However, Main's story starts in the second Folsom administration, when he was introduced to the Montgomery political world as a page for State Representative Bryant McLendon of Union Springs. The responsibility of a page was to run errands for the legislators. The privilege was access to the actual floor of the legislative body. The benefit was to witness history as it was evolving. In addition to the responsibility, privilege, and the benefit, a page was paid a small sum of money.

For Main, the experience of twice a week "skipping" school to go to Montgomery with Representative Bryant was indeed a treat and a learning experience in Alabama politics.

A few years later, he had the opportunity to serve as a page for Senator Andrews, who was indeed, Main said, one of the most colorful and charming Southern gentlemen he ever knew. A typical Andrews display of Southern charm occurred when camellias were in bloom. Andrews would present a fellow senator with a camellia bloom with a personalized salutation such as, "I saw this camellia from my breakfast table this morning and thought of your beautiful wife's pink cheeks," etc. This ritual was repeated at each legislative session, and no one seemed to notice that the other senators also had camellia blooms.

During Main's time as a Senate page, there were filibusters that lasted all day and night, wonderful meals in fancy places with powerful people, and the opportunity to hear many interesting conversations. However, he recalls that his most exciting experience was an incident with his page pay check.

Over lunch break one day, Senator Andrews, Lieutenant Governor Boutwell, and Main were walking from the legislative end of the Capitol to the governor's office on the opposite end to take Governor Patterson to lunch. As they walked, Senator Andrews spied Main's check and quickly took it into his possession. He said this would reimburse him for chauffeuring Main on trips from Union Springs to Montgomery.

When they arrived at the governor's office, Boutwell explained to Patterson that they had a serious case that needed resolving—whether Andrews was legally entitled to keep Main's check. So the four of them piled into Patterson's car and drove one block down Dexter Avenue to the Supreme Court Building. (How was Main to know Patterson, Boutwell, and Andrews were going to pick up Chief Justice Livingston for lunch?)

When they arrived at the Supreme Court, the party trooped into the chief justice's office and Lieutenant Governor Boutwell explained the need for a special trial on the "serious" case concerning Main's page check and Senator Andrews's levy on it. The delegation promptly retired to the Supreme Court's main courtroom for the trial.

Governor Patterson represented Senator Andrews and Lieutenant Governor Boutwell represented Main. The hearing lasted for only a few minutes before Chief Justice Livingston ruled from the bench that 1) Senator Andrews had to return Main's check; 2) Senator Andrews had to let Main continue as a page for another term; and 3) Senator Andrews, in satisfaction of court costs, must pay for the group's lunch at the Elite.

The governor, lieutenant governor, chief justice, a powerful state senator, and a senate page then piled into the car and went to lunch at the Elite.

Where else but in Alabama in the 1950s could a young boy have such an experience?

AT THIS WRITING IN early 2015, Governor Patterson was still alive and in good health at age 93. He lives and raises goats on the same land he was born and raised on in Goldville, Tallapoosa County.

3

George Wallace

When George Wallace was born in rural Alabama in 1919, he was destined to become the greatest politician in Alabama history. He went on to become the king of Alabama politics and the longest-serving governor in Alabama history.

Wallace loved politics. Even as a child he used to listen to radio broadcasts of Huey Long, the Louisiana demagogue known as the "Kingfish."

As a boy growing up, he also heard stories about Augustin G. Clayton of Georgia, a secessionist of the 1800s. He was an advocate of "states rights." The town of Clayton, the seat of Barbour County, was named after him. Wallace would later trumpet Clayton's states' rights theories in presidential forays throughout the country.

Over the years I've often heard the same story from old timers, I would ask them, "Do you remember the Depression?" They would reply, "Yeah, I do, do you know you couldn't tell any difference, we were poor before the Depression and we were poor during." Indeed, Southerners lived off the land. They grew their own crops, had very little disposable money, and didn't own stocks.

Everybody was poor, but very few Southerners were jumping out of tall buildings. They were hard-working and happy. Their favorite pastime was listening to the Grand Ole Opry on Saturday night and to politicians.

The South had Huey Long, Gene Talmadge, and Theodore Bilbo. George Wallace grew up in this world. He was about 10 years old when the Great Depression set in. By 10 his favorite pastime and passion in life was politics. It would remain with him for life.

Actually Wallace was better off financially than most rural Alabamians of that era. His family roots on both sides went back in Barbour County. His daddy owned some land and farmed, and his granddaddy, G. O. Wallace, was a country doctor. Many a doctor in rural Alabama would not be paid in money, but folks would give them chickens and vegetables for their service. Therefore, Wallace's grandfather being a doctor assured young Wallace that he would not starve even if he was poor.

Wallace had a typical childhood in southeast Alabama. He grew up swimming in the Pea River in cutoff overalls. He picked blackberries and picked up pecans and sold them on "halves." He also picked cotton.

His love for politics emerged early. At age 13 he got involved in his first political race. He campaigned for Fred Gibson for secretary of state. He knocked on every door in Clio for Gibson. His man lost statewide but carried Clio overwhelmingly.

Wallace then became a page in the legislature. Chauncey Sparks was governor and was from Barbour County. He helped Wallace get his first page appointment.

By this time George knew politics was his life. He was determined that he was going to be governor one day.

Wallace was always a fighter. At 15 he was a champion bantamweight Golden Gloves boxer, beating an 18-year-old in the title fight in Montgomery. He won, but while he was walking in downtown Montgomery after the fight, a policeman stopped him and questioned him because his face was such a mess that he thought someone needed to be arrested. George won the Alabama Bantamweight Boxing Championship. At Barbour County High School he was quarterback of the football team and was also elected senior class president.

Like most aspiring Alabama politicos of his era, he went to the University of Alabama. When George arrived, he had only a suit of clothes on his back and a cardboard suitcase in his hand. He had been in Tuscaloosa only two months when his father died and the mortgage holders foreclosed on all his mother's farm property except the family home in Clio. Wallace waited on tables, drove a taxi, and worked as a clerk. He was also captain of the freshman baseball team, captain of the boxing team, and president of the Spirit Committee.

When he graduated, he stayed in Tuscaloosa and went right on to law school. When Wallace finished law school in 1942, he was so broke he sold all the clothes he could spare to get $4.50 to eat on until he found a job. The only job he could find was driving a dump truck for the State Highway Department in Tuscaloosa and worked 11 and a half hours a day for 30 cents an hour.

It was at this time that George met his future wife. George and Lurleen married in May 1943. He met and married her within nine months. She was 15 when they met, had just graduated early from Tuscaloosa County High School, had finished a business school course, and was working as a clerk behind the cosmetics counter at the Kresge's Five and Dime store in Tuscaloosa. She was a thin, pretty girl, the daughter of a shipyard worker.

Wallace was 23 when they met, recently graduated from law school but still lingering in Tuscaloosa and driving a dump truck for the state while he awaited induction into the army.

"CALLING GEORGE WALLACE . . ."

After Wallace got out of the Army, he went straight to Montgomery to ask Governor Chauncey Sparks to help him find a job. George was put on as an assistant attorney general and became close friends with the governor. His stay in Montgomery was shortlived as he had an eye on politics. He took a three-month leave in 1946 and went home to Barbour County to run for the legislature. He beat two prominent opponents.

While the legislature was meeting, George and Lurleen lived in a boarding house in Montgomery. There were mostly railroad men living there at that time. They called George the "Little Fighter" because of his boxing prowess when he was a youngster and his progress as a young legislator.

Wallace was already canny about politics. He always knew he would run for governor. In fact, he had been running for the job all of his life, every waking moment. Like most aspiring gubernatorial candidates, Wallace was not universally known when he started his first run for governor, but he knew how important name identification was. Therefore, he started early building on his name identification.

After his first legislative session, George opened a law office in Clayton and moved his family to an upstairs apartment over the law office. George would then stay at the old Exchange Hotel in downtown Montgomery during the legislative sessions. This was the home to most state legislators and lobbyists in that day. It was a hotbed of politics and many a political deal was consummated on the premises. Wallace used to pay the bellhop a tip every day to walk through the lobby and sing out loudly, "George Wallace, George Wallace, a phone call for George Wallace, calling George Wallace."

Wallace would use this same gimmick at the University of Alabama football games in the Fall. He would get the PA announcer to call out his name, "Calling George Wallace."

He ran for governor in 1958 and lost to John Patterson. He was elected governor in 1962, 1970, 1974, and 1982, and his wife Lurleen was elected in 1966 as his stand-in. By the time he bid his political adieu in 1986, he was arguably the best-known person in Alabama. A poll probably would have indicated that at least 95 percent of all Alabamians knew who George Wallace was. This is a precious commodity in politics. People generally have to know who you are before they will vote for you. By the end of his long tenure most Alabamians were in one of two groups, they either loved Wallace or they hated Wallace. There was no middle ground, but they certainly knew who he was. Most aspiring gubernatorial candidates would love to have even a fourth of Wallace's name identification. Most of them find out in a hurry that they are known by few voters when they start out. They think they are known but they aren't. A benchmark poll usually shocks them with their abysmal anonymity.

". . . Calling George Wallace . . ." He made sure from early on that he would never be anonymous to the voters.

WALLACE AND BIG JIM

During George's five years as a state representative he achieved quite a bit. One of the things he was proudest of was the Wallace Act which gave tax breaks to out-of-state industries if they would move to Alabama. George had the help of Governor Jim Folsom to get the act passed, allowing cities and counties to finance new industry with municipal bonds. It got out-of-state industries interested in coming to Alabama because it exempted them from paying taxes for 40 years. He was also proud of the Wallace Trade School Act which created five trade schools in the state.

George began making a national name for himself before he got out of the legislature. At the Democratic National Convention in 1948 he did not walk out of the Convention with the Dixiecrats who left and formed their own party. George was a loyalist who stayed behind and grabbed the chance to nominate a Southerner for president, Senator Richard Russell of Georgia. Wallace leaped up again to nominate Russell for vice president.

George and Big Jim Folsom formed a mutual bond while Big Jim was Governor and Wallace a young legislator. George got Big Jim to name him to the board of trustees of the all-black Tuskegee Institute.

George and Big Jim did not always agree. During the years when George was seeing which way the political wind was blowing on state's rights and civil rights, Big Jim was preaching equal rights for blacks and shaking hands with blacks. That was taboo and usually the kiss of death for any Southern white politician except Big Jim. Big Jim also made national headlines when he invited New York Representative Adam Clayton Powell, one of three African Americans serving in Congress at that time, to come by the Governor's Mansion for a drink while Powell was in Montgomery to give a speech at what was then Alabama State College. The joke that circulated from this occasion was that it wouldn't have caused such a fuss if Folsom and Powell had drunk bourbon, but drinking Scotch at the governor's mansion was looked on as uppity.

In 1952 Wallace left the legislature and won the office of circuit judge in Barbour County. With a growing family, he realized he had to make a living.

In 1954 Big Jim called in the favors George owed him for the Tuskegee appointment and for his support of the Trade School bill and the Wallace Act. He asked George to be his south Alabama campaign manager. With Wallace's help, Big Jim beat six opponents without a runoff.

Wallace's First Run for Governor

George, meanwhile, was going his own route. He had made enough of a name for himself that when the National Democratic Convention rolled around in 1956, Mississippi Governor J. P. Coleman named him chairman of the Southern delegation on the platform committee. That gave George a chance to make a shambles of the Democrats' civil rights platform position. The result was, as one NAACP leader put it, "The civil rights plank is weak as a wet splinter."

In 1958, the Fighting Little Judge was running for Governor.

Wallace knew instinctively how to feel the pulse of the Alabama electorate. He would say, "If you want to find out who is going to win, go to the barber shops and little country stores, that's the folks you gotta ask."

That is how he knew Jimmy Faulkner of Bay Minette was not the man he had to beat in 1958, it was John Patterson. Most people thought Faulkner was the front-runner, that he was a shoo-in because he was tall and good-looking and a smooth talker. Most folks thought he was going to be the next governor. However, time and time again in the small towns when George told the folks he was Judge Wallace and he was running for governor, the folks would say to him, "How about this fellow John Patterson? What about the man whose daddy got shot?"

John Patterson's father, Albert Patterson, had won the Democratic nomination for state attorney general in 1954. Seventeen days later he was murdered by gangsters in Phenix City. After his daddy's murder, John Patterson was named in his place as the Democratic nominee. After four years as attorney general, Patterson was running for governor and folks still voted for him out of sympathy because the Phenix City mafia had murdered his daddy.

Whether folks would tell George that they were voting for Patterson or for Faulkner, George would say, "If your man doesn't get in the runoff, I'd appreciate it if you'd make me your second choice." However, George knew he was in for trouble from Patterson on election day. "I could possibly get elected if not for his daddy getting shot," George said. "It's like an airplane with everything going fine; suddenly it hits a covey of birds and the plane goes down."

Primaries were in May. It got hot in May so George always tried to stay in north Alabama as much as he could late in the campaign, where the mountains cooled down the temperature. George just naturally knew where he should spend his time. "We should spend more time in DeKalb County, they have all the white votes there," said George. When he was running against Patterson who was from Phenix City, he would go there just to say he had been there. But George would say, "Let's don't spend much time in Phenix City. We got all the votes we're going to get there, whether we go there or not."

During that campaign, George told folks in speeches he was 39 years old, but he was only 38. One day he was asked why he told people he was 39 when he was only 38. He replied that people think you're old enough to be governor in your forties but not in your thirties. "It sounds like I'm old enough if I tell folks I'm 39 and too young if I say 38."

That may have been a sound strategy, but in 1958 it did not give Wallace the edge. He was two years older than Patterson, but Patterson defeated him. This would be George Wallace's only political defeat in an Alabama election, and Wallace himself, as well as commentators and historians, believed the defeat was because Patterson was perceived as the more segregationist candidate. After finishing second, Wallace famously vowed that he would never be "out-segged" again.

Then, having run his "get acquainted" campaign in 1958, he immediately began his campaign for 1962.

The Political Animal

His life was politics 24 hours a day. He was consumed by it. He didn't care what he ate—he had rather shake hands than eat. He didn't care whether he had a dime in the bank or whether he had a roof over his head, his every thought was the next election.

He started running in 1946 and was elected to the state legislature. He was reelected in 1950 and then ran for circuit judge in 1952. He left his judgeship to run for governor in 1958. He lost but never stopped running. He ran every day for four years. He became governor in 1962 and ran for something every two years. He ran for governor in 1962, then president in 1964, then ran his wife in for governor in 1966 since the Alabama Constitution precluded him from succeeding himself. He ran for president again in 1968, then ran for and was elected governor in 1970; then ran for president again in 1972. He was shot and almost died, but it didn't stop him from running for governor and getting elected again in 1974. When he left office in 1978, he waited four years and came back and was elected again in 1982.

That four-year absence from office almost killed him.

Like Bear Bryant, Wallace didn't live long after he retired. Both he and Bryant loved their callings, and they were indeed called or sent down by God for their roles. God decided one day that he was going to make the greatest college football coach in history and send him to Alabama and he sent Bear Bryant. Then he decided he was going to create the greatest Southern politician and he made George Wallace. He gave both the talent but also the love and desire to succeed at their callings. They were focused on their love and everything else was secondary.

The word "political animal" was coined with George Wallace in mind. When you couple this desire with a unique God-given ability to campaign, you have the ingredients for the ultimate political animal. One of the greatest God-given talents that any politician can ever have is the ability to remember names. Wallace was as remarkable at this as any man who ever lived. Many who knew him can tell amazing stories about how unbelievable he was at remembering people and calling them by their name. The best one I ever heard was one by a Geneva County commissioner who was going to see the governor about getting a road completed. The commissioner on the spur of the moment as he was leaving asked his best friend if he wanted to ride with him to see the governor. The friend said he would like to see the governor, so they took off to Montgomery. On the way the commissioner asked his friend if he knew the governor. His friend said, "Not really but I've shook hands with him." This was in 1963, and Wallace was in the first year of his first term.

Back then if you ran for governor it wasn't like it is today when you simply get on TV to campaign—there was no TV and the candidate shook hands 12–16 hours a day and made 12 strong speeches and met thousands of people. Wallace had done this in 1958 when he ran second to Patterson and again in 1962 when he won against Big Jim Folsom and Ryan DeGraffenreid. There is no telling how many people Wallace had met and shaken hands with in these two statewide campaigns.

The two men arrived at the governor's office. Wallace greeted the commissioner by name and asked about his wife by name. The commissioner was impressed by Wallace remembering his wife's name, but it would have been possible for Wallace to have been prepped by an aide on the commissioner and his wife in advance of the appointment. However, can you imagine the shock on the faces of these two men when Wallace looked at the friend of the commissioner—remember that Wallace had no idea that the friend was coming—and as the commissioner started to introduce his friend to Wallace, Wallace stopped him short and said, "I know Bill. I met him at a fish fry in Samson in 1958 when I ran for governor the first time. Bill, how's your wife, Susie?"

Daddy's Still Dead

However, Wallace was evidently better at remembering adults than children. Maybe it was because the children couldn't vote.

A story often told on Wallace occurred in his first run for governor. After a speech, Wallace was speaking to folks and a little boy came up to Wallace to shake his hand. Wallace perfunctorily said to the little boy, "How's your daddy?" The boy responded, "My daddy's dead." Wallace said, "I'm sorry." Then he went on visiting with the crowd and shaking hands. The little boy meandered on and later inadvertently bumped into Wallace again. Wallace looked at the boy and asked him, "How's your daddy?" The little boy responded, "He's still dead."

He'll Pay You

Wallace really didn't care that much about the power or trappings of the office, he just wanted to run. He thrived on shaking hands and getting votes. He didn't care about what time it was or what he had to eat or whether he had anything to eat. In short, he didn't care about making any money. He didn't care if he had a dime to his name. He was oblivious to money. There was never any hint of scandal or corruption around George Wallace himself—his cronies were another story—because he didn't care about money. He surely didn't want to hurt his political career by stealing, and he was convinced that voters liked you better if you were poor.

His cavalier attitude toward money caused him to charge into any campaign, whether gubernatorial or presidential, without regard as to how to pay for the effort. He just figured the money would show up.

McDowell Lee, the longtime secretary of the Alabama senate, told a story that illustrates Wallace's disregard for the particulars of campaign finance. During one of Wallace's early campaigns for governor, he and the other major candidate both employed the help of famous Grand Ole Opry stars to draw and entertain crowds for them. A few weeks earlier, Wallace had Minnie Pearl with him for a big rally in Ozark and Dothan. The good folks in Troy were having a big Chamber event on the Square and inviting gubernatorial candidates to come. They told Wallace they knew he could bring Minnie Pearl to their event. Wallace called Minnie Pearl's husband, who was her agent, and asked if they were available. By chance, they were open for that one night. Wallace told them he would pay to fly them in. Minnie Pearl came and performed and then the time came for them to get paid. The bill was $5,000, a pretty good sum in those days.

Wallace motioned toward Lee and said, "He'll pay you." Lee had to go to a Troy bank and have the $5,000 taken out of his family's farm account at their bank in Clio and wired to him to pay the entertainer.

Wallace never gave it another thought or seemed the least bit concerned about how Minnie Pearl was going to get paid. I imagine McDowell steered clear of more Minnie Pearl appearances during that campaign.

Haleyville Votes Count Just the Same

Wallace often traveled with his main crony, Oscar Harper, in his early campaigns. Every now and then there wouldn't be a car for him to ride in and he had to ride in Harper's new Cadillac. Wallace was as fidgety in that Cadillac as a young'un dressed in fancy duds sitting through a two-hour sermon on a hot day.

Every time they stopped at a country store or a service station George would make a point of getting out and walking around the car, looking at it.

When he had everybody's attention he'd say, "That's not my car, that's his car." Then he'd shake his head and say, "Now I don't even know what kind of car that is. I got an old '54 Ford at home, all wore out, tires all wore out, and this man was nice enough to pick me up and ride me around. This is a nice car. But it isn't my car."

George was always the poor man's governor.

Mountain Brook is the rich folks' city next to Birmingham.

While talking about who voted for him, Wallace said, I'll tell you what you do, they're having a mule show in Haleyville Saturday. You go up there with me and you'll see 4,000 or 5,000 people just massed together everywhere and practically everyone of them for me. You'll see Wallace signs on the cars and Wallace signs on the pickup trucks. You'll see Wallace signs on the mules. You know those 4,000 Haleyville votes count just the same as those 4,000 Mountain Brook votes."

Ralph Adams Was Tight with a Dollar

Ralph Adams was one Wallace crony who was as tight with money as Wallace was unconcerned with it. Adams had been one of George's best friends and advisers since their days together as law school roommates at the University of Alabama.

By the time George was governor, Ralph had also made a name for himself. He was a graduate of Birmingham-Southern College and a graduate of the school of law at the University of Alabama. He had taught at the University of Colorado and had been a judge in Tuscaloosa. He had also served as dean and acting dean of the Air Force Law School at the Air University in Montgomery.

George named Ralph to a couple of jobs. He was the attorney for the State Insurance Department and also headed the state's Selective Service system, but he knew Ralph Adams's big love was education.

When the presidency of Troy State College came open, George knew Ralph would do a good job and put Adams in that position shortly after he took office. Ralph Adams ran the university like a business. The only criticism you might hear would be that Adams used his friendship with George to make what is now Troy University into one of the best schools in the state and nation.

When there was state money going for any education project, Ralph made sure that Troy had a piece of the pie. He started numerous branches of Troy on U.S. Air Force bases so that any Alabamian could join the Air Force, get shipped to California, sent to Germany, come back home to the Florida panhandle to Eglin Air Force Base, and never miss a Troy University class.

It would be a unique challenge to find anyone who was more frugal than Ralph Adams.

Ralph would drive a car until the wheels fell off and would keep driving it if he could find someone to put the wheels back on.

One time Ralph was driving Oscar Harper and Billy Watson to the Governor's Mansion on a pitch-black night in a pouring rain. Billy got a lap full of water because the window wouldn't roll up all the way. Billy asked Adams what kind of car he was driving since they were getting more water inside than outside.

Another time, Ralph had his tie on backwards. When someone mentioned it to him, he replied, "I know. It's my only tie and the other side's dirty." George's security people used to try to loan Adams shaving cream when he would go on a trip with George because he never brought any. He always said no thanks, he would just use the motel's soap.

Frank Long was the middle man between Ralph and millionaire oilman Bart Chamberlain Jr. when the latter donated his big salt-water fishing boat to Troy. Frank knew that Bart needed a tax write-off and Ralph knew that Troy needed a way to keep the legislators happy so they would keep giving Troy money. Taking them deep-sea fishing was a good way to keep them happy.

After the papers were signed giving Troy University a $100,000 fishing boat, Ralph suggested that they all have lunch. They did. Frank and Bart were naturally thinking Troy University would pick up the lunch tab. Sure enough at the end of the lunch, Ralph reached for the checks. "I don't want you fellows buying my lunch," he said. "I'll pay my own." He then took his check out of the stack and returned the other checks to Frank and Bart.

George always depended a lot on Ralph. When Oscar asked George to help a lawyer get appointed as U.S. attorney in Montgomery, George told him the best way was to call Ralph and get him to call U.S. Senator Jim Allen and put in a good word for the lawyer. Senators nominate U.S. attorneys and Ralph's daughter, Kelly, was married to Jim Allen Jr. The lawyer got the appointment because a lot of folks wanted him to be named and George Wallace was one of them.

Ralph, Charles "Mister" Smith III, and Jack Rainer Sr. started Bankers Credit Life Insurance Company. George didn't own any stock. Jack joked about the board meetings that Ralph would just sit there quietly, acting like he was in a daze, until something would come up about money. Ralph would then jump up and say, "What's that? What's that? Let's go over that again."

Ralph kept as tight a rein on Troy University's pocketbook as he did on his own. George used to tease him about the president of a university not even having air conditioning in his car (a bare-bones Chevrolet). The university tried about once a year to buy Ralph a new car and he wouldn't take it, which George knew. After George had griped about Ralph's car not having air conditioning, he was told that it did. "He's got 4-80 air conditioning," Oscar told George. "That's when you roll four windows down and run 80 miles an hour."

A Legislative Genius and Master

George Wallace was definitely a political genius and a master of the legislative process. You might say that he was so successful because he had a lot of experience with being governor and dealing with the legislature. That is true, but it went deeper than that. He worked at it.

During my 16 years in the legislature, he was in a league by himself. My first term was 1982 and Governor Wallace was serving his last term. He treated us legislators like kings. It didn't matter who was in his office, if you were a member of the legislature and you needed to see the Governor about something for your district, he would drop everything and usher you into his office and do anything he could to address your concern or district needs. One day I went down unannounced without an appointment and his secretary told him I was outside. The next thing I knew the door opened and Wallace told me to come in. He had about six Japanese diplomats in his office who were prospective industrial prospects. He asked if I wanted to ask them to leave so we could meet privately. I said, "Governor, no, that's not necessary, I'll be glad to come back." He said, "Okay," but insisted on my staying while they visited. I sat down and he began telling the poor Japanese fellows that I had been a page when I was a little boy and he was in his first term as governor and that now I was his representative since I represented his hometown of Clayton, and he told them who he was kin to in my county and who I was kin to in south Alabama. I'm sure they were amused. Who couldn't help but vote with a guy who gave a lowly member of the House that kind of attention and deference?

At other times he would call my home at supper time and talk for about 30 minutes about a certain bill he was interested in. He would continue to talk long after I had already told him that I would vote with him on his issue. He would tell me to put my two daughters on the phone; they were little at the time, but in his uncanny ability to remember names, he would call them by name and say, "Steve, let me talk to Ginny and let me say hello to little Allyson." He was amazing. He loved to talk on the phone.

He would also constantly have legislators out to the Governor's Mansion for supper. We would eat supper with the governor more than with the lobbyists. He knew your district, your family and relatives, what committee you served on, which program and roads you were interested in. The only thing he didn't know is what time you went to bed, because might call you at six at suppertime or he might call you at 11 when you were asleep.

He knew how to manipulate the legislature better than anyone. One day he had a group of legislators in his office trying to get them to vote with him. His secretary interrupted him to tell him Vice President Mondale was on the phone. The legislators sat quietly while George talked to the vice president for a few minutes and took care of whatever business they had.

Mondale hung up when they got finished. However, George never let on that Mondale had hung up. He pretended to listen a while longer and said, "Look, Mr. Vice President, I'd like to talk to you some more, but I've got a group of representatives and senators in here and I really don't have time."

All the legislators started whispering, "No, Governor, don't do that. Don't hang up on the Vice President. We can wait."

But George just kept talking, "I really appreciate your asking for my help, Mr. Vice President," he said, "but I'm hanging up now. I've got enough problems here in the state of Alabama. I just can't solve the world's problems for you. I've got to talk to these legislators about a problem we've got in the legislature."

He then hung up the phone.

By that time, those legislators were so impressed at how they were more important than the vice president of the United States that George could have gotten anything he wanted from them.

And he did.

The Consummate Politician

As the ultimate politician, Wallace was not above stretching the truth when it came to endearing himself to people based on their locales.

One slow day my legislative seatmate, Seth Hammett, and I were sitting at our desks and talking politics. Wallace would periodically call me and Seth down to his office to simply talk politics. Seth and I were discussing that ritual and I mentioned to Seth, "You know, Wallace often tells me that he would always kick off his campaigns for governor in my home county of Pike."

A smile came across Seth's face and he said, "Steve, he told me that he always begins his campaigns in my home county, Covington."

George Wallace Loved Loyalty

In 1982, most pundits had written him off as he rode into the sunset at the end of his unprecedented third term. However, Wallace would surprise them all and win a fourth and final term in 1982. The irony was that he won that last election only because of strong support from Alabama's black voters. He had a tough Democratic primary battle with Lieutenant Governor George McMillan. Earlier in the year Wallace had gone in his wheelchair to the historic black Dexter Avenue King Memorial Baptist Church in Montgomery and asked for forgiveness from the African American community for his past racism. His conversion and contrition appeared sincere. The black community responded with not only forgiveness but they took a page from the Biblical parable of the prodigal son, rewarded him with their votes, and elected him their governor. Wallace showed his appreciation. He was very loyal to the African American community during that last term, 1982–1986.

Wallace himself respected and appreciated political loyalty.

In 1982 I was elected to my first term in the legislature. My district included Wallace's hometown of Clayton in Barbour County.

I had grown up paging in the Alabama legislature. I had gotten to know

Wallace when he was governor most of that time. He loved to remind me that he had been a page like me when he was a teenager. He had paged for Governor Chauncey Sparks of Barbour County.

It amused him that I—now a grown 30-year-old man rather than a page—had just been elected as his representative.

After he defeated McMillan in the Democratic primary, his election in the fall was assured. Being the Democratic nominee was still a lock for election in Alabama.

He had a viable Republican opponent in Montgomery Mayor Emory Folmar, who had staked out a position as a racist like Wallace had earlier. However, a rich man's racist cannot beat a poor man's racist. I knew the election would not be close.

Meanwhile, a contentious race was brewing for Speaker of the House.

The very conservative Speaker of the House, Joe McCorquodale of Clarke County, was retiring after 12 years. His chief lieutenant was his fellow Black Belt conservative, Rick Manley from Demopolis. Manley was a lawyer and skilled parliamentarian. He was the heir apparent, and the conservative groups led by the Farm Bureau were backing Manley.

At the same time, the Alabama Education Association was feeling its political oats. AEA Executive Secretary Paul Hubbert had built a reputation as the strongest lobbyist on Goat Hill. He had elected and developed a Tuscaloosa teacher/principal named Roy Johnson. He had trained Johnson and made him a legislative leader.

The AEA wanted Roy Johnson to be Speaker. The gigantic battle was on between the two powerful lobbying groups, AEA and Farm Bureau. They were organizing and garnering votes with a devout passion.

Both sides had about 35 votes lined up in the 105-member House and 35 of us remained uncommitted. We were the battleground. I told both sides I was uncommitted—both had endorsed me.

Unbeknownst to them I was committed. I had grown up in the legislature and I knew that the governor had always been involved in electing his man as Speaker. In addition, I knew George Wallace and I knew he was not going to relinquish this power easily. I also knew the governor had a lot of power and patronage. I also was cognizant of the fact that I was going to be Wallace's representative and I knew how much he appreciated loyalty.

I went to Wallace and committed to him early that I was for his choice for Speaker. His smile showed his appreciation and affection for my commitment. He said, "You know, Steve, I've got this race with Emory Folmar before we can get to that, but I appreciate your commitment and we will get with you after the election."

The battle for Speaker raged on. I was bombarded daily.

Wallace disposed of Folmar in the general election. The organizational session was looming with the election of the Speaker first on the agenda. With Wallace's aura and experience, it should have been obvious to both sides that he would be a major player in the Speaker race.

About a week before the vote, my phone rang about midnight, and Governor Wallace said, "Steve, you are one of the first legislators we are calling. Hold on a second, I want you to talk to somebody." He handed the phone to longtime Cullman Representative Tom Drake. Drake was said to be so loyal to Wallace that if Wallace asked him to jump off the top of the Capitol, Drake would have only asked him what time he was supposed to jump.

Drake said, "I am going to be the governor's choice for Speaker. Are you with me?" I said, "Mr. Drake, I don't know you, but if you are the governor's choice, I'm with you." Drake won.

This commitment to Governor Wallace did help me immensely with the Wallace administration. I never had a better relationship with a governor than I did those four years with Wallace. He made me one of his floor leaders and I got just about anything I wanted for my district the entire quadrennium.

We had a warm relationship for the rest of his life. He would call me off the floor to come down to his office to reminisce and talk politics.

HARDBALL WITH "NUDY" COSBY

Of course, Wallace also knew how to play hardball with those who were less enthusiastic about his legislation. He knew how to stroke you and he knew how to punish you.

I will share with you a somewhat funny story about an encounter I witnessed as a freshman legislator. It was about 1983 and Wallace was in his last term as governor. Wallace was beginning to get up in age and as was the case with a lot of men his age who had fought in World War II, his hearing had diminished due to excessive exposure to loud noises. Wallace had been particularly hard hit because he helped load the planes for his entire service career. His hearing had gotten progressively worse over the years. He was basically deaf by this time and you wondered on your visits down to his office if he ever heard a word you said. It really didn't matter much anyway, because he usually did most of the talking. He probably had selective hearing and heard what he wanted to hear.

In early 1983, he and his team decided the state needed more revenue, so he hit the legislators with an avalanche of tax bills which he conveniently called Revenue Enhancement Measures. There was a new tax bill on the calendar every day. He and his lieutenants were monitoring your vote in loyalty with the Wallace Administration.

My best freshman buddy was a car dealer from Talledega named Jim Preuitt. Jim and I had been singled out by Wallace early as his favorite freshmen. I was liked mainly because I was Wallace's home county representative, was young, and he got a kick out of remembering when I was a page about 20 years earlier. Jim had been helping Wallace with his campaign for years. So Jim and I were on the Wallace team. As loyal team members, Jim and I would vote for most of the taxes but some of them we just couldn't go along with. If you weren't voting with the governor, Elvin Stanton and Billy Joe Camp would summon you down to the governor's office for a prayer meeting with the governor. Jim and I wound up there one day for not voting for a tax on gasoline which was earmarked for road building. We were in a group of particularly bad boys who were voting against all of Wallace's taxes. Wallace looked over at us and seemed puzzled by our presence as we were his boys and he assumed we were always with him so he simply dismissed us as being down there by mistake or to give encouragement to some of the renegades. He ignored us so Jim and I settled into a corner out of his sight and sat back to watch his approach to our disobedient colleagues who were not on board for the tax-a-day plan Wallace was promoting. He zeroed in on a well-liked House member from Selma named W. F. "Noopie" Cosby. Noopie had acquired his nickname early in life and I'm not sure that anyone in Selma or anywhere else knew his given name. I had known Noopie since our days at the University of Alabama and thought his parents had named him that.

Wallace, besides being deaf had also gotten prematurely senile because of the tremendous amount of pain killers he had to take every day to even survive because of the devastating gunshot wounds to his body ten years earlier. It was a miracle he had survived, but he had to take a lot of medication to get through the day. He was particularly hazy this day and he called Noopie "Nudy." He must have called him Nudy 20 times. Jim and I began laughing so hard we started crying. It was the most humorous dialogue I ever recall. Wallace said, "Nudy, you need you a road program. Nudy, when I was a legislator I had a road program for Barbour County. Nudy, you need a road program for Dallas County, and Nudy, we need these taxes for our road programs. So, Nudy, here's the way it works here, Nudy, if you vote for my taxes your road program will be my road program and Nudy, if you don't vote for my taxes you won't have a road program and your road program will go to Barbour County. You understand this program, Nudy?"

The whole time Wallace was cajoling poor Noopie about his needing a road program for Dallas County, he would point to me sitting over in the corner with Jim Preuitt and say, "Now, Steve Flowers doesn't need a road program. He will have a road program because he represents Barbour County and believe me Barbour County will have a road program."

He wasn't just joking. He made sure Barbour County was taken care of when it came to roads or anything else for that matter. My first year in the legislature as Barbour County's representative, I was called up to the Capitol every week for a grant announcement. They would get you a big banner with the city and amount of money your town was getting, take your picture with the banner and replica of a check and send it to your paper. I would be in the *Clayton Record* every week. One week it would be $400,000 for a park for Clio, the next week $350,000 for a sewer system for Clayton. Clayton would get $600,000 the next week for roads. All of this money was federal money and the grants came through ADECA and as governor, Wallace had discretion over where the funds would be spent. A good bit of it was being spent in Barbour County and a poor little powerless representative was getting some of the credit for the grants thanks to Governor Wallace looking after his home folks.

He never forgot his roots in Barbour County. He loved his home county.

Helping the Home Folks in Barbour County

Speaking of the *Clayton Record*, it was run by the venerable Barbour County lady named Mrs. Bertie Parrish. The paper had been owned by her family for awhile before she took over running it. It is now owned and run by the third generation, Rebecca Parrish Beasley. Rebecca is Mrs. Bertie's daughter and also the mayor of Clayton. She is married to Billy Beasley who is a pharmacist and Barbour County's current state senator. He is Jere Beasley's younger brother by five years.

One Sunday after he first began running for president, Wallace was appearing on *Meet the Press*. The sophisticated liberal moderators were trying to belittle Wallace as a Southern demagogue and bumpkin. They snobbishly asked Wallace what newspapers and periodicals he read. Wallace, playing along, said, "My favorite paper is the *Clayton Record*. My favorite writer is Mrs. Bertie Parrish."

Oscar Harper tells a humorous story about Wallace's last days in office in 1978. Wallace was not sure if he would ever be at the trough as governor again. So he wanted one last bite at the apple for good old Barbour County before he left.

Oscar Harper was a principal in Wiregrass Construction Company, which paved a lot of highways in the Wallace years.

George always paid attention to the roads when he was driving around. He knew there was a chance folks would vote for you if you paved their roads and kept them up. He was always particular about Barbour County roads, because that's where he came from.

George once told Ray Bass, the Highway Department director, to put a traffic light at an intersection in Barbour County. Ray said, "Governor, there's not enough traffic to justify putting a traffic light there."

George said, "I know. But the folks who live there have wanted a light for years and they've never voted for me. I want to see if they'll vote for me if I put them a light there."

The highway department put a new traffic signal at the country crossroads. After the next election, George studied the returns from the voting place near the intersection and said, "They didn't vote for me. That traffic light didn't make any difference."

When George was going out of office in 1978, and Fob James was coming in, Dan Turner was highway director. Dan found some "maintenance money" which could be used however the governor wanted.

George had some projects all over the state he had promised folks. But he told the highway director to be sure to pave some roads in Barbour County. It was only 60 days or so until George was going out of office and he wanted those roads paved before another administration decided some other county was more important than Barbour.

AND THEN HELP THEM SOME MORE

To further accentuate how Wallace liked to take care of the home folks, you need only to look around his home county and see where the newest state prisons are located.

There is one in Clayton and one in Clio. Both are in Barbour County, and another is just over the line in Union Springs in Bullock County. Bullock and Barbour are in the same judicial circuit. Wallace was the circuit judge in Bullock and Barbour before being elected governor.

During Wallace's last term as governor, an in-depth comprehensive study detailed the state's long-term prison needs. This study had been in the works for almost a decade. The independent study commissioners brought the prison plan to Wallace. The study called for five new prisons in Alabama. In the proposal, the commissioner suggested that the prisons be located strategically across the state so that the prisoners could be close to their homes. Also suggested was that all five prisons would be close if not adjacent to the urban areas of the state such as Jefferson, Mobile, and Madison since the bulk of the prisoners came from the larger cities.

When Wallace got the presentation, he listened as far as the need for five new prisons. He stopped the commission at that point and said, "That's good. We'll have five new prisons. I know where three of them can go. They can go in Union Springs, Clayton, and Clio."

And, that's where they went.

Should I Help My Enemies?

In recent years there have been numerous political trials in Alabama regarding campaign contributions. The question has revolved around the difference between a bribe and a campaign contribution. This is a gray area, today. During the Wallace era, campaign finance was not scrutinized to the extent that it is currently. In fact it would be ludicrous for zealous prosecutors to seek indictments of public officials of yesterday under the lax standards of that time.

These trials remind me of a story during one of Governor Wallace's early terms as governor. It was a slow day and Wallace was having a news conference on mundane issues when out of the blue, a young, upstart, muckraking reporter asked Wallace, "Why do you give all of the state road building and resurfacing contracts to your political cronies and campaign contributors?" Wallace looked at the young writer quizzically and said, "Who do you think I ought to give them to, my enemies?"

The 1965 Special Succession Session

The legislature meets in regular session every year for three and a half months. An extraordinary session can be called by the governor if he deems there is a dire emergency in the state government. This provision in the Constitution gives the governor inherent advantage in a special session. The official proclamation calling for a special session allows the governor to set out specific matters when calling the session and requires the legislators to address those specific issues.

A large number of special sessions were called in earlier years because the legislature met only every other year. Special sessions were part of the norm during the Wallace years. Wallace realized the importance of isolating and focusing on his issues.

The Alabama legislature has seen many epic legislative battles, but none can approach the level of animosity reached in the 1965 special session called to consider a constitutional amendment permitting Alabama's constitutional officers to succeed themselves. At this time governors could serve only one term and could not succeed themselves. Only two governors since 1901 had served more than one term: Bibb Graves and Big Jim Folsom and each had waited out four years before returning for a second term.

Wallace wanted a second term. Therefore, the momentous and historical September 1965 special session called by Wallace is referred to in Alabama political lore as the Succession Session.

To recap, Wallace had lost to John Patterson in 1958 and vowed that he would never be "out-segged" again. He immediately began his campaign for 1962 and won as a strict segregationist. In his January 1963 inaugural address, he vowed "segregation today, segregation tomorrow, and segregation forever." Several events occurred that year. Wallace's "stand in the school house door" to block integration at the University of Alabama, his support of segregation in Birmingham, Tuskegee, and other places, and his fiery rhetoric against civil rights demonstrators and federal judges made him the leading segregationist politician in America (and it was a crowded field). Wallace's newfound national fame emboldened him to enter Democratic presidential primaries in 1964 in Maryland, Indiana, and Wisconsin. Incumbent Lyndon Johnson won the Democratic nomination, but Republican nominee Barry Goldwater, a states' rights supporter, overwhelmingly carried the five Deep South states where race was the dominant issue. Meanwhile, Wallace had captured the issue and was a folk hero to white segregationists.

With the dawning of 1965, attention began to focus on the 1966 governor's race. Three prominent players were already posed to run. Former state senator Ryan DeGraffenreid, who finished second to Wallace in 1962, Alabama Attorney General Richmond Flowers, and Congressman Carl Elliott were also certain to run. Big Jim Folsom was also a probability. All were more progressive than George Wallace.

Wallace realized that he needed to remain governor or the state would lose ground on segregation. Thus, the special session was called for September 30. Wallace was at the peak of his popularity and enjoyed immense support in the house. His succession bill, House Bill 1, was reported favorably from the rules committee on the second legislative day and passed the house on the third legislative day by a vote of 74–23.

Therefore the fight would be in the senate. The battle that took place in the senate was the most fierce and most bitter witnessed in the old Capitol. Seldom in our history has there been such intense tension and drama.

Throughout the session the numbers remained about the same. Wallace had about 18 loyal senators. His floor leaders needed 21 to invoke cloture on the debate. They never got them. The opposition senators were extremely capable. Most were legislative veterans who knew and used the rules to gain parliamentary advantage. The opponents included Vaughn Hill Robison of Montgomery, Joe Smith of Phenix City, Bob Gilchrist of Hartselle, Larry Dumas of Birmingham, and John Tyson of Mobile. A good many of these senators were loyal to DeGraffenreid. Wallace went into each of their districts and threatened these senators with losing road projects and other pet projects. They all remained steadfast.

Finally, on October 22, 1965, the 14th day of the session, Wallace realized he could not get the 21 votes needed for a constitutional amendment. The state senate thus denied him the opportunity to run for a second successive term, but at a price—no senator who opposed Wallace's legislation was reelected in 1966. Some chose not to run, but each one who sought reelection was overwhelmingly defeated.

Wallace ran his wife Lurleen as his proxy, and she won a landslide victory in 1966.

The Bandwagon Effect

Wallace understood the bandwagon effect. He knew that people like to vote for the winner. He would often tell me the he would rather have someone say that he was going to win rather than say that they were going to vote for him. He continued, "If they hear someone say they're going to vote for me, they figure they might have a selfish motive, but to say 'he's going to win' invites everyone to get on the train to victory and vote for the winner." Some country people would describe it as, "I don't want to lose my vote voting for so-and-so, he can't win."

Wallace used a unique political practice to exploit the bandwagon effect. He would employ what used to be called runners. These well-trained runners would only number a handful of men because they had to be perfect for the job. They had to be believable and genuine and look the part. These men would circulate throughout the state during an election year. They might pose as a traveling salesman. The state was full of country stores in those days. These country stores were where politics was talked. They were at the country branch heads. They were the grapevine for the rural community. The barber shops in the county seats were the other stage. Wallace himself would campaign in the barber shops.

Wallace's man would stop at a country store in north Alabama several times, first to talk about the weather and the crops. On his next stop he would talk about football. Finally, after he had won the confidence of the locals in the country store, that he was indeed a wise and well-traveled sage of Alabama, he would go into politics. Folks would ask their well-traveled friend how the governor's race looked throughout the state. He would look them in the eye and say, "It ain't no race, George Wallace is going to clean up. He's going to get all the votes in south Alabama." The north Alabamians would want to get on the bandwagon.

Another Wallace runner would do the same thing in south Alabama. He would say that Wallace is going to get all the votes in north Alabama.

SNOWBIRDS

On an early fall day in Wallace's last term, I was a 31-year-old freshman legislator. Wallace was in his last term. Since I was his home representative and supported him in the legislature, he had made me a floor leader and seemed to like me. As I mentioned earlier, he had known me since I was 12 years old and a page in the legislature during his first term as governor. My relationship gave me access to him. So on this fall day I ambled down to the governor's office one floor down from the house chamber in the Capitol. I walked into the office and the secretary whisked me back to his office pretty quickly. They said he would love to visit with me as he was not having a good day with his health, and would like to reminisce with me about his younger days and first term. It would cheer him up.

He seemed to be in good spirits when I went in, and he had his ever present cigar in the corner of his mouth. Wallace's health had deteriorated badly from the bullet wounds he had endured and his hearing was really bad. My mission that day was to get $10,000 out of his discretionary fund for a Pioneer Museum for my district. He controlled all of the extra pork money we legislators appropriated. So we had to see the governor for our pet-project money. I knew we had put money into the tourism budget for projects like my museum. After listening to his story about politics and earlier days, I got down to business. He led in by asking, "Steve, what did you want today?" I had to shout so Wallace could hear and began by selling the fact that my Pioneer Museum was located on a well-traveled four-lane highway which was a corridor and travel route for Northerners traveling to the Gulf Coast beaches for their winter escape, and that they would stop at our museum and spend tourist money in Alabama.

Therefore, $10,000 of tourism funds for my museum was wise stewardship of Alabama taxpayer money. Wallace still seemed like he didn't hear me well, so I almost shouted that we were catching the snowbirds as they traveled north or south. I had just heard the term snowbird and was loudly and proudly using it. Well, Wallace had not heard the term but he heard me and said, "Steve, what kinds of birds are y'all catching down there?" I knew he was confused so I dropped my snowbird terminology and said, "Governor, we have a lot of Yankees that come through Pike County and we want to stop them at our museum and get them to spend tourist dollars." He looked even more puzzled and looked at me aghast and said, "Steve, what in the world are y'all doing to the Yankees down there in Pike County?" The poor fellow thought I was asking for money to set up a speed trap of some sort for unsuspecting Yankees traveling through Alabama.

He finally gave me the money for the museum but I still think he was a little concerned about how it was going to be spent.

Saying No to the Senate

In most states the ultimate political prize has been to go to the U.S. Senate and die there. There is an old saying that longtime Southern senators are wont to say that "the only way that I'm going to leave the United States Senate is by way of the ballot box or in a pine box."

Being governor of a state is generally considered a prelude or stepping stone to a U.S. Senate seat. Not so in Alabama. The governor's office has always seemed to be the ultimate brass ring.

Wallace could have gone to the U.S. Senate early in his career. In 1966 he had the golden opportunity. He had fought valiantly in 1965 to get the law changed so he could succeed himself. With that door closed, the obvious route for any politician would be to go to the Senate. In 1966 Wallace was at the top of his game. He was at the height of his popularity. Race was the paramount and only issue. He owned the issue. Most blacks could not vote and most whites were segregationists, so he owned the state of Alabama politically. He was the King of Alabama politics, and there was a Senate seat up for election. The venerable John Sparkman was up for election. He was powerful and he was popular but he was no match for George Wallace and he was considered soft on the race issue. Wallace would have easily beaten Sparkman and gone to the Senate. He chose instead to run his wife for governor. Lurleen trounced an illustrious field of candidates.

After Wallace was shot in his presidential bid in 1972, he survived but he was left a paraplegic. For the rest of his life his health was ruined and he was relegated to constant pain and confined to a wheelchair.

In 1978 Alabama had not only one but both Senate seats vacant. Wallace was ending his third term as governor and had nowhere to go politically. It was obvious that Wallace should take one of the open seats. It was his for the asking. His close personal aide and friend, Elvin Stanton, related the scenario to me. Stanton said that Wallace was going to run, but at the last minute, he told Elvin, "Let's go to Washington and look around." They went together to the Capitol and surveyed the terrain.

It occurred to Wallace that his life would be difficult at best maneuvering the steps and corridors of the Capitol. He just didn't want to leave Alabama. He wanted to be near his doctors. He wanted to die in Alabama, not Washington. The bottom line is that George Wallace just didn't want to be a United States senator. He liked being governor of Alabama.

One More Campaign

When Wallace left the governor's office in 1978 and chose voluntarily not to go to the Senate, many folks assumed his remarkable political life had come to an end. But Wallace's political obituary had not yet been written. He arose from the grave four years later to win his fourth and final term as governor.

The bullet wounds inflicted on Wallace by the crazed assassin Arthur

Bremer in 1972 had taken a devastating toll on Wallace's health. He was confined to a wheelchair, paralyzed from the waist down. He was always in constant pain. Therefore, he was on heavy medication. His condition caused peripheral health problems and he took numerous pills and painkillers to survive each day. He had numerous maladies in addition to his pain. He had lost his remarkable memory for names and his hearing had continued to decline. In short, the extensive medication had dulled his senses and made him prematurely senile and very emotional. He was given to crying unexpectedly and lingeringly.

Yet I do believe that Wallace knew deep down when he left the governor's mansion in 1978 that he would return in 1982.

Between 1978 and 1982, Wallace made his famous visit to the historic Dexter Avenue King Memorial Baptist Church. He told a packed church that he was sorry for his past racist rhetoric. He confessed that he knew that his strident racist diatribes had caused violence, discord, and death, not to mention the strained race relations he had sown with his constant haranguing of the issue. His contrition seemed sincere. The black audience believed him. It resonated throughout the state. The black community accepted Wallace's apology. Seventeen years after the passage of the Voting Rights Act, which Wallace had opposed, they rewarded him with their vote. It was the black community and statewide black vote that elected George Wallace to his fourth and final term as governor in 1982. There is no mistaking this fact. The election results were illuminating. The black vote unquestionably elected Wallace.

Many Wallace naysayers contend that Wallace's apology and pleas for forgiveness were orchestrated and calculated. Indeed, that would have been the Wallace way. There is no question that if you were a student of Alabama politics and George Wallace you knew that George Wallace would do or say anything to be elected governor. He was a total pragmatic political animal.

However, in this case, it is my belief that Wallace's remorse was genuine and heartfelt.

One day late in his last term, I was visiting with him in his office and it occurred to me that there was something strange about the decor. Usually people have pictures of their children and grandchildren surrounding them or on their desk areas. Wallace had four children and lots of grandchildren. Strangely, the only picture on his desk was a picture of a little black girl. Out of curiosity I asked the governor who that little girl black girl was in the picture. He started crying and said, "Steve, that little black girl came down here to the Capitol with her school class from Birmingham and hugged my neck and told me she loved me and gave me her picture."

I believe that Wallace was truly remorseful for his fiery racist past.

Just before eight o'clock on the evening of Labor Day, down in Mobile, the long line of people passing by the window of the limousine finally ended, and George Wallace slumped back into the deep-cushioned corner of the backseat, hidden from public view. "Ah sure hope that's all," he sighed wearily . . .

"You want the window up?" his old pal Oscar Harper asked solicitously from the other corner of the car.

"Huh?"

"Ah said it's almost time to go on up to the stage, idn't it?"

Wallace did not answer. Tilting his head slightly, he peered through the window of the limousine toward the several thousand people . . .

"It's a damned good crowd," Harper suggested.

"What?"

"Ah said it's a good crowd, a nice crowd."

Wallace merely grunted.

"They all gonna be glad to see yuh, Jo'ge."

"Huh?"

"These folks," Harper shouted. "All these folks'll be glad to see you again, Guv'nuh."

Wallace looked quizzically across the impressive width of the car, staring hard at his faithful crony of so many, many years. "Oscuh," he said, quite earnestly, "What you don't seem to understand is that most of these folks'll be dee-lighted to git shed uh me." He slumped even deeper into the soft corner of the Lincoln and waved his cold cigar in the direction of the distant crowd. "Yessuh, Oscuh," he concluded in a faint, faraway voice, "they'll be verrah, verruh happy when ol' Jo'ge Wallace is gone . . ."

—From an article by James Wooten, *Esquire*, November 7, 1978

Wallace's Last Hurrah

Oscar Harper tells the story of Wallace's last hurrah very well.

Most folks would have bet you when George went out of office as governor two months after that article in *Esquire* that he was finished politically. He was tired, and he was in pain.

You wouldn't have found me betting George Wallace wouldn't be on the ballot again. No, siree. "Never say never," George always said and I always believed him.

He decided to run again in 1982 because his close friends all over the state kept calling him and visiting him and telling him how the state was going down the drain without him.

When Fob James announced he wasn't running for governor again, that left a wide-open field. Attorney General Bill Baxley was the front runner, but he had made a public statement that he'd never run against George Wallace and he was stuck with it. Baxley had to withdraw from the governor's race and run for lieutenant governor.

Baxley and George both won, which was no surprise.

George's last term as governor almost killed him. He was in and out of the hospital so much that we worried constantly about him getting some infection and it running wild.

Doctors told us he was in unbelievably good health for a paraplegic. Toward the end, however, when it came time to decide whether to run for reelection or not in 1986, none of us knew whether he would run.

We knew George Jr. would have a lot to do with the decision. George Jr. wanted to run for treasurer and George wanted to help him out. Could he help George Jr. if he was running for governor himself? That was one of the big questions in his own mind. Another big question was whether his health would hold up during a 14-hour-a-day campaign.

Wallace was trying to decide whether to run. The advice he got from most people whose jobs were at stake was that he should run again. The people who cared the most for him were urging him to make up his own mind, to do what was best for him. They didn't know what was best for him; nobody did.

On the one hand, the mansion was the only home he'd ever really known. He was comfortable there. On the other hand was the pain, always the pain. He never had a minute in his life when pain didn't throb through the lower half of his body. When he went to Denver for the operation that was supposed to relieve the pain, he had hope. When he left Denver and the pain went with him he left the hope behind. He vowed it was the last time he would voluntarily go through any surgery again, whatever the reason.

As a young legislator with Governor George Wallace, 1983.

Denver is where George first started thinking about leaving the governor's office for good.

We had a time trying to figure out what George was gonna do. One day he called all his department heads together at a luncheon and asked them not to make any commitments about who they would support for governor.

That sure sounded like he was running, didn't it?

On the day George planned his news conference to announce his decision, he called Mike Jemison, his longtime Trooper bodyguard and confidant, to come up to the room in the Governor's Mansion that had been fixed up as a therapy room. George said, "Just stay with me. That way nobody will bother me."

Two blue folders were on George's lap, one on each knee. One was marked "Run." The other was marked "Don't run." Each contained a speech.

"Have you made up your mind?" Mike asked.

George shook his head. He had not. They sat for three and a half hours.

Finally, Mike said, "We've got to go. Which folder do I bring?"

George paused. "Bring them both."

Mike helped get George into the waiting van and they drove to the Capitol, where news media and friends waited in a crowd. Mike opened the door and started to get out. "Mike, stay in here a minute," George said. Mike sat down.

"It's the hardest decision I've ever had to make," George said. "There are so many people depending on me." He sat for a moment. Then his eyes filled with tears. "If I run again, I know it will kill me, Mike," George said. He took one of the blue file folders from Mike and nodded for him to open the door of the van.

As Mike unloaded George in his wheelchair the media converged upon him. Elvin Stanton walked to George's side and glanced at Mike, a question in his eyes. Mike answered with a slow shake of his head from side to side.

I was standing there at the edge of the crowd, watching Mike and watching Elvin. I knew what the head shake meant. It meant George Corley Wallace was saying goodbye to the only life he had ever known or loved.

I was there on that spring day of 1986. He wheeled his chair next to my desk in the old Capitol chamber where he began his career 40 years earlier as a 28-year-old state representative from Barbour County. It was nostalgic and moving. I knew I was witnessing history as Wallace tearfully wished us all a fond adieu.

Always the Governor

When George Wallace was elected in 1962, he started a virtual monopoly on the governor's office that lasted more than two decades. Alabama voters elected Wallace for an unprecedented four terms: 1962, 1970, 1974, and 1982, and basically as defacto governor in 1966 for the administration of his wife, Lurleen Burns Wallace. During the same period he ran for president unsuccessfully four times. There was hardly an election during the 25-year span that Wallace was not on the ballot. He ran for governor as a Democrat and nationally on different party labels. He was basically a segregationist and states' rights populist.

In Alabama, he was either loved or hated. He had tremendous charisma and a God-given gift for remembering names. His biggest achievements were in road construction, education—especially junior colleges and trade schools—and industrial development.

In the twilight of his career, he shifted his racial views and won a last term in 1982. Opinions are divided on whether the shift was from conviction or convenience.

Also in 1982, I was elected, at age 30, to my first term in the legislature.

I had first met George Wallace when I was an 11-year-old page in 1963 in the first months of his first term. My mentor and best buddy was Mr. Gardner Bassett, who had served as my county's representative for 24 years. Mr. Gardner took me in to meet Governor Wallace. Wallace told me that he also had been a page from Barbour County as a young boy. Mr. Gardner told the governor that I loved politics like they did and that when he, Mr. Gardner, retired I was going to follow him in his house seat, which I did. Governor Wallace never forgot that conversation.

Fast forward 20 years and Wallace made me a floor leader and gave me almost everything I wanted for my district. I had total access to the governor and one day I was visiting with him and he retold me a familiar story. It started with, "Steve, you know I'm kin to all the Shepherds and Flemings in the northern part of Pike County. You know Miss Janie Wallace, the librarian in Brundidge, is my aunt. You know I was born in Clio and those folks in Clayton love me. I am very popular in Brundidge and Troy, too." He would ask me about every barber in Troy by name. He loved to campaign in barber shops and beauty shops. "You know, Steve, I remember when you were a page boy. I was a page boy like you."

On this particular day, he got a faraway, smiling, nostalgic look on his face and said to me, "Steve, how old are you now?" I said, "Governor, I'm 30 years old. I'm your home county representative. I'm not a page anymore." He smiled, took a pull on his ever-present cigar and said, "I've been governor most all your life." I smiled back and said, "Governor, you sure have. I guess you'll always be governor of Alabama."

4

Lurleen Wallace

Our only woman governor was Lurleen Burns Wallace. Many historians count her 1966 election as governor as one of George Wallace's victories. They simply say he won the governor's office five times, when in fact he only won four and Lurleen won one.

It was no secret that she was running as a stand-in for her husband. He was prohibited by the State Constitution from running for reelection in 1966. He was at the height of his popularity and he tried valiantly to get the legislature to change the constitution but they rebuked him.

Lurleen Wallace was a quiet, sweet lady. She did not like the limelight or politics the way that George did—nobody in the world did. She did warm to it and made a very good governor after she was elected. However, she lived less than two years after she took office. She visited the state's mental hospital in her native Tuscaloosa County soon after she was inaugurated. She was so moved by the deplorable conditions that she made it her mission to improve the mental health facilities in the state. She gave one of the most moving speeches ever delivered before a legislature that resulted in passage of a major bond issue to support mental health.

She was also instrumental in the creation of a major cancer center at UAB. It came to pass after her death.

She became beloved by Alabamians. She showed such a grace and courage as she battled against cancer. When she died the outpouring of sympathy from people throughout the state was unparalleled. Thousands of people filed by her open casket in the Capitol Rotunda.

Schools let out all over the state and school children came to Montgomery from all over the state to pay their respect for our only Lady Governor. My editor, Randall Williams, told me that he was in Montgomery for an FFA meeting at the time of Lurleen's funeral. His FFA advisor at LaFayette

High School, Mr. Leonard Brown, drove the FFA boys by Greenwood Cemetery, where she was to be buried. Randall said he remembers that the street leading to the cemetery was lined with flower arrangements for what seemed like miles.

Probably as memorable as her legacy as governor is her remarkable victory for governor in 1966. The magnitude of her landslide was unprecedented.

Allow me to share the details of that race with you. In order to set the stage for her colossal victory, I will give you a short eight-year history leading up to 1966.

If race was a major issue in the 1958 between John Patterson and George Wallace, then you ain't seen nothing. Being the racist candidate in 1962 was the only way to be elected governor. With this issue in hand and Wallace's love for campaigning and remembering names, he would have beaten anybody that year.

Big Jim was really no match for Wallace because Big Jim had always been soft on the race issue. He was a true progressive liberal who would not succumb to racial demagoging, but Big Jim had succumbed to alcohol. Leading up to the governor's race in 1962, while Wallace had been campaigning 12 to 16 hours a day, 7 days a week, for four years, Big Jim sat home. Wallace would have won even if Big Jim had not embarrassed himself on live TV the night before the election.

A secondary story developed during the 1962 campaign. A star was born. Ryan DeGraffenreid was a smart, handsome, articulate, Tuscaloosa State Senator and lawyer. His family had been a prominent Tuscaloosa political family for generations but young Ryan DeGraffenreid truly had the makings of an Alabama governor. However, when he entered the 1962 governor's race the pundits wrote him off as an also ran. They said it was a Folsom versus Wallace race, but DeGraffenreid had charisma and captivated all the silk-stocking voters who would be Republicans today. He was quietly moving up in popularity leading up to the May Democratic primary.

The night before the election, DeGraffenreid, Wallace, and Folsom each had 30-minute television shows. Wallace appeared first and did all right but he was used to the stump and country campaigning so the new medium of television felt uncomfortable to him. But he did not hurt himself.

Ryan DeGraffenreid came on next and he was a sensation. He took to the camera like a duck to water. He was the new kind of candidate. He had John Kennedy-like appeal and he mastered the new medium of television. He helped himself a lot. Alabamians saw a candidate that they liked. Then Big Jim came on obviously inebriated and sunk himself, although it was a very colorful show.

Wallace won, but the surprise of the election was that Big Jim finished third. Ryan DeGraffenreid came in second and would face Wallace in the runoff. Wallace was elected governor, but DeGraffenreid had run a brilliant get-acquainted race and a star had been born.

The 1966 governor's race had two stories: the Ryan DeGraffenreid story and the Lurleen Wallace story. Ryan DeGraffenreid had become the man to beat in 1966. He took a page from the George Wallace playbook and copied Wallace's work habits from four years earlier. He worked the state nonstop from one end to the other. He worked as hard as Wallace but was even more organized. Old timers say he had a precinct and box captain lined up in every box and hamlet in Alabama. It was an unbelievable organization for that era.

During the summer of 1965, one of the most titanic sessions in state senate history occurred. Wallace called a special session to get the legislature to change the Constitution and do away with the one-term limit to allow him to succeed himself. It was called the Succession Session and is discussed in more detail in the George Wallace chapter. The bill Wallace wanted passed the House easily, but some strong-willed state senators withstood the most powerful pressure ever put on legislators. They refused to buckle in to the brazen and strong-armed Wallace power play. Wallace could not get the majority he needed in the Senate. Many of those senators were committed to DeGraffenreid. They had served with him and were loyal to him. It cost many of them their political careers. Wallace went after them with a vengeance. He was at the height of his popularity. The race issue was at its peak and at a fever pitch and Wallace owned the race issue.

With Wallace out of the race, DeGraffenreid appeared invincible. He campaigned tirelessly even though he had only token opposition. It was a cold windy night in February of 1966 and he was to make a speech up around Sand Mountain. He had a campaign plane and he and his pilot were advised not to try to make the flight to the event. DeGraffenreid refused to stop. He boarded his plane at Fort Payne and within minutes after takeoff his plane crashed into a mountain and he and his pilot were killed instantly. DeGraffenreid would have been governor in a cakewalk but it was now a new ball game with less than ten weeks until the May election.

George Wallace mulled it over for a few weeks, then the amazing story of his wife Lurleen Wallace running for governor came to fruition. George would be her number one advisor.

The idea of George Wallace running his wife, Lurleen, as his proxy had been tossed out by a few of his cronies as a joke but Lurleen would never have run if DeGraffenreid was still alive and running. But after he tragically died, a real vacuum existed and the Wallace name was still magic. After a few weeks the idea grew on Wallace. He made calls to every county in the state and began to realize that dog might hunt.

Wallace had captured control of the race issue and that was the issue in 1966. He was known as the foremost segregationist in Alabama and the most pronounced in the nation. His inaugural speech in 1963 declaring, "segregation today, segregation tomorrow, and segregation forever," had endeared him to the white Alabama electorate, and at the same time very few blacks were yet registered to vote.

Wallace was also one of the most masterful politicians ever born. His love of campaigning and ability to remember names was unmatched. Politics was his life and Lurleen saved his life because he could not have lived without politics.

Lurleen was a genuinely sweet lady. Her humble background as a dime store clerk in Northport endeared her to Alabamians, most of whom could relate to her. She was gracious and sincere and people fell in love with her. Lurleen had been diagnosed with cancer two years prior to the 1966 election. Although it seemed to be in remission, her health was not excellent. The campaigning was a challenge to her. She did not cherish the spotlight the way George did. Instead, she preferred her quiet time.

Wallace's total devotion to politics had taken a toll on their marriage and quality of life. Lurleen had been mother and father to four children.

However, after Lurleen agreed to run it seemed to grow on her. She got better day after day. She was a quick study. She grew in political skills on the stump. As the crowds grew you could feel the momentum and surge of popularity that she and George were experiencing. She seemed to thrill to it.

Lurleen's landslide victory in May was astonishing. She set records of historic proportions for vote-getting, some of which still stand 48 years later. Most astoundingly she defeated nine male opponents without a runoff and it was quite a lineup of opponents. Left in the carnage was an illustrious field of proven political vote-getters.

Lurleen received 400,000 votes. Alabama Attorney General Richmond Flowers finished second, having received the black vote. Jasper Congressman Carl Elliott finished a distant third. Morgan County State Senator Bob Gilchrist finished fourth (he tried unsuccessfully to assume the DeGraffenreid organization). Dothan businessman Charles Woods ran fifth. Two former governors, John Patterson and Big Jim Folsom, finished sixth and seventh. State Agricultural Commissioner A. W. Todd ran eighth.

She then went on to trounce the most popular Republican in Alabama, Jim Martin, in November by a two-to-one margin. Martin was a first-time Republican congressman from Gadsden who had been elected in 1964. He had all but beaten Lister Hill for a U.S. Senate seat in 1962. He was the strongest Republican in Alabama in 1966 but he was no match for the Wallaces. He was a segregationist, but a poor man's segregationist would beat a rich man's segregationist every time.

Lurleen Wallace was a very popular lady in 1966. The state fell in love with her. She was not only a sweet and beloved lady; she was also a good governor for the 18 months she served before she succumbed to cancer.

5

Albert Brewer

One of the finest men ever to serve in Alabama government was Albert Brewer. He was among the highest-caliber individuals to rise to the governor's office.

Brewer hailed from Morgan County in the heart of the Tennessee Valley. He was first elected to the legislature in 1958 at the very young age of 28. He was identified early as a rising star. In fact, his star was meteoric. In his second term in 1962 he was elected Speaker of the House at age 32, an unheard of feat. Besides being on a fast track politically by his mid-30s, he was also considered one of the best attorneys in Decatur.

He was a kind, considerate, and genuinely sincere man with a pleasant and contagious smile and countenance that would melt the most hardened enemy. Once you met Albert Brewer you immediately warmed to him. He became especially dear to me. When I first met Governor Brewer, I was a 12-year-old page from Troy and Brewer was Speaker of the House. My mentor, sponsor, and best buddy was my state representative from Troy, Gardner Bassett. Mr. Gardner was in his 70s and he loved Brewer. Since Mr. Gardner and I were close, he got me acquainted with the young Speaker. Brewer graciously took me under his wing and would let me run special errands for him and occasionally let me sit next to him in the presiding officer's chair. This pleased Mr. Gardner because he had told Brewer of my love for politics and that when he, Mr. Gardner, retired that I would run for and take his House seat, and that's exactly what eventually happened. So it was no secret to Brewer that I aspired to get into politics and eventually run for the legislature. He and Mr. Gardner would share legislative stories and history with me. When Brewer became lieutenant governor in 1966, he took me over to the Senate with him to be head of the Senate pages. So I was able to work in the legislature during the summer while growing up.

Work the Country First

One day Brewer said, "I want to tell you a campaign secret." He began his lesson by stating that when you get ready to run for the legislature, you should start your campaign in the country. He then explained why. It was based on the old bandwagon theory. He said people in the rural towns and hamlets have more time on their hands, they like politics better and they gossip more, and they appreciate your interest more. They want to be asked for their vote. Therefore, if you work the rural communities, they talk about your being there and they will commit to you early, and—at that time—if a rural person told you they were going to vote for you, you could take it to the bank. So if you got there first you would wrap up that area early and forever. But the big plus was that whenever any person from that rural box came into the larger towns or county seats to shop or get their hair cut, and the city folks would ask how is politics out your way, the rural man would say, "I don't know about the other races, but that Brewer boy is going to get all the votes up here for the open legislative seat." The bandwagon domino theory was on. The city folks assumed that if all the country folks were for someone they were bound to win in a landslide so they better get on board. That was a good lesson. I took his advice in my first race. It worked, I got 82 percent over two opponents.

The 1970 Wallace versus Brewer Race

Many historians and political scientists point to certain political races and years as watershed events in a state's course or history. That year and race in Alabama was the 1970 gubernatorial contest between George Wallace and Albert Brewer. It was an epic battle.

Albert Brewer was the most clean-cut politician to grace the Capitol. He was a prince of a fellow, likeable, with a winning smile. He came as a legislator in the freshman class of 1958 that the late Bob Ingram referred to as the greatest ever. A lawyer by profession, Brewer quickly learned the ropes, and after only four years experience he became Speaker of the House in 1963, Wallace's first term as governor. It should be noted that he would not have been elected Speaker without Wallace's blessing. After four years as Speaker, he ran for lieutenant governor as the Wallace team's candidate.

Wallace's wife, Lurleen, carried the state in a landslide in 1966; Brewer beat two state senators, Neil Metcalf and John Tyson, without a runoff.

Lurleen Wallace had cancer when she was elected and died two years later. Brewer ascended to the governor's office. He continued Lurleen's passionate work, upgrading Alabama's mental health facilities, but he also took on some progressive programs of his own. He was very popular among legislators in both houses. He had strong friendships built by personal relationship. He was widely respected for his abilities, honesty, integrity, and loyalty—including to Wallace.

However, Wallace had made the race issue into his calling card and had drawn national attention to Alabama. We had gotten a very negative image nationwide as a backwoods, race-driven island. It was hurting economic development. He ran for president as a states' rights candidate in 1964 and ran as the Southern segregation candidate in 1968. Wallace became a household word synonymous with racebaiting. When his wife died in 1968, he was running for president.

Brewer had made business and governmental issues paramount and downplayed the race issue. The state was at a crossroads. The business community in Alabama wanted a noncontroversial, progressive, "New South" governor like Albert Brewer. Wallace supposedly told Brewer he did not intend to run in 1970. Brewer committed himself to running. At the last minute, Wallace changed his mind and decided to run. The race was on.

Early on it was apparent who was on which side. The business community and middle- to upper-income whites, primarily in the suburbs of Montgomery, Birmingham, and Huntsville were with Brewer, along with 300,000 to 400,000 new black voters registered by the 1965 Voting Rights Act. So the battle lines were drawn with black voters, liberal whites, and Republicans—there was still no real Republican Party in Alabama at that time—united for Brewer, and the traditional Alabama white Democrats were backing George Wallace.

Brewer led in the Democratic primary by a small margin. The runoff was to be in early June, so the scene was set for three weeks of brutal campaigning, and brutal it was. With Wallace's political life on the line, he pulled out all the stops.

Brewer's slogan "We need a full-time governor" resonated with swing voters because they knew that Wallace had been running for president full-time.

Wallace countered in the runoff by begging for forgiveness and promising never to run for president again. Wallace spoke 10 times a day at courthouse rallies all over rural Alabama. Wallace also ran some of the most negative TV ads in our state's history, saying that a vote for Brewer would turn the state over to the "Black Bloc Vote." There were also vicious flyers attacking Brewer and his family.

Wallace came from behind to prevail. He was on a plane to Wisconsin the next day campaigning for the presidential nomination in 1972.

The $400,000 of Republican Money to Brewer

There are several stories surrounding how the $400,000 came to Alabama to try to beat George Wallace in the 1970 governor's race. Two things are for sure—it came, and $400,000 was a lot of money in 1970. It probably accounted for at least a third of the money raised and spent by Brewer in his attempt to beat Wallace.

The Watergate hearings confirmed that the Richard Nixon reelection committee sent the money to Alabama to beat Wallace. The late Bob Ingram told the story this way in his book, *That's the Way I Saw It,* and gave me permission to reprint it:

Perhaps no political story has been the subject of more talk during the past two decades than the $400,000 in Republican money contributed to the campaign for Governor Albert Brewer in 1970. Most of the stories about this contribution were incorrect; if for no other reason than posterity's sake, the time has come to set the record straight. To tell it like it happened.

Since it is my story, since I am telling it, I am going to take the license to set a few ground rules. Some of the participants in this story are still in and around Alabama politics and Alabama government. They may or may not want their names mentioned. I will not mention their names. As a matter of fact, their names are not that important to the story.

Another thing I would like to say at the very beginning. I will take a position on this campaign contribution which will be sneered at by some of you, That's all right, too. My position is this—the $400,000 contributed by the Republicans *to the Brewer Campaign in 1970 was perhaps the "cleanest" contribution, in a political sense, that any candidate could receive. What do I mean by "cleanest?" To explain necessitates that I give you a brief course in the financing of a political campaign, particularly, a campaign for governor of Alabama.*

First, it costs an indecent amount of money to make a serious race for governor in Alabama. I am not talking about tens or thousands of dollars. I'm talking about millions of dollars. Where does this kind of money go? Obviously you have enormous travel expenses, hotel and meals, salaries for full-time workers, office space, telephone and other utilities. But far and away the major expense is advertising—newspaper, radio, but mostly television. A recent example to underscore this point—on one day in the 1986 gubernatorial primary campaign, the Fob James staff purchased $750,000 in TV time. That "buy," as it is called in the trade, was made at one time. And if you don't know this, the candidates must pay for their advertising in advance.

Second, an obvious question would be, where does this kind of money come from? How does the candidate raise this kind of money? If you think it comes from the little old lady who drops $1, $5, or even $10 into a collection plate of sorts, if you think it comes from the people who mail $10, $25, or even $50 to the campaign, you are terribly naive.

The money that fuels a gubernatorial campaign comes from the major contributors—those who give $5,000 or $10,000 or $25,000. It comes from asphalt dealers and heavy equipment dealers and contractors and architects and lawyers, It comes from the suppliers of all manner of goods . . . it comes from banks and businesses . . . and of course it comes from a myriad of political action committees representing every known special interest you can think of and a few you would never think of.

And as diverse as these major contributors might be, they have one thing in common—they all expect some sort of return on their investment. If you think they are contributing that kind of money simply for good government, then you are a couple of bricks shy of a full load.

Some of these big-buck contributors expect to share in the spoils of victory in a monetary way. The state buys a lot of asphalt to build new roads and to resurface old ones . . . the state does a lot of construction, and architects are needed for all these projects . . . there is a lot of legal work that has to be farmed out to private firms . . . there are a lot of deposits to be made in banks, not to mention the lucrative bond issues which attract undue attention from the major banks. We are not suggesting anything illegal or unethical, only the practical application of an old political rule—them that help bake the pie get to eat it.

While some of these major contributors hope to be rewarded in a financial sense, others, particularly the PACs, are looking for a "friend" in the governor's office, one who understands the problems facing particular special interests.

But the point I seek to make is quite simple—it may not be visible in every instance, but there is a string (or strings) attached to these big contributions. There were absolutely no strings attached to the $400,000 contribution made by the Republicans to the Albert Brewer campaign. Nobody at the White House wanted a job or a state deposit or an architectural contract. All they wanted to do was to defeat George Wallace in his campaign for governor. I say it again, politically speaking, the $400,000 was a squeaky clean contribution.

Anyway, why this enormous interest on the part of the national Republicans to defeat George Wallace? What business was it of theirs as to who was the governor of Alabama?

Let's back up two years to the 1968 presidential campaign. Richard Nixon was the nominee of the Republican Party. Hubert Humphrey was the Democratic nominee. Also in that contest was George C. Wallace of Alabama, running as a third-party candidate under the banner of the American Independent Party. What we had was the liberal Humphrey, the conservative Nixon, and the ultra-conservative Wallace.

You remember the outcome. Nixon was elected, but Wallace earned a niche in American history by polling almost 10,000,000 votes, more than any third-party candidate had polled in history. Not remembered by many, but the far more significant numbers in that election were the electoral votes won by the three candidates. Nixon won 301 electoral votes, Humphrey got 191 votes, and Wallace got 46 electoral votes. He carried the states of Alabama, Arkansas, Georgia, Louisiana, and Mississippi and those five states represented 45 electoral votes. He picked up an additional vote from a presidential elector in North Carolina.

But consider this: What would have happened if Wallace had been able to carry the Southern states of Tennessee, South Carolina, and Florida in that 1968 election, three states which Nixon carried by relatively narrow margins? If

Wallace had won those states, Nixon would have been denied their 35 electoral votes, and he would not have had the required 269 electoral votes to win the election. Instead, the election would have been decided by the U.S. House of Representatives, which at the time was overwhelmingly Democratic. Humphrey unquestionably would have been elected President.

Governor Wallace has been quoted on more than one occasion to the effect that his third-party candidacy prevented the liberal Humphrey from being elected. How Wallace could make such a claim is beyond my comprehension. His position that he took votes away from Humphrey is so politically illogical that it scarcely merits a rebuttal. Every vote Wallace got . . . and most certainly every vote he got in the Southern states . . . would have gone to Nixon had Wallace not been on the ballot. Nixon swept Dixie by a landslide. Wallace did not prevent Humphrey from being elected President in 1968, he almost elected him.

In 1970 Nixon and his staff were already preparing for his 1972 race for reelection. No Democrat had emerged who appeared to be a serious threat, but the Nixon people, remembering what had almost happened in 1968, were looking for a way to keep Wallace and his third-party movement out of the '72 campaign. They came to an obvious conclusion—if Wallace was defeated in his race for governor of Alabama it would certainly lessen the likelihood that he would be a presidential candidate in 1972. If his own people rejected him in Alabama, they reasoned, how could he expect the American people to vote for him? Also, without the considerable advantages of the office of governor, from which to run, Wallace could not likely wage an effective national campaign. Lastly, there was at least some evidence that Wallace was beatable in Alabama. Some professional polls showed that incumbent Brewer had an excellent chance of winning a full term (as late as March 1970, only two months before the primary, the Brewer poll and the Wallace poll showed Brewer leading by a huge 50 percent to 41 percent margin).

It was against that background that in the spring of 1970 the decision was made in Washington to funnel funds into the Brewer campaign. I do not know when or how the first contact was made, but sometime in late March or early April I remember hearing that "some Republicans in Washington" were going to raise some money for the Brewer campaign.

My recollection is that it was only a few days later that Brewer called me to his office, told me that some money had been raised and that he wanted me to pick it up. He did not know how much it was not how it had been raised. He then gave me the bizarre plan I was to follow in picking up the money. I was to walk into the lobby of the Sherry Netherlands Hotel in New York City at 11:45 a.m. on a specific date . . . I don't remember the date but I think it was early April. A man would be seated in the lobby of that hotel with a briefcase in his lap. I was to approach him and ask, "Are you Mr. Jensen of Baltimore?" If he was my contact, he would reply, "No, I'm Mr. Jensen of Detroit."

I thought then and I still think that this little scenario was a bit silly, but subsequent developments in Washington caused me to better understand the mentality of some of the people around Richard Nixon.

The more I thought about the trip to New York and picking up what I presumed would be a large amount of cash—just how large, I didn't know—the more uneasy I got. Call it cowardice if you like, but I decided I would be a lot more comfortable if someone went with me. I asked an associate of mine to accompany me. I told him all that I knew about our mission—that some Washington Republicans had raised some money for the Brewer campaign and I was to pick it up. Let me add here, in case you are wondering, all of the expenses for me and my associate on this trip were paid by the campaign.

Something else was bothering me about this trip. I have been in the lobbies of countless hotels, and invariably there have been a dozen or more men seated with briefcases in their laps. How was I to know which man seated in the lobby of the Sherry Netherlands would be my mysterious contact, "Mr. Jensen"? That proved to be an unnecessary fear. Shortly after we checked into our own hotel, about three blocks down Fifth Avenue from the Sherry Netherlands, I decided to make a "scouting" trip of the pick-up point. To my enormous relief, I discovered that the Sherry Netherlands had no lobby. It is much like an apartment building. As I walked through the door, on my left was a small registration desk, to the right a restaurant, and to the rear was a narrow hall where several elevators opened. There was one chair in that hall, just down from the registration desk. With only one chair to worry about, I figured I would have no problem finding my man. I didn't.

At precisely 11:45 a.m. on the appointed day I walked into the Sherry Netherlands Hotel. Sure enough, a tall man, a dour expression on his face, was seated in that one chair, He had a briefcase in his lap. It was time for me to go through the little charade.

"Are you Mr. Jensen from Baltimore," I asked, trying to keep a straight face.

"No, I'm Mr. Jensen from Detroit," he replied. If he saw any humor in this exchange, it didn't show.

I'm not sure what I said next, I think I said something to the effect that I understood that he had something for me. He suggested we go into the restaurant. For some unaccountable reason, even though it was but minutes before noon, the restaurant was not open. The entrance into the dining area was blocked by a heavy rope. "Mr. Jensen" unhooked the rope and we sat down in a circular booth in the corner. Immediately an irritated uniformed man, perhaps the head waiter, came over and told us the restaurant was not open and for us to leave. Tartly, "Mr. Jensen" told him we would leave when we had completed our business.

Then came a crisis.

"Where's your briefcase?" he asked.

"I didn't bring one." I replied, beginning to panic just a bit. "I figured you would give me that one."

"I'm not going to give you my briefcase," he snapped back.

He then opened the briefcase revealing stacks of money. Underneath the bills was a large brown manila envelope, perhaps 11x14 inches, with a metal clasp. You have seen hundreds of them. He began stuffing the money into that envelope. Standing no more than 20 feet from us was the waiter who had ordered us to leave, and with him were a half-dozen other waiters. I sensed that every one of them could see what was going on and were already contemplating how they would take that envelope from me and dispose of my body.

Finally, it seemed like an eternity, "Mr. Jensen" transferred all the money into the envelope. Without so much as a word, he closed his briefcase, stepped over the rope blocking the entrance to the dining room, and strode briskly out of the hotel. He had to walk fast to beat me to the door.

I had insisted that my associate accompany me for the pick-up. He was standing outside of the hotel, appearing as nonchalant as he could. I nodded to him, and we headed back down Fifth Avenue. As long as I live, I will never forget that scene. It was now noon, the lunch hour, and it seemed there must have been a million people heading straight toward me on that sidewalk. And I knew *for an absolute fact that every one of them knew what I had in that envelope. I was so concerned about the throng of envelope snatchers that at one intersection I was almost hit by a taxi turning right off of Fifth Avenue. I immediately envisioned what might have happened—the cab knocks me to the ground, the manila envelope is ripped open, and all those $100 bills are scattered down the street. That would have been a show.*

It didn't happen, thank goodness. After the longest three-block walk in my life we finally reached our hotel room. I locked the door, chained it, even considered pushing a dresser in front of the door. Only then did I open the envelope and count the money. It added up to $100,000. I was astounded. I had no idea what the contribution would be, but I expected maybe $25,000, certainly not $100,000.

The remainder of the trip was a nightmare. When we went to eat, I didn't dare leave the money in my hotel room. Fortunately, my colleague had brought his briefcase, so I put the money in it. I carried that briefcase with me to the dining room and never let go of it. There, too, I sensed that all eyes in that restaurant were focused on the briefcase. When we boarded the Delta flight to return to Montgomery, needless to say I didn't check that briefcase. When I took my seat on the plane a pretty young stewardess asked if she could put the briefcase in the overhead rack. I nearly had a stroke at the suggestion. No way was I going to let go of that briefcase.

At this point in this story some of you are saying, wait a minute, we thought the Republican contribution to Brewer was $400,000. It was, but all I ever picked up, all I ever saw, was $100,000. In fact, this was to give me a loophole, if you please, when the story finally surfaced about the Republican money going to the Brewer campaign. I was asked countless times by various members of the media if I did not go to New York and pick up $400,000. I could truthfully deny the charge. I did not pick up $400,000 . . . I picked up $100,000. In 1978 Bill Baxley, then a candidate for governor in which Brewer was also a contender, publicly accused me of picking up the $400,000. He even had the dates of the New York trip and the hotel where I stayed. But he was $300,000 wrong on how much I picked up.

All of which leads to an obvious question—when and where was that $300,000 picked up? Some of you will chuckle at this story, but my family and close friends will not be surprised. I detest flying. I am the original white-knuckle *flyer. The first time I flew across country in a jet I remained buckled up in my seat the entire trip, not once going to the bathroom for fear that walking up and down the aisle would surely cause the plane to go into a dive. I might add that when we finally landed on the West Coast I gave a new meaning to that old political expression about "hitting the ground running." To the men's room, that is. But back to the story.*

Some weeks after my trip to New York, Brewer told me another pick-up was to be made, and this time it was to be in Los Angeles. I didn't tell him so at the time, but there was no way I was going to make that trip unless I could go by Greyhound. I came up with an acceptable excuse, something about pressing business matters, and another campaign staff member made that pick-up. The contribution this time totaled $150,000. Still later, it might have been during the run-off but I am not sure, yet another pick-up was arranged, again, it was in Los Angeles, and again I begged off. The same staff member made this second trip as well and again he picked up $150,000.

It was not until four years later, during the Watergate hearings in 1974, that I first learned where the $400,000 had come from. I had assumed that the money had been raised in 1970 by some of the White House people. I figured they got on the phone, called some of their rich supporters, explained to them the good political sense of trying to defeat Wallace, and raised the money that way. That was not the case. It was brought out at the congressional hearing that a great deal of money had been left over from Nixon's race for President in 1968. It had subsequently been given to the Committee to Re-Elect the President (with the unfortunate acronym of CREEP). It was from this fund that the $400,000 had come.

White House aide John Dean had confirmed this during his testimony. He was being quizzed on how some of the CREEP money was spent, and he mentioned that $400,000 had been given to George Wallace for his campaign for governor in 1970. Senator Herman Talmadge of Georgia was on the committee, and he almost fell out of his chair when he heard that.

"You surely don't mean that $400,000 was given to help elect George Wallace, do you?" Talmadge asked.

"No, I meant to say it was given to the man who was running against Wallace . . . I can't remember his name," Dean replied.

From that day forward some people in Alabama—notably critics of Brewer—have referred to the $400,000 contribution as "Watergate Money." In fact, this expression has been used so often that no doubt many Alabamians have concluded there was a connection between the contribution and the Watergate break-in. As a matter of fact, the contribution was made in 1970, more than two years before the break-in at the Watergate.

One final note to this story. It was during those same Watergate hearings on TV that I learned who "Mr. Jensen of Detroit" really was. I was watching the hearings one day when suddenly there he was—the man seated in that chair in the Sherry Netherlands Hotel, the man who wouldn't give me his briefcase. It was Herbert Kalmback, the personal attorney for Richard Nixon.

OSCAR HARPER TELLS A different version of the story in his book, *Me 'N' George*, and he also gave me permission to reprint the story:

Albert Brewer was sworn in as governor after Lurleen Wallace died. He served out the rest of her term in office and made it no secret that he wanted to run for a term of his own in 1970.

Of course, he didn't want to run against George Wallace. Nobody did. The problem was that nobody knew if George Wallace was going to run again. George always said he wouldn't let anyone know until he had to, because you would wear yourself out in a campaign if you "jumped in too early." George said you needed to keep the voters eager, wondering if you are going to run, because it would keep their enthusiasm up.

Brewer went ahead and announced that he was running before George publicly told anyone what he was going to do. After Brewer announced his plans to run for governor, George jumped into the race. Immediately, Brewer came down with a case of sour grapes. He told everyone in the state that George had broken his word, that he had said in private that he was not going to run again for governor in 1970. George told me it didn't happen that way.

He was so mad he paid Brewer a call at the mansion to set things straight when he heard what Brewer was telling folks.

"I didn't say it," George told him, "and if I said it, I'm withdrawing it."

Meanwhile . . . some of George's biggest campaign workers joined up with Brewer.

You can speculate all day about why a lot of top Wallace folks declared they were for Brewer. Maybe they really believed that George was not going to run or maybe they thought George was going to run but Brewer might beat him. Perhaps they figured that after working for Brewer, they owed him loyalty. Who knows?

About the time George jumped into the race, a Montgomery man named Bob Wilder, who was close to Louisiana Senator Russell Long, was playing golf at a swanky golf course where he ran into two people who were close to Richard Nixon.

I wasn't there, of course, but Wilder told folks back in Montgomery one of the men he met playing golf was Bebe Rebozo . . . pretty much known as Richard Nixon's best friend. The son of a Cuban-born cigar maker, Rebozo had known Nixon since 1951 and lived next door to the president in Key Biscayne, Florida. In fact, Nixon had been Rebozo's first customer when Rebozo started the Key Biscayne Bank & Trust Co. Nixon was issued savings account No. 1.

Well, Wilder got to talking pretty seriously with Nixon's friends, who allowed as how Nixon was very interested in helping Brewer defeat George Wallace.

It wasn't that Nixon cared whether Albert Brewer won the race or not. Nixon just wanted to defeat George to take the steam out of George's presidential race. If George won for governor, then went on to run on a third-party ticket for president, Nixon figured George would be taking votes away from the Republicans, not the Democrats.

Wilder wasn't close to Brewer himself, but he volunteered to go back to Montgomery and arrange a meeting between a representative of Nixon and some folks who were close to Brewer.

When he got back to Montgomery, Wilder called a Montgomery attorney who was known for being able to put things together and asked him to set up the meeting. The attorney called two of Brewer's men, Drexel Cook and Alton Turner, and they agreed to meet at Wilder's house in Montgomery.

Nixon's southeastern campaign manager, a man from South Carolina, was at the meeting for Nixon. The Montgomery attorney who had set up the meeting was there, too, but he said when he realized they were talking about laundering boocoodles of money, he told them to count him out on future get-togethers. He knew more than he wanted to know already . . .

They decided that day at the meeting that Jim Bob Solomon would be the one to pick the money up in California. Jim Bob was the nephew of Henry

Steagall, who came from George's part of the state and had been a loyal George Wallace man from the word go. Jim Bob had been a legal adviser for the finance department under Brewer since 1969. The Brewer folks knew he could be trusted.

It was all real hush-hush when Jim Bob picked up that suitcase with that $400,000 cash in it. He didn't even introduce himself to the man who brought it and vice versa. They picked each other out because of a prearranged signal on what they would wear to identify themselves.

Jim Bob got the money and brought it back to Alabama and handed it over to the folks he was suppose to hand it over to. The $400,000 donation came to light when Congress investigated the Watergate scandal. In January 1974 Rebozo was one of the five witnesses called before the Senate Watergate committee. They were interested in contributions he had received, not contributions he had given anybody. In the next four years, the Watergate Special Prosecution Force conducted a 16-month investigation into Rebozo which an Associated Press story in March 1978 called a "wild goose chase."

The story stated: "Before the probed ended, prosecutors chased suspicions or allegations of a million-dollar cash donation to Nixon from Arab oilmen and that Nixon kept a multimillion dollar slush fund in a secret bank in the Bahamas. No proof was found."

Some of the allegations were made by a man the committee decided was a known con man. Not much came out of the Watergate hearings about the $400,000. Jim Bob's name wasn't mentioned, but it came out that the man who gave Jim Bob the money was Nixon's personal attorney, Herbert Kalmbach.

What happened to the $400,000 once it got to the point where it should have been used for Brewer's campaign?

Brewer, in a confusing confession, announced he didn't know anything about the $400,000 supposedly given to his campaign until news of it surfaced in the Watergate testimony.

Whatever version you want to believe, one thing is for certain. The money came to Brewer from Nixon and $400,000 was a lot of money in 1970.

6

Other Governors

Fob James and the 1978 Governor's Race

When longtime observers of Alabama politics get together and the subject of Alabama's past governor's races comes up, the one mentioned first and most often is the 1978 race. It was truly one for the record books.

The 1978 governor's race between the three heavyweights, former Governor Albert Brewer, Attorney General Bill Baxley, and Lieutenant Governor Jere Beasley, was expected to be titanic. The press called them the "Three B's." Republicans then were still insignificant in statewide politics; the winner of the Democratic primary would be governor.

Meanwhile, over in east Alabama, a little-known former Auburn halfback named Fob James strolled into the governor's race. Fob's entry evoked little interest, only curiosity as to why he would want to enter the fray against three well-known major players. Fob was exposed as a card-carrying Republican whose only political experience had been as a member of the Lee County Republican Executive Committee, but even a political novice like Fob knew he could not win as a Republican so he qualified to run as a Democrat along with the Three B's.

Fob had become wealthy by starting and running a barbell manufacturing company in Opelika. When Fob signed up to run for governor, the press wrote him off as a rich gadfly who simply chose politics rather than golf as his pastime. Little did they know the fact he was rich and had a lot of time on his hands could spell trouble for the average political opponent who had to worry about fundraising and feeding his family while running a full-time campaign.

Fob realized he was no political professional like the Three B's, who had spent their entire political adulthoods in public office, so he sought professional advice. He had the money to think big and wanted to know who the best political consultant in the South was. It was an easy answer: Deloss Walker, a political public relations genius who lived in Memphis, Tennessee. His track record for electing governors of Southern states was 5-0. The scenario was the same for all five upset victories. He took an obscure candidate and got him elected governor over a well-known incumbent or favorite. He had just taken an unknown school board member named Dale Bumpers and made him governor of Arkansas. Deloss Walker was the most renowned and expensive political guru in the country in 1977.

Fob quietly sought out Walker, who at first refused to take Fob's race. Walker's first impression was that even he could not mold Fob into a winner against three well-financed, experienced thoroughbreds. Fob persisted, convincing Walker that he had unlimited personal money to spend. Walker relented, knowing he might risk blemishing his unbeaten record but at least he would make a lot of money off poor old Fob. Walker's one condition for taking the race was that Fob must do exactly what he said. He must be scripted and never deviate from Walker's ads and speeches.

With Governor Fob James, center, and longtime Troy Mayor Jimmy Lunsford, left.

At the time Fob announced in the spring of 1978, nobody knew he had already secured the genius Walker and been to political school. Brewer, Baxley, and Beasley ignored Fob. Baxley even praised him saying, "Fob would be a good governor. Too bad he's not a serious candidate." Those words would come back to haunt Baxley.

Walker's initial polling showed that Fob actually had some name identification from being an Auburn football player in the 1950s. It also picked up that Auburn alumni yearned for an Auburn man to become governor instead of it always going to a University of Alabama alumnus. However, Fob's best attribute was that he always followed Walker's script. No matter what question Fob was asked, he answered it with the same pat answer, "I'm for getting back to the basics, reading, writing, and arithmetic."

He traveled the state in a yellow school bus while letting the Three B's tear each other up. Baxley, Beasley, and Brewer spent all their time and money attacking each other with negative ads, while Fob ran positive ads evoking his clean image. By mid-May, most Alabamians had seen so many negative ads and mudslinging by the Three B's they were of the opinion that all three had probably shot their mothers in a bar fight, but they liked old Fob James, even if they thought his name was "Bob James."

It was too late for the Three B's when they saw a poll about a week before the election showing Fob ahead of all three of them. Baxley refused to believe it and kept hammering at Beasley and Brewer, ignoring Fob. When the votes were counted Fob was in first place. Baxley finished second because black voters were with him. Brewer was third and Beasley finished fifth behind State Senator Sid McDonald.

Fob easily beat Baxley in the runoff. After all, what could Baxley say? He had run all over the state for three months saying Fob would make a good governor. Fob James had pulled off one of the most amazing upset victories in the history of Alabama politics. The Fob James story of the 1978 governor's race is truly one for the record books.

Fob did not seek reelection in 1982. However, he tried for a comeback in 1986 and 1990 and failed. But in 1994 he ran as a Republican and won, thus becoming the only person in Alabama history to be elected governor as a Democrat and as a Republican.

Guy Hunt

If 1964 was the pivotal year that Alabama became a Republican state on the national level, then 1986 was the watershed year that Alabamians started voting Republican for governor. It was caused by the arrogance of the state Democratic Party.

In 1964, when Alabama and the other Southern states voted straight Republican for Barry Goldwater, five GOP congressmen were elected, sweeping out veteran Democratic congressmen with a combined 100 years of seniority. In the same election, a lot of novice and unsuspecting local Republican candidates were swept into office. One of those was Guy Hunt, who had signed up to run as the GOP candidate for probate judge of Cullman County. He won and commenced to become one of the most stalwart Republicans in the state. Perry Hooper Sr. was similarly elected probate judge in Montgomery, and he, too, would be heard from again later in state politics.

Hunt labored in the rural Alabama Republican vineyards for years. He became a Ronald Reagan disciple and continued his yeoman efforts at building the conservative party's brand throughout north-central Alabama.

In 1986, Hunt again was in the right place at the right time. His years of loyalty to the Republican cause culminated with his being the token Republican nominee for governor. He was not given much of a chance as there had not been a Republican governor in the state since Reconstruction.

That was about to change. The Democrats shot themselves in the foot and an angered Alabama electorate elected Hunt.

In 1978 Fob James sent the Three B's—Brewer, Beasley, and Baxley—packing. Brewer and Beasley were permanently exiled to Buck's Pocket, the mythical destination for defeated Alabama gubernatorial candidates. However, Bill Baxley resurrected his political career by bouncing back to be elected lieutenant governor in 1982, while George Wallace was winning his fifth and final term as governor. Meanwhile, another player arrived on the state political scene. Charlie Graddick was elected as a fiery, tough lock-'em-up-and-throw-away-the-key attorney general. Graddick had previously been a district attorney in Mobile.

When Wallace bowed out from seeking reelection in 1986, it appeared the race was between Baxley, the lieutenant governor, and Graddick, the attorney general. Former Governor Fob James (still a Democrat at that point) was also in the race. It also appeared there was a clear ideological divide. The moderates and liberals in Alabama were for Baxley and the archconservatives were for Graddick (who later became a Republican). Baxley had the solid support of black voters, labor, and progressives. Graddick had the hard-core conservatives, including most of the Republican voters in Alabama.

The Republicans had gone to a primary by 1986, which Guy Hunt won, but very few Alabamians, even Republicans, participated. It was still assumed that winning the Democratic primary was tantamount to election. The Alabama Democratic primary would draw almost a million voters while the GOP primary drew fewer than 50,000, so obviously most Republican-leaning voters felt that for their vote to count they had to vote in the Democratic primary.

Graddick and James went after each other with a vengeance in the crowded Democratic primary, while Baxley mostly ignored both. Baxley came out on top but did not receive enough votes to avoid a runoff. Baxley says he had hoped to be in a runoff with James, because polls showed Baxley was the second choice of Graddick supporters. But on primary election night, Graddick became Baxley's runoff opponent, and he went on television proclaiming, "Bill, circle your wagons, because we're coming after you."

And by the "we" who were "coming," Graddick meant Republicans as well. He encouraged Republicans to come out to vote for him in the runoff. They did and that is why he won. This was not something new; it had been happening for decades. Brewer would have never led Wallace in 1970 without Republican voters. Fob would have never won the Democratic primary and thus become governor in 1978 without Republican voters. Basically, Alabama had been a no-party state. We still have no party registration law. So how do you police people weaving in and out of primaries without a mechanism in place for saying you are a Democrat, Republican, or Independent?

The difference in 1986 was that Republicans had held a primary for the first time. The Alabama State Democratic Committee thus passed the

With Governor Guy Hunt signing Tort Reform legislation.

"Radney Resolution" stating that if you voted in the Republican primary, thus helping to nominate the Republican slate for the November general election, you could not then vote in the Democratic primary runoff to help choose the Democratic slate for November.

After Graddick defeated Baxley by fewer than 9,000 votes in the runoff primary, the Democratic Party did the unthinkable. They convened the hierarchy of the party, who clearly favored Baxley, and declared Baxley the Democratic nominee because they calculated that Graddick had won the runoff only because at least 10,000 Republican crossovers had voted. The Democrats paraded experts in front of their committee to testify that Baxley would have won in a Democrats-only contest. They brazenly chose Baxley as the nominee despite the fact that Graddick had clearly gotten the most votes.

This move went against the grain of the vast majority of Alabama voters, even though a Graddick legal challenge to the Democratic Party procedure failed before both a three-judge federal court and the Alabama Supreme Court. Nonetheless, many voters felt Graddick had gotten the most votes and should be the nominee. The Democratic Party leadership sloughed it off. They assumed that the Democratic nominee would win regardless. After all, there had not been a Republican governor of Alabama in 100 years. In addition the Republicans had nominated an unknown Cullman County probate judge named Guy Hunt with no money and no name identification.

The Democratic leaders guessed wrong. The backlash was enormous. The bold handpicking of a nominee who had not received the most votes, was a wrong that needed to be righted. Baxley did not help his case by ignoring Hunt and dismissing him as a simpleton. He mocked Hunt saying he was unqualified because he only had a high school education. Baxley, as politically astute as he was, should have realized that he was insulting the majority of Alabama voters who themselves only possessed high school educations. This created a backlash of its own.

There is an old George Wallace political theory that declares more people vote against someone than for someone. This was never more applicable than in 1986. The Democratic Party's undemocratic decision to name Bill Baxley as their nominee even though he did not get the most votes in the primary so incensed Alabamians' sense of fairness and honesty that they would have voted for Mickey Mouse if he had been the Republican nominee.

When the votes were counted in the November general election, Guy Hunt was elected. Alabama had its first Republican governor in 100 years. The 1986 governor's race will go down in history as a red-letter year.

Helen Hunt

Guy and Helen Hunt were childhood sweethearts in rural Cullman County. Helen assumed that she and Guy would have a happy rural religious life on their small north Alabama farm. Her expectations were met as she raised their children and kept their family home. They lived a very simple life. Guy was a Primitive Baptist preacher in their community.

Hunt was uneducated but he was not ignorant. After he was elected governor, he surrounded himself with very smart and capable people. He quickly grasped the political spectrum of Montgomery and set out to sail a conservative ship of state. He was wise enough to keep his agenda simple and achievable. The need for tort reform was the paramount conservative business mission. He set his sights on that goal and did not deviate.

Hunt took a page from the George Wallace playbook. Wallace was a master at courting and working the legislature. In fact, Wallace was so adept that one month during my freshman year in the legislature I ate more meals with Wallace at the governor's mansion than I did with my family. Hunt, like Wallace, would invite legislators out to the governor's mansion for dinner. He made it his mission to befriend and entertain those of us who were members of the conservative and pro-business wing of the State House of Representatives.

One night I was seated at the table with the Governor and Mrs. Helen. Hunt was at the head of the table and Mrs. Helen was at the opposite end. I was seated next to Mrs. Helen and visited with her during the meal. I have known some saintly women over my life but this lady exuded a genuine sweetness and Christian demeanor that was unmatched. You could tell that you were in the presence of a truly humble lady.

Mrs. Helen was totally undeterred by the grandeur of being First Lady of Alabama. It was obvious that she would have much rather been cooking dinner at her modest home in Cullman County than living in the governor's mansion with a host of servants at her beck and call.

My mama taught me to thank your host for dinner. Therefore, at the end of the evening I looked for Mrs. Helen to thank her for the meal but she had disappeared. I asked the servants where she had gone and one of them directed me to the kitchen. As I entered the kitchen, to my amazement Mrs. Helen was washing the dishes while four maids stood and watched her. The sweet First Lady was so accustomed to taking care of her own cooking and washing that she could not bring herself to allow someone else to wait on her. The privileges and deference bestowed on the First Lady were completely outside of her comfort zone.

Helen Hunt was probably the sweetest and most genuine First Lady Alabama has ever known.

Jim Folsom Jr.

James E. Folsom Jr. was literally born in the Governor's Mansion. His father, the legendary two-term Alabama Governor James E. "Big Jim" Folsom Sr. was in office when "Little Jim" was born on May 14, 1949, in Montgomery. One could argue that Jim Jr. enjoyed a more successful and illustrious political career than his famous father. However, there is no question that Little Jim's career was launched because of his name and the following that Big Jim had earned among the rural enclaves of Alabama.

With Governor Jim Folsom, Jr.

Little Jim's last successful campaign was for lieutenant governor in 2006. It was a razor-thin win over Luther Strange. That race had several angles from a political historian's perspective, first of all Big Luther Strange stands 6'9". The last state politician that tall was Big Jim Folsom. However, Big Jim wore a larger shoe, a size 17 to Luther's 15 (though Luther has a son with a size 17 foot).

Little Jim adroitly ran one of the most effective ads in state history the last week of the campaign to eke out his victory. He ran an ad showing Luther playing tennis at the Mountain Brook Country Club. He knew that the Mountain Brook silk-stocking image would not sit well with the anti-big city, country folks around the state. I'm convinced that there were still enough old Big Jim loyalists left in the state that voted for Little Jim that day. I said the day after that 2006 election and since then that Big Jim won that race for Little Jim from the grave.

Jim Jr. was elected lieutenant governor of Alabama three times. He was elected to the State Public Service Commission twice and was governor for two years. Big Jim did not have that many wins. He was elected governor twice, once in 1946 and again in 1954.

Folsom was elected to the Alabama Public Service Commission in 1978 and reelected in 1982. In 1980 he defeated incumbent Donald W. Stewart in the Democratic Senate primary, but narrowly lost the general election to Republican Jeremiah Denton. Jim Folsom, Jr won the first of his three terms as lieutenant governor in 1986. He won a second term in 1990. During that term he assumed the governorship from Guy Hunt when Hunt was removed from office, convicted of state ethics law violations with regard to funds involved in his second inaugural ceremonies.

Only weeks after Folsom assumed the office, State officials were approached by Mercedes-Benz about the possibility of locating its first manufacturing plant outside Germany in Alabama. Over the following months, Folsom led Alabama's efforts to recruit the facility, culminating in an October 1993 announcement that Alabama had beaten 30 other states for the coveted facility. The prestige of the Mercedes plant opened the door for future automotive plants to locate in the state.

In 1994 he ran for a full term as governor. Despite his record he was narrowly defeated by former Governor Fob James. In 2006, Folsom re-entered state politics, running again as the Democratic nominee for lieutenant governor. He defeated Republican Luther Strange in the general election.

He lost in his bid for a record fourth term as lieutenant governor in 2010 to Kay Ivey. He was swept away in a GOP tidal wave that year. The Republican tsunami took out every Democrat in statewide constitutional office. Jim Folsom Jr. was considered the best thoroughbred in the Democratic Party stable. Little Jim has been let out to pasture like every other Democrat in the state.

Folsom is married to the former Marsha Guthrie, they have two grown children, and reside in Cullman. Marsha Guthrie Folsom is the daughter of Big Jim's best friend. Her father served one term in the legislature and was a devoted Big Jim man.

Marsha is a few years younger than Jim. They both grew up in Cullman and knew how close their father's were. Marsha was actually closer in age and friendship to Jim's younger sister, Bama. Bama was a beautiful girl. She looked a lot like her mother Jamelle.

Bama and I paged together in the State Senate when we were in high school. She and Jim both went to Jacksonville State.

Marsha went to the University of Alabama. We were in school together at the same time at Alabama. We were political friends. She was very outstanding at the University. It was assumed that she would go into politics. Most observers say unequivocally that Marsha is the best politician in the family.

They look like a Hollywood couple. Marsha is sweet and pretty while Jim is strikingly movie starlike handsome. Their children of course are attractive.

Big Jim was proud of Little Jim's political success.

Don Siegelman

Those of us who grew up in and around Alabama politics have coined a descriptive term for a person who is obsessed with seeking political office constantly and tirelessly without reservation or concern for their physical, mental or financial welfare. They will run for high elected office at all cost. The term we use to describe those people is named for the man who best exemplified that obsession, George Wallace. Therefore, someone who is driven by obsession to win high public office has the "George Wallace Syndrome." The Alabama baby boomer who was eaten up with the George Wallace Syndrome more than any other I know was Don Siegelman. Siegelman ran nonstop since he was a student at the University of Alabama in the 1960s. He was successful. He was president of the student government at Alabama and went on to become Alabama's secretary of state, attorney general, lieutenant governor and finally his life dream of governor. There is an old political saying that you don't ever want to get into a race with someone who wants it more than you and will out work you. Siegelman was never outworked. He was relentless and focused on the ultimate prize that many a young politician in Alabama aspired to and that's the Governor's chair. He captured the brass ring.

Siegelman reminded me so much of George Wallace, he truly deserves the award for having the Wallace Syndrome. He and Wallace were both so consumed with politics and being governor that neither one of them could tell you what they were eating when you had lunch with them. Eating was a sideline to any political discussion they were having and calling lunch. They ate because they had to eat to survive.

Siegelman was always a little more liberal than most Alabamians. Therefore, he grew up admiring the more progressive Alabama political icons.

He admired our progressive New Deal Democrats such as Lister Hill, John Sparkman, and Carl Elliott, but the utmost idol in administration for young liberal politicians of my era was James E. "Big Jim" Folsom. Big Jim was truly a progressive on fiscal and social issues.

Siegelman had a remarkably similar career and educational background as Bill Clinton; both were almost the same age; both went to prestige law schools—Clinton to Yale and Siegelman to Georgetown. They both went on to do postgraduate work at Oxford in England. Then they both started running for office right away. Clinton ran for Congress but narrowly lost, then was elected attorney general, and two years later was elected governor of Arkansas. Siegelman ran for secretary of state and then on up the Alabama political ladder to attorney general, lieutenant governor and governor.

SIEGELMAN MEETS BIG JIM

As Siegelman was beginning his first foray into Alabama politics, he was campaigning hard all day for Secretary of State in early 1978 and wound up his day late in Cullman. Big Jim, in his later years, camped out at a truck stop along the interstate at Cullman. Big Jim was drinking coffee and Siegelman spotted his lifelong hero and liberal idol, Big Jim, and went over to introduce himself. Siegelman gave Big Jim his spiel and what he was doing and how his campaign for Secretary of State was going. He gave Big Jim the story of his pedigree concerning all of his education degrees, University of Alabama student government president, Georgetown law school and Oxford in England.

Big Jim listened intently to the young politician and sipped on his coffee. Now, you've got to realize that even though Big Jim was a progressive on fiscal and race matters, he was pretty down home when it came to country politics, patronage, and homespun talking to folks. Big Jim was also pretty pragmatic and plain spoken.

He said, "Boy, are you asking my advice about your campaign?" Siegelman said, "Sure I am, Governor." Big Jim said, "Well, first of all you need to change your name, ain't nobody in Opp going to vote for some boy named Siegelman. First of all you can't say it, secondly it don't sound like a good regular Alabama Baptist or Methodist name, and you better tell folks you went to school at Oxford High School in Calhoun County and not some place in England and thirdly, don't you know you can't steal any money in that job?"

Bob Riley

Bob Riley was Alabama's 52nd governor and served two terms. He had previously served six years in the U.S. Congress from the 3rd District. He was born and raised in Ashland in Clay County where his family had ranched and farmed for six generations. Riley was a successful businessman prior to going to Congress. He had close ties to the Business Council of Alabama during both his terms as governor. Like a good many Alabama governors, he was a graduate of the University of Alabama and a Southern Baptist.

Riley took office in January 2003 after surviving one of the most bruising gubernatorial elections in history. His razor-thin margin over Don Siegelman hardly gave him a mandate for major accomplishment in state government. He and Siegelman had so pulverized each other in campaign ads that most voters wondered why both were not in jail—ironically a cloud was brewing over Siegelman and he indeed would be heading for jail.

As Riley took the reins of state government his only political experience was his previous six years in Congress. He had no experience in state government and both branches of the legislature were overwhelmingly Democratic. Although partisan acrimony was not yet as pronounced as in Washington, partisanship had arrived in Montgomery and the Democratic legislature and the powers that controlled the legislature did not want a Republican governor to succeed.

For reasons that nobody can figure out, Riley immediately set out to commit political suicide. Both the general fund and education fund were in the red and facing a crisis. Even though the general public did not believe this perennial cry of wolf, Riley saw the figures and did buy into the crisis mentality.

Riley, who was a Reagan small-government fiscal conservative, went in the opposite direction than his idol would have. Instead of asking for massive cuts in government spending, Riley offered the biggest tax increase in state history, $1.2 billion to be exact. The most unbelievable approach was that the plan he offered and that was enacted by an eager legislature placed the entire tax burden on Republicans. The most onerous part of the tax burden was directed at the special interests that had backed Riley the most in his race for governor. It was as though he took a rifle and aimed the tax at his supporters, starting with those who had most loyally backed him. It was a blunder of monumental proportions. Voters defeated his proposal by a 3–1 margin.

At the end of Riley's first year in office he appeared to be a lame duck. Most pundits wrote his chances for reelection as slim or none. Siegelman, who had never stopped running, was exuberant. Fellow Republicans were also eyeing the 2006 governor's race to succeed Riley. The governor's office had been a musical chair since 1994. No incumbent governor had won reelection in the last three races and Riley seemed on course to follow that trend.

The most logical challenger to Riley was Lieutenant Governor Lucy Baxley who had served two successful terms as state treasurer and had been elected the first female lieutenant governor in state history. She received the most votes of any statewide candidate in her 2002 race for the state's second-highest office and had great name identification. She was simply known as "Lucy."

Lucy sat back and quietly watched Riley self-destruct. She took no positions on the tax debacle or anything else. She did not have to because there was no power in the lieutenant governor's office.

Riley, to his credit, took his setback in stride with great resilience. He quickly recovered and his next three years were very Republican. He espoused less government and lower taxes. He cut ribbons and smiled and handled crises like hurricanes with aplomb and confidence. Riley looked gubernatorial. In fact his handling of Hurricane Katrina in August 2005 marked a turning point in his political recovery. His positives shot up dramatically at that point and continued to skyrocket.

Ironically, Lucy had to make a decision to run at this same time. The polling numbers she saw in July 2005 revealed that she could beat Riley.

She pulled the trigger around the same time as Hurricane Katrina. Riley turned the tide about a month later and he never looked back. His numbers escalated. He trounced former Chief Justice Roy Moore 70–30 percent in the GOP primary. Lucy defeated Don Siegelman who was under indictment and was actually convicted during the primary of ethics violations. Lucy's 60–40 margin over a hapless Siegelman portended that she was not as strong as once thought.

Once the dust settled after the June primaries, polling and other indications showed that Riley would be tough to beat in the fall. The first polls showed him with a double-digit lead over Lucy. As the summer ended and the fall campaign began in September his lead in the polls had grown to 20 points. It went as high as 25 points as late as mid-October. Riley's insurmountable lead in the polls transpired into an avalanche-sized campaign fundraising advantage. He outspent the underdog Lucy Baxley by a 4–1 margin. He ran an aggressive, well-managed, 21st-century campaign spearheaded by some of the best and most expensive political consultants in America. His positive, happy, confident personality, and charisma were captured and reflected in his ads. It resulted in a landslide victory over Democrat Lucy Baxley.

He had a somewhat lackluster second term. He left the cupboard bare, so to speak, for the next governor, fellow Republican Dr. Robert Bentley.

Robert Bentley

Dr. Robert Bentley was elected governor in the November 2010 general election. But you might say he was elected in the Republican primary runoff that June because Alabama has become such a one-party Republican state that winning the Republican nomination is now tantamount to election in the Heart of Dixie. He became the first person to move directly from the legislature to the governor's office in this century.

Bentley was born on a farm in rural Shelby County near Columbiana where he was a straight-A student and student body president. His Republican roots came out in the 1950s presidential contests. At that time, all elected officials in Alabama were Democrats and the state voted Democratic for president. The future doctor and governor, Robert Bentley, was the campaign manager for Republican presidential candidate Dwight "Ike" Eisenhower. Nobody can ever claim that they are more Republican or have been a Republican longer than Robert Bentley.

He went on to the University of Alabama and graduated with honors. He married Diane Jones from Montgomery. He went on to medical school at UAB. He had a stint in the Air Force as a doctor. Then he set up practice in Tuscaloosa. He built an astounding career as a dermatologist in that region; his medical group was one of the largest in the state. He and Diane raised four boys and they have six grandchildren, all girls. He was also a deacon and leader in his Baptist church in Tuscaloosa. He was a well-respected physician and leader in his community and was financially secure. At age 60 he ran for and was elected to the State House of Representatives in 2002. He served two terms, a total of eight years. He retired from his medical practice and decided to run for governor of Alabama. Very few gave him much of a chance to be elected Alabama's 53rd governor. He proved us all wrong. As the race began, he was considered a nice guy but a dark horse.

The Republican field for governor began to form early. They all figured that the winner of the GOP primary would have a cakewalk to the Governor's office because they assumed that an aloof, intellectual, mild-mannered, Harvard-educated African American congressman named Artur Davis would be their Democratic opponent. In the Heart of Dixie that is called a free pass. In basketball vernacular it is referred to as a slam dunk. Every major GOP player saw a clear shot at being governor. The only hurdle they faced was to win the Republican primary.

As the race began in earnest in mid-2009, most so-called experts projected a Bradley Byrne and Tim James runoff simply because these two had the money. Bradley Byrne was a 55-year-old Fairhope lawyer, former state school board member, two-term state senator, and chancellor of the state junior college system. He began running two years in advance of the election. Byrne became the anointed candidate of the Big Business community. It was also known that he was Governor Riley's choice. With these credentials he took on the mantle of frontrunner.

Tim James, the son of former Governor Fob James, had made a half-hearted run for governor in 2002 when Riley was first elected. He ran poorly but really did not put a lot of effort into that race. James changed his tune in 2010 and gave it his all. Being a former Auburn football player like his dad, he gave it the old-fashioned college try. He campaigned full-time for two years, spent $2 million of his own money, and brought in the best professional staff that money could buy. He was determined to give it his best effort.

From the onset the wild card in the field was former Chief Justice Roy Moore. He would be relegated to being a one-issue candidate. Moore's famous stance as the Ten Commandments Judge made him the darling of the religious right. These voters comprise approximately 25 percent of the GOP primary vote in Alabama. Therefore, early polling showed Moore was going to get 20–25 percent and no more. However, he would probably not make the runoff with this threshold limitation and very little money. Therefore, the other serious players would have to work around Moore's capture of 20 percent of the vote from the get-go.

Dr. Robert Bentley appeared to be relegated to becoming a likeable also-ran. He was expected to finish in a respectable fourth place.

As the race began, Bradley Byrne forged to the front with his overwhelming money edge. He was the candidate of the Big Mules and they put their money where their mouth was and delivered for Byrne. He wound up raising and spending $7 million.

The race appeared to be Byrne's to lose. However, as is the case in politics, funny things happen on the way to a coronation. Byrne's career had been built around not only opposing but openly lambasting Dr. Paul Hubbert and the AEA. Byrne had picked on the wrong enemy.

Eight governors had come and gone since Dr. Hubbert's famous David vs. Goliath victory over George Wallace in the 1970s. Dr. Hubbert had rendered every governor hapless and irrelevant in the budget process. His strength was derived from controlling the legislature. He usually could care less who was governor because the governor played second fiddle to him when it came to education dollars. Therefore, it surprised the Byrne team when Hubbert decided to destroy Byrne.

Bradley Byrne made his announcement for governor looking down Dexter Avenue at the AEA building and attacking Dr. Hubbert's omnipotent control of Alabama government. He threw down the gauntlet and declared that the dethroning of King Hubbert would be the hallmark of his tenure as governor. This was like waving a red flag in front of a raging bull.

Most people assumed that Hubbert would simply ignore Byrne's rhetoric and continue to bestow his political action committee largesse onto the legislative battles. However, Byrne's bold attack on Hubbert and his herd of teachers angered the king. He figured a governor could be allowed to play in the governor's sandbox, but Hubbert was not about to allow someone to kick sand on him in his own sandbox.

Hubbert created a conduit PAC to funnel AEA money to pummel Byrne with attack ads. Hubbert not only spent a ton of money to derail Byrne, the ads were well-designed and effective. They created havoc for Byrne and ultimately destroyed him.

Byrne assumed that Tim James was his competition so he began attacking James with negative ads and James hit back. Byrne was getting hit from two sides. In the meantime, the mild-mannered, kindly Dr. Bentley was smiling and remaining positive with his campaign. Bentley's simple and positive television ads, saying "Alabama is hurting and we need a doctor," resonated with voters even if he did not have the resources to run the ads as often as James and Byrne played their negative spots. However, what hit home more than any message in the entire campaign was Bentley humbly and sincerely looking into the camera and saying to Alabamians that if elected he would not take a salary as governor. These two ads were as effective as any in Alabama political history.

Polls had shown Bentley as the most likeable candidate in the race. His Achilles heel was that voters did not think he could win. He had shown an incremental upward momentum the entire campaign. However, in the last two weeks he caught fire as Byrne and James continued attacking each other. The fallout created by Byrne's and James's negative campaigns was that voters did not accrue to either of the aggressors. Instead, every vote Byrne and James peeled off of each other with negative ads went to the good Dr. Bentley.

Interviewing Governor Robert Bentley, 2014.

When the votes were counted from the June 1 GOP primary, Bradley Byrne led with 28 percent and Dr. Bentley and Tim James were in a dead heat with 25 percent each. Roy Moore finished fourth with 18 percent. After a recount to determine who finished second between James and Bentley, the good doctor prevailed by 166 votes. Therefore, the runoff was set between Bradley Byrne and Robert Bentley.

A cursory look at the polling data could portend a Bentley victory. Both James's and Moore's voters overwhelmingly favored Bentley. AEA continued to hammer Byrne in the runoff, which allowed Bentley to stay positive in his own ads. He simply smiled and continued to run his no-salary ad while AEA did the dirty work.

Bentley won easily in the July 13 runoff. He had emerged as the GOP nominee with two amazing anomalies. He spent $1.8 million compared to Bradley Byrne's $7 million, which is an amazing 4 to 1 advantage overcome by the underdog. In addition, Bentley ran an entire campaign with no negative ads.

As Bentley entered the fall fray against his Democratic opponent Ron

Sparks, he had the lowest negative ratings of any candidate in recent history. Very few people disliked the doctor from Tuscaloosa. Therefore, he was the odds-on favorite to win the governor's race on November 2.

There were no surprises in the general election campaign. The Republican establishment embraced Dr. Bentley and bestowed their financial support on their GOP standard-bearer. He was able to outspend his Democratic foe by a 4–1 advantage. Dr. Bentley's 58–42 margin victory over Ron Sparks appeared easy. It was made even easier by the Republican tidal wave that swept Republicans into every state office. Bentley would have won regardless, but the Republican tsunami made his victory bigger. Dr. Bentley became Alabama's 53rd Governor.

Bentley Wins Second Term in 2014

During the 2010 governor's race, I continuously made the statement that whoever won would be a one-term governor. My prophecy was based on the fact that the state was flat broke and it would take a lot of tough decisions and probably tax increases to fix the mess.

Former Governor Bob Riley was not helping his successor any with what seemed to be a concerted mission to spend every cent in an already barren cupboard. There was nothing in the state rainy day funds and all the federal stimulus money from Washington was gone. Unlike the federal government that can just print money, the state constitutionally has to live within its means.

Therefore, the new governor, Dr. Robert Bentley, inherited a ship of state that was like the *Titanic* about five minutes before it hit the iceberg. However, the good doctor from Tuscaloosa took the helm of state government with the same positive attitude that had resonated during his campaign for the office. He had connected with the Alabama electorate during his come-from-behind capture of the state's political brass ring. He began his four-year adventure by declaring he would not offer any tax increases to resolve the state's budget woes. This same mantra was espoused by his friends and former colleagues in the new super-majority ultra-conservative legislature elected with him during the 2010 elections.

Dr. Bentley rolled up his sleeves and went to work, although he went to work at below minimum wage. In fact, he received no wages for being governor during his entire four-year term, living up to his campaign promise of not taking a salary until the state reached full employment.

His primary goal was to create new jobs. He made that the focus of his first four years. He indeed had some success. He helped lure several high-profile high-paying manufacturing plants to the state. He was not flashy or ego driven but came across to fellow Alabamians as a good guy and a hardworking, underpaid governor. He was seen as a plow horse, not a show horse.

He further endeared himself to Alabamians with his outstanding service during devastating tornadoes that came through the state about two years into his tenure. He handled the catastrophe with aplomb and a sincere empathy that was evident. Indeed, the tornadoes hammered his home area. The worst damage and casualties resulted in and around Tuscaloosa.

Dr. Bentley had made it known early that he would seek a second term. It became obvious that my prognostication four years earlier, that whoever was elected in 2010 would be a one-term governor, was going to come back to haunt me.

A cursory look at the initial polling for 2014 revealed that I was indeed going to have to eat my words. Bentley had an overwhelming and unprecedented approval rating, driven by an incredible trustworthiness factor. Folks simply liked the old doctor from Tuscaloosa. He was like an old shoe. He felt good to them. Therefore, it became obvious early on that he was going to coast to reelection and he did. Incumbents have an inherent advantage in all elections but popular ones really do. Thus, the 2014 election shaped up as a very dull year for Alabama politics. Bentley was perceived as unbeatable, so the election became uneventful.

He received token opposition in the GOP primary. Two obscure people qualified. Bentley trounced them with an amazing 90 percent of the vote. He then went on to trample the Democratic nominee, Parker Griffith, by a record-breaking 64–36 margin, further relegating the Democratic Party to minority and uphill status in statewide elections.

Bentley's landslide reelection victory was also remarkable in that he won so overwhelmingly without running one negative ad.

7

Two Who Never Made It—Baxley and Hubbert

Bill Baxley

There is a great movie entitled *The Summer of '42*. The summer of 1942 was not a normal long, hot, mint-julep-sipping summer for Alabama. We, like the rest of the nation, had been thrown into the throes of the most ferocious world war in human history. The Japanese had bombed Pearl Harbor on December 7, 1941, and within hours we were in World War II. By summer we were in combat in Europe and the Pacific. We were a sleeping giant that had been awakened. Our state along with the nation was concentrated on saving our nation and way of life.

The City of Dothan was a sleepy farming community in the southeast corner of Alabama. It was the hub of the Wiregrass area and the peanut-producing capital of the world. However, in the summer of 1942 it was being transformed from an agriculture peanut economy to a war economy. Our power-laden Congressional delegation was loyal to Franklin Delano Roosevelt. Their loyalty and seniority made the United States Army select Fort Rucker as a major military training facility. This military operation became the largest employer in the Wiregrass region and remains so today. In June of 1942, during this upheaval, William J. Baxley was one year old. He was the son of Keener and Lema Baxley.

Keener Baxley was a very respected circuit judge in Dothan. The Baxleys were a prominent family and among the earliest settlers of Houston County, one of the last counties organized in Alabama. Most of the prominent fami-

With longtime friend Bill Baxley while Bill was Lieutenant Governor and I was a freshman State Representative, 1983.

lies in Dothan and Houston County, like the Baxleys, can trace their roots from southeast Georgia. There is a Baxley, Georgia, settled by their ancestors. Even though not wealthy, the Baxleys were an upper-class, well-respected family. Keener Baxley was revered as a man of exemplary character and integrity.

Young Bill Baxley grew up loving law, politics, and baseball. He grew up around his daddy's courtroom in Dothan and learned to love the law and lawyering. There was probably never any doubt that he would be a lawyer by profession if he didn't make it as a major league baseball player, which was every young boy's dream at that time. Bill was probably a better student than a baseball player. He was brilliant academically. He even skipped a grade and finished high school at age 15. He entered the University of Alabama at age 16 and cruised through. He was active politically and socially at the Capstone. He went on to the University of Alabama Law School and after graduation returned home to Dothan. He was elected district attorney of the judicial district containing Houston and Henry counties at the ripe old age of 25. He prosecuted the wayward felons of Dothan in his daddy's courtroom.

At the age of 28, Bill Baxley ran for attorney general of Alabama in 1970. He beat longtime Attorney General McDonald Gallion in the May Democratic primary and went on in the November general election, at age 29, to become the youngest person ever elected a state attorney general in the history of the United States. His meteoric rise at such a young age made him fodder for national publications like *Time* magazine which featured him as one of the brightest rising stars in the nation. His brilliance gave new meaning to the word prodigy.

The 1970 governor's race between George Wallace and Albert Brewer overshadowed any other political race in Alabama. It was a titanic war that wallowed in the throes of race-baiting politics and is considered the most classic, bitter, and pivotal gubernatorial battle in our state history. In fact, the attack ads that Wallace used against Brewer in his come-from-behind victory that year have been labeled the most overtly racist ads in American history.

The attorney general's race was below the radar screen. It was considered an upset that a 28-year-old Wiregrass district attorney beat a veteran McDonald Gallion in a close race. Therefore, it was not apparent to the voters that they had elected a true progressive liberal as their attorney general. Baxley had openly and unashamedly courted liberals, labor, and blacks to win the race. He didn't do it for expediency but because his heart was in it. Baxley was a true progressive Southern Democrat.

Baxley never shirked from his populist beliefs and held his principles of egalitarianism above his personal success politically. At first glance you would wonder why Baxley was so progressive both economically and on the race issue, being that he was born into a privileged, upper-class, prominent family headed by a father who was a conservative circuit judge. However, when you delve into Alabama political history, you discover that the Wiregrass region from which Baxley hailed has always been progressive. It gave large pluralities to the populist Big Jim Folsom and as early as the late 1800s voted with the north Alabama yeoman farmers for Reuben Kolb over the landed gentry Black Belt farmers. The Wiregrass has always aligned with north Alabama politically, and being the son of the Wiregrass made him sympathetic to the underdog and downtrodden.

Baxley's political idol was Big Jim Folsom. He was Big Jim personified

20 years later. Baxley's political philosophy may have been obscured during his campaign, however, he immediately dispelled any doubt that he was a liberal. He sued every Big Mule in sight including U.S. Steel and Alabama Power over pollution and other environmental concerns. He openly embraced, courted, and built an overt friendship with labor leaders and black leaders such as Joe Reed. He was certainly a contrast to our racist Governor, George Wallace, who had dominated our state politics for the past decade using the race issue which was the premier issue.

Ironically, Wallace loved Baxley. They had a special friendship and spoke on the phone constantly. Wallace's cronies and legislative leaders who were avowed racists disliked and distrusted Baxley, but Wallace who demagoged the race issue for his political advantage was really a true populist progressive like Baxley and Big Jim. However, unlike Wallace, Folsom and Baxley were racial progressives and proud of it. Wallace was cut from the same cloth only on economic issues.

In the spring of 1972, Baxley was 31 years old and into his second year as attorney general. Jere Beasley was a 36-year-old lieutenant governor. They were rivals with the state awaiting their showdown. Wallace had barely escaped with a slim tainted victory over Albert Brewer in 1970. He had gone to every hamlet in Alabama and begged that "if you elect me Governor of Alabama I will never run for president again. I only want to be Governor." Brewer had killed him with a slogan, "Alabama needs a full-time Governor," an obvious reference to the fact that Wallace was never in the state being governor but was only using the state title and state coffers to constantly run for president. After he slipped by Brewer in the primary, he conveniently forgot his promise and was on a plane to Wisconsin the next day running for president in 1972.

The people of Alabama did not forget his shallow political promise. He was considered dead by most political observers. So, in May of 1972, all Three B's, Baxley, Beasley, and Brewer, were planning to run for governor in 1974. They were all committed. They felt Wallace was finished. In mid-May a nut named Arthur Bremer gunned Wallace down in the parking lot of a Laurel, Maryland, shopping mall as Wallace was finishing a presidential campaign speech. Wallace's body was riddled with bullets. Most people would have died, but he survived, though he would be paralyzed and in a wheelchair for life.

Wallace's forays into the presidential races and his disregard, absenteeism, and total neglect of his duties as governor of Alabama had made him vulnerable for reelection as governor in 1974. However, the assassination attempt and seeing Wallace in a wheelchair evoked such sympathy from Alabamians that it became apparent that the bullet wounds may have ruined Wallace's personal life but it had saved his political life. The sympathy vote for Wallace in 1974 would be too great to overcome. All Three B's, Brewer, Beasley, and Baxley sensed it by early 1973. They all pulled back and set their sights for 1978. It gave advantage to Baxley and Beasley who were young anyway and would benefit from the delay. Brewer was the loser, he was a generation older than Beasley and Baxley and would be out of the limelight for six more years. Baxley and Beasley never stopped running, the collision would occur in 1978 rather than 1974.

The two could not have been any more different. Beasley was an arch conservative who had cut his political teeth campaigning for the very conservative lieutenant governor and late United States Senator, Jim Allen, while Baxley was following in the steps of Big Jim Folsom. If Big Jim epitomized the word uninhibited, Baxley epitomized the word flamboyant. Beasley was the perfect family man and Baxley was the prototypical bachelor. Baxley pretty much lived the same lifestyle as a 34-year-old bachelor attorney general that he had lived as a 21-year-old bachelor University of Alabama Law student.

During his second term as attorney general, Baxley took a junket to Las Vegas. Baxley who has a genius IQ level also has a photographic memory. This photographic memory allowed him to win hundreds of thousands of dollars at blackjack at the Las Vegas casinos before they asked him to quit playing as they do when they discover a genius is breaking their bank. When he got back to Alabama, the media asked him about his exploits. He answered them with vintage Big Jim Folsom candor and said proudly, "Yes, I beat the Las Vegas casinos. You boys know I like to gamble and have a good time. If you wanted a monk for attorney general, you should have elected a monk." Baxley's flamboyant lifestyle became common knowledge. However, there was never any hint of corruption or scandal in his duties as a public official.

Bill Baxley and His Baldwin County Buddies

In his first race for attorney general in 1970, Bill Baxley was only 28 and only a few years removed from his fraternity days at the University of Alabama and still a bachelor. It was safe to say that he had as much a penchant for Schlitz beer as he did for politics. His drinking and partying would have to be subdued during the campaign. Wiser heads pulled him aside and told him that he would have to curtail his drinking during the campaign. Baxley had indeed completely abstained from alcohol the entire campaign. However, the last week of the campaign, it was toward the end of the day and he was campaigning in rural Baldwin County. He was hot, tired, and thirsty. He succumbed to the urge of beer. He stopped at what appeared to be a popular beer joint in the area. He proceeded to have an all night binge with his new Baldwin County buddies. They loved Baxley. The fact that a young candidate for attorney general of Alabama would spend all night drinking beer with them endeared Baxley to them.

A few days later, Baxley won the attorney general's race by a slim margin over the veteran McDonald Gallion. It was an upset.

Out of curiosity, Baxley wondered how he did in Baldwin County. As he perused the return totals, the results from Baldwin County basically mirrored the vote from throughout the rest of the state. However, one box stood out. In the box where he spent the night drinking, he carried it over 4-to-1. Obviously, his Baldwin County beer drinking buddies turned out for Baxley.

Squatlow and Baxley

Bill Baxley like most politicians had his favorite stories or jokes. One that Baxley told repeatedly throughout the years was about an old guy named Squatlow.

I'm not sure whether this story or joke is true or not, but it could very well be true.

Squatlow was nicknamed that because he would squat down close to the ground whenever he would talk with folks. You've seen old guys who do that. Squat down while they talk. Old Squatlow would hunker down with a chew of tobacco in his mouth and gossip and swap stories all day.

Baxley was a young district attorney for Houston and Henry counties. Houston is a fairly large county. Dothan is the county seat. Houston had about 90 percent of the people in the circuit with Henry County being the home to the rest. Baxley was a youthful 25-year-old DA and would travel to court on occasion in Henry County to prosecute the few criminals they had in Henry County.

Baxley like most politicians would stop at a country store and drink a Coke with the rural folks in the area. Henry County is a very sparsely populated rural county in the Wiregrass with two small towns, Abbeville and Headland. Abbeville happens to be the county seat. This story takes place in the early 1960s about the time of the Cuban Missile Crisis.

Squatlow had a mechanic shop/gas station/grocery store in the obscure community of Tumbleton in Henry County. His whole world was no bigger than that county. The biggest places he had ever been were Abbeville and Headland with a population of about 1,000 people each.

Well, they may have been back in the woods, but they knew about the Cuban Missile Crisis and the standoff between the United States and Russia. It was a scary situation. I think most people were afraid that a nuclear war was imminent. The whole world was on edge.

During the week of this crisis, Baxley was traveling to court in Henry County. He stopped by Squatlow's store in Tumbleton. Squatlow and all the folks in the little community were scared. This was obviously the topic of conversation that day.

Old Squatlow hunkered down in his lowest squatting position and just shook his head. "You know, I've been thinking about it all night, and I just know those damn Russians are going to bomb Abbeville. Yeah, they gonna drop one of them atom bombs right on Abbeville."

Baxley looked at Squatlow and said, "Squatlow, why in the world would the Russians drop a bomb on Abbeville, Alabama?"

Squatlow looked at Baxley like he was the most stupid person he had ever seen. He shook his head at how ignorant this young, 25-year-old lawyer was.

He looked at Baxley and said, "Boy, don't you know nothing? Don't you know that Abbeville is the county seat of Henry County?"

Mac McArthur

Even though he is a relatively young man, Mac McArthur knows Alabama politics as well as anybody. He has lots of tales and experiences.

Mac grew up in Ashford in Houston County in the Wiregrass. His family had been involved in county politics for generations. The McArthurs were mainstays of Houston County politics.

He knows all the legendary tales surrounding the local politics of that area from his childhood days and he knows most of the statewide stories as well. He has been a participant on the state stage for most of his life

Mac was always close to Bill Baxley. The Baxleys and McArthurs both being longtime Houston County families, their histories are intertwined.

Keener Baxley

Bill Baxley's father was a revered Circuit Judge in Houston County. Prior to going on the bench, Keener Baxley was the District Attorney. Keener Baxley was an austere and stern proper man. He was like an old man when he was young. Keener was up for reelection as District Attorney. He had fielded a tough, serious opponent. A young man named Martin, who was also from a prominent Dothan family, had just come home from the war. He was a military hero. Keener had been too old to go to the war. Old Keener was campaigning in a country store one day and the proprietor said to Keener, "That young Martin boy is a good boy. He is a nice, clean-cut, family man, and he's a real war hero. He's a really nice young man." Keener calmly replied, "Yes, he is. He is every bit as great as you say. I admire the boy and like him. You are absolutely right. So, why would you want to ruin a nice young man and get him into politics. You need an old son-of-a-bitch like me for this job."

Bill Baxley followed his father's lead and became district attorney for Houston County and Henry County as a young 25-year-old. He prosecuted cases before his father who was the circuit judge. They say Keener was tougher on Bill than any other lawyer who entered his courtroom.

Mac McArthur became Bill Baxley's right-hand man. Mac was only 11 when Bill was first elected attorney general of Alabama in 1970. He began working for Baxley when he finished law school and Baxley became lieutenant governor. Mac was 24 and Baxley himself was only 42 although he had already been attorney general for eight years and lost a governor's race in 1978 and been elected lieutenant governor in 1982. He had four statewide races under his belt by the time he was 42 years old.

Mac knows all the Baxley stories from 1983 on because he was Baxley's right-hand man.

Baxley's Chilton County Man

In the 1986 governor's race between Baxley and Charlie Graddick, Baxley got a couple of calls from folks in Chilton County that he had a problem with the man he had chosen to be his campaign manager. Baxley sent young Mac up to Chilton County to check it out. Mac got there about 8:30 in the morning and went into the store of their campaign man. It was a dilapidated old filling station in bad need of repair and customers. When Mac entered he saw an immediate problem. Their man was not just their campaign manager, he was everybody's. He had a menagerie of campaign material for every candidate he was for in every race. He had material for his lieutenant governor and attorney general candidates as well as all of his local favorites. It is a cardinal rule in Alabama politics to never get involved in another race. However, their man's choice of mixing multiple races was not their biggest problem. Their man met Mac with a bottle of whiskey half gone. It was 9 a.m. and the man was already drunk. Their campaign manager was the biggest drunk in a dry county. Chilton County is one of the most conservative counties in the state with a church on every corner.

Mac had to scurry around and get Baxley a new man for Chilton County.

Baxley and Wallace

Not many folks know that George Wallace and Bill Baxley were close friends. Wallace thought of Baxley as a protégé although both were perceived differently by the public. They appeared to be strange bedfellows as Wallace was perceived as an arch conservative racist and Baxley was an open progressive on the race issue.

They developed a friendship and close working relationship during the four years period from 1982 to 1986 while Wallace was Governor and

Baxley was lieutenant governor. It was no secret that Wallace was in bad health during this time. The bullet wounds from the 1972 assassination attempt had taken a toll on the Governor. Most insiders thought Wallace would not make it through his term.

Mac became the go-between between Wallace and Baxley. Mac would go see the Governor about every week and discuss with Wallace the progress in the legislature and how Baxley felt about things in the Senate. Wallace was not as out of it as it appeared. He knew what was going on and he heard all the rumors. He looked at Mac on day and said, "I know the reason you and Baxley check on me so often is you think I'm going to die, don't you?"

Mac and Wallace both liked Cigars

Anybody who knows Mac McArthur or knew George Wallace, know that both loved good cigars. Both Wallace and Mac have a stogie in their mouth, especially when they are talking politics. Wallace appreciated this penchant for cigars that his young political friend, Mac, had, like him. They were cigar buddies you might say.

Mac like Baxley loves baseball. Baxley used to make an annual trek to the World Series.

Wallace knew of Baxley's and Mac's journey to major league parks and cities and asked them to shop around and bring him back some good cigars from their trips.

Mac was going to Florida for Spring Training to see his beloved Boston Red Sox. They were playing the Detroit Tigers in a weekend, Spring Training series at the Tiger's Spring Training domain of Winter Haven.

This is near Tampa and Mac and his entourage were going to eat at the famous Columbia Restaurant in Tampa. The restaurant is near an old warehouse district. It had about six tobacco warehouses nearby where they rolled tobacco. These were fine Cuban cigar warehouses.

Mac ambled over to one and as he was meandering met an old Cuban proprietor who spoke broken English. Mac and the Cuban were able to converse. When the Cuban learned that Mac was from Alabama, the Cuban told him that he loved George Wallace and had voted for him for president. Mac tells the Cuban he not only knows Wallace but is his close friend and actually the reason he was there was to shop around for some cigars for the Governor. Upon hearing this, the Cuban goes back and opens a vault and proudly presents Mac with an exclusive box of Cuban cigars for the Governor.

He says, "You give those to the Governor." Then he looks at Mac ruefully and gives him a less expensive box of Cuban cigars and says, "These are for you, because if I don't give you some, you will steal the Governor's cigars for yourself."

Baxley and Wallace and the 1986 Governor's Race

Most insiders knew that Wallace favored Baxley over Graddick in the 1986 Governor's Race. As mentioned, Baxley and Wallace had become close and Baxley was Wallace's protégé and Wallace became Baxley's confidant.

After Graddick had gotten more votes than Baxley in the Democratic runoff in 1986, and the Democratic Party hierarchy went behind closed doors and picked Baxley to be the nominee, Baxley was not deaf to the negative reaction from the public. I don't think he realized how mad people were at the affront. He would find out pretty soon. An unknown Republican named Guy Hunt would trounce him in the Fall over the egregious arrogant move by the Democratic Party.

One day shortly after the selection process, Baxley was having some reservations over the coup. So he called Wallace and had a heart-to-heart talk with the King of Alabama politics. Baxley asked Wallace his opinion and what he would do. Wallace, the ultimate politician, told Baxley, "Bill you know what they call a governor who gets handpicked behind closed doors?"

Baxley said, "No, what?"

Wallace said, "They call him Governor."

Paul Ray Hubbert

Paul Ray Hubbert was born on Christmas Day in 1935 in the small rural crossroads of Hubbertville in Fayette County. The community was named for his family, who were the original and primary settlers.

Dr. Hubbert left an indelible mark on Alabama political history. The most enduring political giant in Alabama political history in my lifetime was George Wallace. Next to Wallace would be Senator Richard Shelby and Dr. Paul Hubbert.

Ironically, Dr. Hubbert made his mark as a political icon by defeating George Wallace in a pivotal legislative battle at the height of Wallace's power and popularity. Wallace was asking his legislature to divert education retirement dollars to mental health to avoid a federal takeover. Wallace called the young head of the AEA to his office to inform him of his plans. Hubbert looked Wallace directly in the eye and told him over my dead body you will.

Hubbert beat Wallace. He earned his spurs in that legendary western gun battle. That built his reputation. He went on to become the fastest draw on Goat Hill. He was an icon for over 42 years. He was so powerful that he was commonly referred to as "Governor."

Hubbert left Hubbertville in the 1950s with the idea that education would be his ticket away from picking cotton for the rest of his life. Similar to when Bear Bryant was asked during the pinnacle of his career what motivated him to become the greatest college football coach of all time, he said, "I didn't want to spend the rest of my life plowing cotton behind a mule." Regardless of what motivated Hubbert, he became the greatest educator in Alabama history.

In the course of his journey, Hubbert made the life of every Alabama educator better by his achievements. Over four decades from 1969 to 2011, Paul Hubbert was the best friend every schoolteacher in Alabama ever had.

He was superintendent of the Troy City School System in 1969. He was only 33 with a brilliant future ahead of him. The Alabama Education Association was a fledgling, toothless, social club run by the school superintendents in the state. Over 30 applicants applied for the vacancy as head of the association. Hubbert had not been one of the applicants. They came to him. He had been fishing with his friend and neighbor, Pike County Tax Collector Fred Dykes, when they called. At first, he turned them down.

Eventually, he acquiesced and took over the reins of the low key AEA. He immediately merged the all white teachers' organization with its black counterpart. He and Joe Reed were on course to make that union one of the greatest powers in Alabama politics. At that time in 1969 there were 30,000 members. When Hubbert retired in 2011, there were 100,000 members of the AEA.

Hubbert became a political kingmaker over the years. He would pump close to $10 million into legislative races throughout the state. By virtue of this largesse, he controlled the legislature during the 1970s, 80s and 90s, the way George Wallace did during the 1960s.

Hubbert and the AEA elected so many members of the legislature during that reign that many, if not most of them, owed their seat to him. Hubbert would boldly and brashly sit in the Capitol balcony and direct legislators' votes by pointing to his eye for a yes and to his nose for a no vote.

Hubbert was easily the most powerful lobbyist in state political history. Even though people facetiously called him "Governor," he yearned to be the real governor. He was the Democratic candidate for governor in 1990, but lost to Republican incumbent Governor Guy Hunt. He ran again in 1994 and lost the Democratic nomination to incumbent Governor Jim Folsom

Dr. Hubbert was first diagnosed with a liver problem in 1972. In 1989, it was widely publicized when he was flown to Pittsburgh, Pennsylvania, for a liver transplant. He was one of the longest-surviving liver transplant recipients in the world. He was hospitalized in October 2014 following a fall. He died 12 days later at age 78.

Dr. Paul Hubbert was a man of integrity. He grew up in an era when your word was your bond. These qualities were his trademark and what made him so effective. He was a devoted husband. He and his wife Ann were a team. He was also a beloved father and grandfather. He loved his family and fishing. He obviously loved public education and educators. He will go down in Alabama political history as a giant.

My Paul Hubbert Story

When I arrived at the Capitol in 1982 as a freshman legislator, Hubbert had already made his mark as the most powerful and prolific lobbyist on Goat Hill. The AEA and Farm Bureau (now ALFA) were the two most powerful groups. They were natural rivals ideologically, and they usually backed different candidates in legislative races. Fortunately, my race had been easy and it appeared early on that I would win handily and they both endorsed me. They sensed my victory and both wanted to bet on the winning horse. Therefore, since the two giants had both backed me as well, I felt somewhat independent, almost as if neither of them had supported me.

One day I was walking into the Capitol and the legendary Dr. Hubbert approached me and said we are having a legislator's reception next week and we hope you will be able to come by and by the way, we are having beef tenderloin, which I thought only my wife and mother knew was my favorite food, but eerily, Hubbert knew this and he also said, by the way, several of your former teachers will be there and how he knew that I will never know. As he departed, he asked about my five-year-old daughter, Ginny, and asked how she was doing in kindergarten in Troy. Needless to say, I was impressed. He had actually been the superintendent of the Troy City Schools in 1969, my senior year in High School, but had moved on to take over the helm of the AEA in 1970 as a very young man. He was only 33 when he took over the sleepy professional organization. He had built it into the most powerful group in the state in 12 short years. Through his prowess, it is still one of the most powerful groups in the state, and for many years he was one of the most powerful men in state politics.

We had a very cordial relationship during the four years of my first term. I was not expecting to get an opponent in my first reelection race in 1986. I had garnered 82 percent of the vote in my first race against two opponents and my reelectability numbers were very high. However, at the last moment, I got an opponent. It caught me somewhat by surprise. It appeared that I had been too zealous a supporter of tort reform and had aligned with the business interests too much to suit the plaintiff trial lawyers. They usually reserved their campaign bucks for Senate races, but they had targeted about a dozen House members who had been instrumental in passage of

Tort reform and they were out for revenge. They spent big bucks against us and defeated five out of the 12. Hubbert and the AEA generally teamed up with the trial lawyers and backed the same candidates and pooled their money and expertise.

A day or two after I realized I was going to be a target, Hubbert came to my office to see me. He told me what was happening in the most kind and fatherly fashion you could imagine. He got his record book out and told me that I had not supported him and the AEA and his teachers as much as he had wanted and that I had earned a failing grade. He said, "If I could beat you I would but we have polled your district and you can't be beaten" He said, "I could get in there with the trial lawyers, but all it would do was upset my teachers and you and I would have hard feelings and you're still going to be back next year." He said, "I want you to remember I've done you a favor." I did remember. It stuck indelibly in my memory for the rest of my legislative career. I went on to get 70 percent of the vote over my opponent. I never had an opponent again, neither Democratic nor Republican, and I also voted with Paul Hubbert 100 percent of the time for the rest of my career. He had made a friend that day.

There are many, many members of the House and Senate who can recount similar stories. That's why he had amassed the power he had. He will be remembered as the greatest lobbyist to ever grace Goat Hill.

A similar story is told by a veteran state senator from Jefferson County. Hubbert had supported him heavily in his first race. In the very first year of his initial term, a critical vote came up in the Education Committee where he had been assigned. Dr. Hubbert came to him, and told him how he needed his vote. The new senator, feeling his oats, told Dr. Hubbert that he could not support him on the issue. The issue was actually important to many retired teachers. The day came for the vote. Sitting in the committee room, directly across from the Jefferson County senator, was his favorite, most beloved, and cherished former teacher. She had taught him in the 3rd grade. He worshiped her. Dr. Hubbert had gotten her to Montgomery and placed her perfectly. The senator voted with Dr. Hubbert and the AEA.

Bringing Home the Bacon

Dr. Paul Hubbert also knew how to bring home the bacon for Alabama school teachers. He did it with power and grace for more than three decades. He built the AEA into the most powerful group on Goat Hill. When he took over in 1970, it was little more than a sleepy professional group controlled by the superintendents and politely ignored by the legislature.

The AEA is not a one-man show, but take Paul Hubbert out of the equation and it would have been nothing more than a one-horse show. The AEA will always be a powerful organization in future years because Hubbert has made it a gorilla, but with him not there it will never be the same. He was the key to the power. His knowledge of politics and the legislative process will never be matched. He knew every intricate detail of parliamentary procedure. He knew exactly how much money was in each pot at all times, and how his teachers could get part of it.

But further than that, he knew every legislator and every senator like the back of his hand. He knew what made them tick. He knew their habits, their church affiliation, their wife and children's names, what was important to them, what was important to their district, whether or not they could be defeated, how much he had given to their campaigns in the past and if need be who their third-grade teacher was and if need be he would bring her to the Capitol to make sure they voted right. He will probably never be rivaled.

Paul Hubbert—the King of Goat Hill

Many of you have asked why was Paul Hubbert such a power in state government, and in addition, was his power perceived or overrated by the media or was it real? The answer to the second question is, "Yes, it was real." He was unquestionably the most powerful person in state government when it came to education and education dollars which now account for two-thirds of all state tax dollars. Hubbert had total control over the funds and all the inherent power surrounding these public dollars. The governor was second. Dr. Hubbert usurped this power and made the governor irrelevant in the process. The cartoons and jokes that allude to Hubbert directing the legislature on how to vote on education issues with a thumbs-up or thumbs-down signal from his balcony perch overlooking the House Chamber are accurate.

The AEA's support is essential to a legislative race. They owed their seats more to Hubbert than they did to any governor. Hubbert was there when they were first elected, probably 20 years earlier with money, campaign workers, polling and advice, and he has been there with the same essential resources every four years, making sure that the legislator is reelected. Hubbert's team of support was enough to win by itself. The legislator knew that if he was loyal to Hubbert, Hubbert would be loyal to him. Dr. Hubbert understood the golden rule of politics—you stay true to your friends through thick and thin, especially the ones that Dr. Hubbert referred to as those "that will stick with you and help you when your ox gets in the ditch." The legislator in turn believes in the adage, "You dance with the one that brung you."

The legislator knows that Hubbert was there with him long before anyone even heard of the governor and he will be with him long after the governor is gone. A governor is limited to four years or maybe eight. Hubbert was King of Goat Hill for 42 years. That's why he was referred to as the "Governor." He was simply more powerful than the governor in the legislative arena which is where the real power is because that is where the money is appropriated. "He who controls the gold makes the rules." Hubbert made the rules when it came to education dollars. He was omnipotent over these funds for many years. Hubbert ran roughshod over every governor for the last three and a half decades. Bob Riley, Don Siegelman, Fob James, Jim Folsom Jr, Guy Hunt, and, yes, George Wallace all played second fiddle to Hubbert.

How did Paul Ray Hubbert from Hubbertville in rural Fayette County garner this much influence? The pivotal year and battle that made Paul Hubbert the King of Goat Hill was 1971 when David, a 35-year-old educator named Paul Hubbert, took on the Goliath of Alabama politics, George Wallace, in the heyday of his political power. It was a remarkable David vs. Goliath victory that propelled Dr. Paul Hubbert to stardom and power in Alabama politics. Hubbert became the King of Goat Hill after that monumental conquest and he never relinquished his crown.

Dr. Hubbert had earned a Ph.D. from the University of Alabama at a young age, became a school administrator in Tuscaloosa, and at age 30 became the superintendent of Troy City Schools. The Alabama Education Association was a toothless, social organization run by school superintendents in 1969. They were without an executive director and he was approached to take the position even though 30 others had applied. After turning it down several times, he finally acquiesced to take over the reins of AEA. It has never been the same. At 33, he became the executive secretary and quickly merged with the sister black organization of teachers headed by a 31-year-old Joe Reed. The Reed and Hubbert partnership began in 1969. That merger was a bold move in an Alabama boiling with racial tension and fighting integration.

Even though they had no financial resources at that time, they stepped out and for the first time endorsed a gubernatorial candidate. They openly endorsed the progressive Albert Brewer over George Wallace in the 1970 governor's race. Wallace came from behind to edge Brewer in the runoff in the bitterest and most racist battle in our political lore.

Wallace believed in repaying his enemies. It was early 1971, and Hubbert had just hired former State Senator Joe Goodwyn, to help him politically. Wallace called Goodwyn and Hubbert out to the Governor's Mansion. He subtly asked Hubbert, "Don't y'all have about $300 million over in the Teacher's Retirement System?" Hubbert said, "Yes, Governor, that's about right." "Well, you know," Wallace continued, "that carpet-bagging, scala-wagging, federal judge Frank Johnson has ordered us to update our mental health facilities and the going cost is $35 million, what do you think of us borrowing some of your money to pay for this problem?" Hubbert said, "I don't mind lending the state the money as long as we get paid the same return."

Wallace had dropped a hint. Goodwyn told Hubbert after the meeting, "I don't think you've heard the last of that." Sure enough, a month later Wallace called Hubbert to a meeting in the Governor's office. Hubbert had to fly back from a national educators' convention in Detroit. He came into the Governor's office like a gladiator into a lion's den. Wallace had the entire House Ways and Means and the Senate Finance and Taxation committees awaiting Hubbert. Wallace danced up and down the room extolling the need to use the education dollars to support mental health. After the tirade, a bold 35-year-old Hubbert looked him squarely in the eyes and told him, "Over my dead body." Hubbert rallied the state teachers like they had never been rallied before. They got their backs up over their retirement fund being raided.

Wallace continued with his plan when the legislature convened in May. Hubbert rallied his troops. There were 400 to 600 teachers a day descending on the legislature. Wallace dug in deeper. He attacked Hubbert, but neither Hubbert nor his throng of educators backed off. Now there were close to a thousand teachers a day coming to Goat Hill. They were dubbed Hubbert's Herd, a nod to Arnie's Army, the passionate followers of the legendary golfer Arnold Palmer. Representative Pete Mathews, the Wallace floor leader, said, "I've been in the legislature 18 years. During that time I have dealt with every kind of pressure group, but I have never seen anything like when the teachers found out someone was going to fool around with their retirement funds. When I came home and went to the post office they were there, they were at church, and when I went home I couldn't find a parking place in my yard. Now that gets your attention." When the vote was finally taken, the teachers and Dr. Hubbert had beaten George Wallace in his prime by a vote of 92–9.

A frantic Wallace called Mathews and said, "Move to reconsider." Mathews retorted, "Reconsider, hell, we done lost five of our nine."

That was the day Paul Hubbert earned his spurs.

8

And Frank Johnson: The 'Real Governor' of Alabama

Frank M. Johnson Jr. was the most prominent federal judge in America when it comes to civil rights. While serving as the U.S. District Court Judge of the Middle District of Alabama from 1955 through 1979, he handed down a good many of the landmark civil rights court decisions.

Johnson was one judge who applied the principles of the U.S. Supreme Court's School desegregation decision in *Brown v. Board of Education*. He made history in 1956 when he and another judge overturned a City of Montgomery ordinance requiring segregation on city buses. That decision gave the budding civil rights movement an encouraging victory and helped catapult Martin Luther King Jr. to the forefront as a civil rights leader.

Johnson's judicial decisions brought death threats to him and his family from whites that opposed integration. He was vilified by most white Alabamians at that time and became George Wallace's favorite whipping boy. Wallace referred to him as a "lying, scalawagging, carpetbagging integrationist."

Frank Minis Johnson Jr. was born October 30, 1918, in Delmar, a town in northern Alabama's Winston County. The county in which Johnson spent his youth was a Republican stronghold in an overwhelmingly Democratic state; in fact, it attempted to remain neutral during the Civil War.

In contrast to the rich planters of the Black Belt region in south Alabama, the people who settled north Alabama were small farmers who migrated to the Tennessee Valley of north Alabama from North Carolina or simply moved down from the hill country of Tennessee. The land they settled was hilly and not as conducive to growing cotton. Rather than large plantations and slaves, the fiercely independent hill-country farmers had forty acres and a mule.

Therefore when the winds of division between the North and the South began to blow in the 1850s, an obvious political difference between north and south Alabamians arose. In 1860 there were only 14 slave owners in Winston County. With the election of Abraham Lincoln, the crucial decision of secession arose. Contrary to what most present-day Alabamians think, it was not an easy, unified decision that we should leave the Union.

A secession convention was held in January 1861 in Montgomery. The vote was extremely close. The delegates split 54–46 for secession. The Black Belters from south Alabama were for creating a confederacy of Southern states to protect their slave ownership and way of life. The hill farmers from north Alabama preferred to wait and see what their cousins from Tennessee were going to do. These north Alabamians voted against secession from the Union at that time.

Shortly after the secession convention, citizens of Winston County met at a local establishment, Looney's Tavern. These yeoman farmers of the hills were obviously reluctant to leave the union for the cause of the planter and his slaves. Legend has it that on July 4, 1861, the good people of Winston County decided to secede from Alabama and remain in the Union. Thus they basically ignored the Civil War the best they could and in their minds never left the Union but remained independent. That's why they are known in Alabama political history and folklore as the "Free State of Winston."

That same sort of independent streak was later attributed to the Johnson family. Frank Minis Johnson Sr., served as one of the few Republicans in the Alabama state legislature in the first half of the 20th century. His son, Frank Jr., studied law at the University of Alabama, where he was friends with and a classmate of future governor George Wallace.

Wallace was always crazy about Johnson's wife, Ruth Jenkins Johnson. He would go by and eat at their apartment during law school, raving about how good Ruth Johnson could cook vegetables. When Wallace got his first paycheck after he graduated from law school, he bought some vegetables and had a cook to fix them and invited the Johnsons to his place to eat.

One time at a University of Alabama football game, while Wallace and Johnson were both in law school, Glen Curlee (a future district attorney) got excited and slapped a policeman on the head. The policeman thought

Curlee was drunk and threw him in the paddy wagon.

It took both Wallace and Johnson to keep Curlee out of jail. Wallace swore he hadn't seen Curlee take a drink all afternoon and Johnson convinced the judge that Curlee wasn't a drunk but was the fine upstanding president of the law school student body.

They were so convincing that when the judge took Wallace, Johnson, and Curlee home with him, and offered Wallace and Johnson beers, he didn't offer Curlee anything but coffee and Coke.

Of course, later, Johnson's and Wallace's politics and ideologies made them adversaries.

Frank Minis Johnson Jr. graduated at the top of his law school class in 1943, then he distinguished himself during World War II as a U.S. Army officer. Wounded in the Normandy invasion, he received numerous decorations including the Purple Heart with Oak Leaf Cluster and the Bronze Star. Upon completing his military service in 1946, Johnson returned home to Winston County, settling in Jasper, where he co-founded a law firm and quickly earned a reputation as an outstanding defense lawyer. Although the Democratic Party dominated Southern politics at the time, Johnson became active in the Republican Party, attending the party's national convention in 1948. In 1952, Johnson worked as a state manager for the presidential campaign of Republican Dwight D. Eisenhower. After Eisenhower became president, he awarded Johnson with the post of U.S. Attorney for the Northern District of Alabama. And in 1955, Eisenhower named Johnson as a district judge for the Middle District of Alabama. At age 37, Johnson was the country's youngest federal judge.

In 1955–56, shortly after taking his seat on the bench, Johnson became involved in a formative event of the civil rights movement. Rosa Parks was arrested for violating a Montgomery ordinance requiring racial segregation on the city's buses. In response the African American community organized a boycott of the Montgomery bus system and nominated Reverend Martin Luther King Jr. as its leader. In addition, bus boycott lawyer Fred Gray challenged the city ordinance in Johnson's federal district court. Citing the U.S. Supreme Court's reasoning in *Brown v. Board of Education,* Johnson and U.S. Circuit Judge Richard T. Rives, members of a three-judge panel, ruled that the Montgomery ordinance violated the due process and equal protection clauses of the 14th Amendment.

The ruling was the first of many by Johnson, either alone or as part of a three-judge panel, which eliminated racial segregation in public accommodations such as parks, libraries, bus stations, and airports during the 1950s and 1960s. In many instances, Johnson's decisions were the first of their kind, earning him a national reputation as a firm defender of civil rights.

Johnson's rulings in support of integration often put him at odds with his old friend and classmate George Wallace. In 1959, Wallace was a state circuit judge when a federal commission began investigating discrimination against black voters in Alabama. Johnson ordered all voting records to be turned over to the federal officials. George Wallace angrily announced that he would personally keep these records from the prying eyes of national officials and Judge Johnson quickly responded by threatening to put Wallace in jail for contempt of court. Hoping to avoid a long jail sentence, Wallace met privately with Johnson, but Johnson made it clear that if Wallace did not turn over the records, he would be sent to jail for as long as possible. It was the last time the two men would ever speak privately. In the end, Wallace distributed the records to members of the grand jury and then quietly suggested that they give the records to federal investigators. Out of the other side of his mouth, Wallace publicly declared that he had defied the court order.

In 1963, after Wallace became governor, Johnson and Wallace would clash again over the issue of desegregation decrees issued by the federal courts in regard to Alabama's blatant opposition. Wallace and Johnson also clashed in 1965 over King's Selma-to-Montgomery march for civil rights. After Wallace stopped the march, Johnson issued a court order allowing it to proceed. The march was credited with sparking passage of the Voting Rights Act of 1965.

Soon after the Selma march, Johnson tried a celebrated case involving the murder of Viola Liuzzo, a white civil rights worker who had been shot to death while riding in her car with an African American. After an all-white state court jury acquitted three Ku Klux Klan members of the murder, federal prosecutors brought a case against the Klansmen in Johnson's court. Johnson skillfully maneuvered to avoid a deadlocked jury, and the trial resulted in the conviction of the Klan members for violation of the slain woman's civil rights.

Johnson's rulings on voting rights cleared the way for African Americans to vote on an equal basis with whites. In several decisions during the 1960s, Johnson developed the "freeze" doctrine, by which African Americans were allowed to vote as long as their qualifications matched those of the least qualified white. The doctrine was later incorporated into the Voting Rights Act. In addition, Johnson also struck down state laws barring blacks and women from juries.

In 1977, President Jimmy Carter nominated Johnson to become director of the FBI, but a heart condition prevented Johnson from taking the job. Surgery improved Johnson's health and he remained on the federal bench. In 1979 Carter appointed Johnson to the U.S. Fifth Circuit Court of Appeals (in 1981, expansion of the court system split the old Fifth Circuit and made him part of the newly created 11th Circuit).

Johnson retired to senior status in 1991. He received many honors and awards, including honorary doctorates of law from Notre Dame, Princeton, Alabama, Boston, Yale, Mercer, and Tuskegee Institute. The federal courthouse in Montgomery is now named in his honor. Judge Johnson died in 1999.

Part II

Congressmen and Senators

9

Alabama's Three Greatest Senators

Many observers of today's political scene are cognizant of the pinnacle of power reached by our senior U.S. Senator, Richard Shelby of Tuscaloosa. He began his fifth sixth-year term in January 2011 and is completing his 29th year in the Senate at the end of 2015. Shelby is easily one of the most influential political figures in the nation and is generally considered one of the ten most influential senators in Washington. He serves on the powerful Senate Appropriations Committee and is chairman of the Banking Committee. It is from this powerful perch controlling the federal purse strings that he has bestowed much of the federal largesse into Alabama's projects. Shelby has also served as chairman of the Intelligence Committee.

Prior to going to the Senate, Shelby served eight years in the U.S. House of Representatives (1978–86) and eight years in the Alabama Senate (1970–78). He has never lost an election. Tall and striking, he even looks like a U.S. Senator. He is a regular guest on many national television news shows and is an excellent ambassador for Alabama. He exemplifies a confident conservative image that casts a positive image on Alabama. From a cursory observation, Shelby would be considered Alabama's greatest U.S. senator. At age 80, Shelby has not yet written the final passage in his senate legacy. He plans to run for a sixth term in 2016. He may wind up in a league of his own.

However, I would submit into the discussion the names of Lister Hill and John Sparkman. They served in tandem for more than 20 years and were respected giants on Capitol Hill. Our Hill-Sparkman team was unsurpassed in power and prestige from 1946 to 1970. They were admired not only in Alabama and the South but throughout the nation. Shelby has in my opinion arrived in their league. Shelby is not bashful about wielding his power. He loves the Senate and he knows how to bring home the bacon. Hill and Sparkman were more reserved.

Lister Hill was considered one of the greatest U.S. senators during his 30-year career. A moderate and the ultimate Southern gentleman, he was chairman of the Senate Labor and Public Welfare Committee as well as a ranking member of the Appropriations Committee. He is known throughout the nation as the father of most of America's rural hospitals, through his authorship and stewardship of the Hill-Burton Act.

John Sparkman, like Shelby, made his presence known as chairman of the Senate Banking Committee for more than a decade. Sparkman served an amazing 42 years in the U.S. Senate. He was the Democratic nominee for vice president in 1952.

Therefore, the three greatest senators in Alabama history are Lister Hill, John Sparkman, and Richard Shelby.

Richard Shelby

Richard Shelby currently reigns as Alabama's most prominent political figure. Shelby has had a perfectly scripted rise to political power and acclaim.

He grew up in Birmingham and went to undergraduate and law school at the University of Alabama. He made Tuscaloosa his home. He became a successful attorney soon after finishing law school. Along with his law practice he began a title company in Tuscaloosa. He still owns the company which has been very profitable over the years. In 1970, at age 35, he entered politics and beat an incumbent state senator in his initial race. He represented the Tuscaloosa area in the state senate with distinction for eight years. He ran for an open seat in Congress in 1978 and won. He served eight years as a Congressman. In 1986 he rolled the dice, gave up his safe congressional seat and took on an incumbent U.S. senator.

Shelby Beats Denton in 1986

In 1986, Shelby was a 50-year-old congressman, a Democrat who had a stellar conservative voting record. He was safe in his U.S. House seat.

Therefore, his decision to challenge an incumbent U.S. senator was a gamble. His friends cautioned him that it was an uphill battle and he shouldn't risk his safe House seat. His basic reply was. "I'm one of 435 in Congress; given the rules of seniority, it will be 20 more years before I can chair a committee or subcommittee. They don't even know my name up here. Ten years ago practicing law in Tuscaloosa I was making three times what I make as a congressman. I'm either going to the Senate and be somebody or I'm going home and make money." He has done both. He has gone to the U.S. Senate *and* made a lot of money, having amassed considerable wealth in real estate investments and through his title company in Tuscaloosa.

One factor that the average political observer is not aware of is that Shelby probably sensed that his congressional district was destined to be the first African American district after reapportionment in 1990. That is what happened to Shelby's 7th District.

Although it would be a daunting task for Shelby to upset an incumbent, U.S. Senator Jeremiah Denton had written the textbook on how to lose a Senate seat during his six-year term. Denton was elected as Alabama's first Republican Senator since Reconstruction in 1980. He was swept into office on the coattails of Ronald Reagan who carried Alabama in a landslide. Alabamians knew very little about Denton except that he had been a naval officer and a well-known POW in the Vietnam War. His patriotic hero reputation sold well in Alabama, especially with Reagan headed to the White House.

Yet Shelby beat Denton. It was close and Shelby had to spend some of his personal money the last week of the campaign to carry out the upset, but Alabama has been the better for Richard Shelby's 1986 gamble. He was reelected in 1992, 1998, 2004, and 2010.

I had the opportunity to fly back from Washington with and visit with Shelby a few years after his 1986 victory. He told me the inside story of the last six days of that campaign that illustrates how important money and media are in today's modern politics.

When he decided to run against Denton, he knew the importance of money to a campaign. He also knew that it was essential to get the best media guru regardless of the price. Therefore, he spared no expense and got the best pollsters and media people in America. About six days out, he was six

With U.S. Senator Richard Shelby.

points behind. The pollster told him to put $100,000 of TV ads in the Birmingham market using a certain ad and it would raise him two points. He did it and it did. The next day the media man and the pollster told him to spend $50,000 on TV ads in the Mobile market using a certain ad and it would give him a one-point boost. He did it and it did. The next day the pollster told him to run a certain ad in the Huntsville market and spend $60,000 and it would raise him a point. He did it and it did. Two days out the pollster told him to run a certain ad in both Birmingham and in Montgomery and it would raise him by three points. He did it and it did.

He won by one point.

I suspect the ad suggested by the pollster and the media guys was the one where Denton was saying he didn't have time to come home and kiss babies' butts.

SHELBY HAS MADE HIS MARK

When I am an old man and I reminisce and tell stories of years ago to young listeners, I will love to tell that I lived during the era of the two greatest Alabamians of their respective professions. No one will ever rival in Alabama the supremacy of Paul "Bear" Bryant in college football or of George Wallace in politics. Their feats and accomplishments and records speak for themselves. God simply sat down one day and said, "I'm going to make the greatest football coach in history and the greatest Alabama politician in history and I'm going to send them down to Alabama to live in the same era." I was fortunate enough to know them both, especially Wallace.

Nobody can reach the pinnacle of success in their worlds as those two did. However, two other men will also go down in the history of greatness in Alabama politics and will be long remembered as legends: Richard Shelby has reached the zenith of power as our greatest U.S. senator, and the late Dr. Paul Hubbert made his mark as the most powerful and prolific lobbyist in Alabama history.

We said more earlier about Hubbert, but I have seen Senator Shelby's power wielded from Washington numerous times over the years. I have also seen it personally and uniquely. I consider Shelby a friend and mentor. Indeed, in 1986 when Shelby made his first race for the Senate he asked me and my best friend, Keith Watkins, to be his campaign managers in Pike County. We agreed and he beat Denton in Pike County. I had become friends with Congressman Shelby because I was in politics. He had gotten to know Keith through law practice. Little did he know that Keith and I were best friends, had grown up together, and were only two months apart in age.

One day several years ago, Keith, who had a successful general law practice in Troy, was asked by another lawyer to ask Shelby to support him for an open federal judgeship. Keith made a call to Shelby to endorse the fellow for the powerful and prestigious position. Shelby returned Keith's call that night about 8 o'clock. Shelby immediately replied that he wanted Keith to be the nominee for the judgeship. Keith stammered and told Shelby that he would get back to him the next day. Keith then called me and asked me what I thought. He confided that he was making a little more in his law practice than he would as a federal judge. My advice was that you don't turn down a federal judgeship. Shelby recommended Keith for the position the next day and the rest is history. Keith won easy confirmation and has been on the federal bench for close to 10 years in the U.S. Middle District in Montgomery.

Lister Hill

As a youngster growing up in Troy, I was keenly interested in politics, government, and history. I marveled at the prestige and power of our two

U.S. Senators, Lister Hill and John Sparkman. In 1965, Hill was in the twilight of his career and was finishing his final six-year term. He had been in Congress for more than 40 years. Sparkman had been in Washington for 30 years. They were powerful, masterful, and very respected men. The Southern senators wielded enormous power. The Eastland-Stennis team from Mississippi was strong and the Russell-Talmadge team from Georgia was tremendously powerful, but our Hill-Sparkman tandem was equal to the task. Their rise to power was undergirded by their years of seniority, accentuated with their brilliant legislative abilities, their deep love for Alabama, and their knowledge and belief that their constituents and state came first. It registered with me that these two great men would take time to tend to the minute details of serving their constituents. I would write them a letter as a boy and would get an answer almost by return mail. They understood the importance of staying in touch with their people.

Senator Lister Hill looked like a U.S. senator. His chiseled features depicted his strong character. Hill had been born to privilege into one of the most prominent families in Montgomery. He was the son of one of the most distinguished surgeons, Dr. Luther Hill. Young Dr. Hill was the first American surgeon to successfully suture the human heart. Hoping that their son would follow his father into medicine, the parents named him Joseph Lister after the famous English physician who was the first person to advocate and practice widespread use of antiseptics.

Young Hill entered the University of Alabama at age 16 and became the student government president. He received his law degree from Alabama and came home to Montgomery to practice law in 1916 at age 22 and was elected to the U.S. Congress at the ripe old age of 28. He served in the U.S. House for 16 years (1923–38) and rose to chair the House Military Affairs Committee. He became a stalwart supporter of President Roosevelt's New Deal. When the president nominated Alabama's Senator Hugo Black to the U.S. Supreme Court, Hill left his House seat and ran for the Senate.

He won that 1938 race decisively and began his 30-year tenure in the Senate. When he retired in 1968, he had served 46 years in the House and Senate, the longest tenure of any Alabamian.

His accomplishments were memorable. Senator Hill had his prints on most major legislation throughout his 30 years. He was instrumental in establishing the TVA, the Rural Telephone Act, the Vocational Education Act, the GI Bill, and the National Defense Act. As chairman of the Labor and Public Welfare Committee, he headed and passed legislation on veterans' education and labor relations and was an impassioned advocate for libraries.

He was a larger-than-life figure in Washington, but Senator Hill's greatest legacy was his landmark legislation in the field of public health. Senator Hill was recognized as the most instrumental man in Congress in gaining greatly increased support for medical research at the nation's medical schools. The great medical center at the University of Alabama at Birmingham exists because of Lister Hill. Probably the best-known legislation which bears his name is the Hospital and Health Care Construction Act of 1946, better known as the Hill-Burton Act. Through this legislation, most of the rural hospitals in America and Alabama were built.

Senator Lister Hill is probably our greatest U.S. senator.

John Sparkman

Senator Sparkman was not born into privilege like Senator Hill. Sparkman was born on an unpretentious tenant farm near Hartselle in Morgan County. He had 10 brothers and sisters. In 1917, by making a cotton crop and netting $75, he was able to enroll in the University of Alabama. At Alabama, he was editor of the *Crimson and White*, and like Hill, he was president of the student body, while at the same time he worked his way through school shoveling coal and feeding furnaces. After graduation from Alabama's law school, he practiced law in Huntsville for 12 years before being elected to Congress in 1936. Like Hill, he supported Roosevelt's New Deal. The passage of the TVA Act was a tremendous boost for his north Alabama Tennessee Valley district.

In 1946 Sparkman had served his north Alabama congressional district well, having been elected to five terms. He had been instrumental in New Deal passage of TVA and REA programs as well as farm assistance legislation. In 1946, Senator John Bankhead died in office. This created a unique situation for Sparkman. He sought the vacant seat, yet remained on the ballot for his House seat. He beat the field handily with strong backing of labor unions who were then in their heyday in Alabama politics. He was also backed by Senator Hill. Sparkman won both races at the same time, making him the only person in American history to accomplish this feat. He immediately resigned from the House. He went on to serve five terms in the Senate, 1946–76, the same amount of time as Senator Lister Hill.

In 1952, Sparkman pulled his 1946 trick again, simultaneously running for reelection to his Senate seat and for vice president as the nominee of the Democratic Party and running mate of Governor Adlai Stevenson of Illinois. To date, this is the only time in history that a native-born Alabamian has been a nominee for president or vice president as a major party candidate. Stevenson went down in defeat to the popular Republican candidate, General Dwight Eisenhower, but the Democratic Sparkman-Stevenson ticket carried Alabama.

Senator Sparkman rose to power and prominence in the Senate. He made his mark as the father of federal housing for the poor. The Alabama junior senator was chairman of the Senate Banking Committee as well as its Housing Subcommittee. Sparkman was the author of practically every major housing bill since World War II, and is also known as the father of the Small Business Administration. He was also the ranking majority member of the Senate Foreign Relations Committee.

For more than two decades, 1946–68, John Sparkman and Lister Hill performed as a team with almost identical positions on the issues which faced the nation. As their seniority increased so did their influence and power. They had exceptional legislative skills and were held in deep respect by their colleagues and constituents. Both men were Methodists. This denomination, even though considerably smaller than the Southern Baptists and Church of Christ in Alabama, has seemed to dominate the state's political landscape, especially high offices such as U.S. senator and even governor. Both men served as president of the student body of the University of Alabama and helped to start what is known as the political "machine" at UA.

They were both giants in the United States Senate.

10

Others in Alabama's Congressional Delegation

Representative Bob Jones

No discussion about the First Monday Trade Days of Scottsboro would be complete without mentioning their most famous political native son, Bob Jones. Jones was born in Scottsboro in 1912. He grew up during the Depression and the New Deal. He served in the Navy during World War II and was elected to Congress in 1946 to the seat previously held by John Sparkman, serving his Tennessee Valley district for 30 years. He became a power in Congress and eventually chaired the House Public Works and Transportation Committee. He brought home the bacon to the Tennessee Valley.

As a boy growing up in Jackson County, he saw how significantly FDR's New Deal had helped transform his native region. He continued that transformation. He was instrumental in maintaining and expanding the vital TVA projects. He also played a major role with his predecessor, Senator John Sparkman, in securing Huntsville as the location of Redstone Arsenal and Marshall Space Flight Center. When Sparkman left the Tennessee Valley congressional district open to go to the Senate in 1946, Jones's home county of Jackson gave him over 90 percent of its vote, allowing him to lead the large field of candidates. This support garnered by Jones in the 1946 special election for Congress is a prime example of "friends and neighbors politics" in Alabama.

Jones arrived in Congress in 1947 in the same freshman class as Richard M. Nixon and John F. Kennedy. Jones and Kennedy became fast friends and fishing buddies. Jones loved to fish and had another high-profile fishing buddy in New York politician Nelson Rockefeller.

Jones was never seriously challenged for reelection in his 15 terms and steadily made his way up the seniority ladder. He rose to the chairmanships of Public Works under the tutelage of the legendary Speaker of the House Sam Rayburn. Mr. Sam was a Texan and took a liking to the young Alabama congressman. Mr. Sam gave Jones his famous advice, "To get along you have to go along." He further told Jones, "You sit over there and be totally quiet. Don't say a word or much less make a speech for about four years and vote with me and you'll go somewhere." Mr. Sam's advice paid off for Bob Jones.

Jones was mentored by Sam Rayburn, but he became a House committee chairman under the Speakership of Carl Albert of Oklahoma.

He knew a lot of presidents including Harry Truman, Dwight Eisenhower, John Kennedy, Lyndon Johnson, Richard Nixon, and Jimmy Carter. One day late in Jones's life a reporter asked him how many presidents he had served under. He replied, "I didn't serve under any; I served with six."

One of the best tellers of Alabama political stories is Jackson County's former Representative John Robinson, who served 20 years in the Alabama House and was close friends with Bob Jones. Robinson would drive Jones around north Alabama after Jones had retired from Congress. Jones was especially proud of being a sponsor of the Interstate Highway Act that President Dwight Eisenhower built during his two administrations in the 1950s. Even though Jones was a staunch Democrat, he liked and supported Eisenhower. The Interstate Highway Program is said to be one of the most important, largest, and costly projects ever undertaken by the United States government. Eisenhower got the concept from the Germans. He had seen what the Autobahn Project had done for Germany's transportation and progress. As chairman of the House Public Works Committee, Jones had worked hand-in-hand with the popular Ike to make the project a success.

One day as Robinson and Jones were riding down the road, they got onto an Interstate and saw the famous Blue Star Highway designation identifying an Interstate Highway. The highways were named the five-star highways after the five-star General Eisenhower.

Robinson absently asked Jones why they named the Interstate Highways after Eisenhower. Jones looked at Robinson in amazement and said, "Hell, because he was the president of the United States. Who do you think they should name it after?"

Representative Albert Rains

Albert Rains was one of Alabama's great congressmen. He served in Congress for 20 years. His district has been significantly altered, but at the time it was a blend of what in 2015 are the third and fourth districts. He always represented his beloved hometown of Gadsden, the largest city in his district, which benefited greatly from Rains's rise to power. Rains was a progressive Yellow Dog national Democrat.

Our entire congressional delegation was once made up of progressive if not liberal Democrats, many of whom came to Congress during FDR's time and were New Deal disciples, especially those from north Alabama. The entire North Alabama/Tennessee Valley reaped the rewards of the adage, "Them that help bake the pie get to eat it."

Rains fit that pattern though he came along later. His career paralleled that of his friend and neighbor, Bob Jones. Their districts adjoined, they were the most powerful members of Alabama's congressional delegation during their era, and they worked together and voted together. The Tennessee Valley and northeast Alabama areas were enhanced by the tandem of Rains and Jones. Rains went to Congress in 1945 and stayed 20 years, Jones in 1947 and stayed 30 years. During his 20 years, Rains missed exactly 0 of 1,990 roll call votes in the House.

Rains always told his young friend Bobby Junkins, who became probate judge of Etowah County, that he wanted to go out a winner. Rains may have been prophetic when he chose not to seek reelection in 1964. His friend Bob Jones survived the Goldwater landslide that year, but a number of other Alabama congressmen did not.

Rains's legacy is still felt all over his district, but especially in Gadsden. There is a magnificent library he built for the city along with numerous city buildings, one that was attached to money for an airport and is located seven miles from the Gadsden airport. There is a terrible curve in Interstate 59 between Fort Payne and Gadsden, because Rains found out the road was going to bypass Gadsden and stepped in to change it. The dam on Weiss Lake was moved back 100 yards so it could be in Cherokee County, a favor to Rains's wife's family.

One day Bobby Junkins was driving Mr. Rains to an event after the congressman had retired, and all of a sudden the former congressman started laughing. Bobby asked the congressman what was so funny, and he had recalled a colorful event the day he had met with President John F. Kennedy to help the president with some legislation. The president had rewarded the congressman with ten new post offices in his district. They had just passed by one of them, and it had brought back a fond memory for Rains.

Rains was a short, erudite man. He made a good bit of money during his time in Congress and afterwards in the banking business. Like a good many other congressmen of that era, he also owned a stake in several radio stations, thanks to assistance and deference from the FCC. John Sparkman owned several in Huntsville and north Alabama. Lyndon Johnson owned the biggest one in Austin, Texas. Johnson made sure the FCC did not grant any new licenses for Austin. His radio station expanded into television as well and was quite lucrative for Lyndon and Lady Bird. There was no Ethics Law at that time.

Rains died at age 89. Junkins was a pallbearer and observed that the other pallbearers were so old they could barely lift Rains's coffin up the steps of the First Baptist Church of Gadsden. Howell Heflin often commented that the problem with living a long time is that you outlive all your peers and it diminishes the turnout at your funeral.

However, that was not the case at Senator Heflin's funeral in Tuscumbia. I attended the event and every famous major U.S. Senator flew in from all over the country. You should have seen the number of private jets parked at the Quad Cities Airport. It was one hell of a turnout for Heflin, an ol' Judge/Senator on his way to heaven.

Representative Carl Elliott

Carl Elliott was a progressive Democratic congressman from Jasper. He served with distinction for 16 years before losing his seat in the 1964 Democratic Primary, which was the second election held under the "9/8 Plan" implemented after Alabama lost a U.S. House seat due to Congressional redistricting after the 1960 census. Under this plan, candidates nominated in the nine House districts Alabama had in the 1950s then ran statewide for the eight House seats Alabama was entitled to after redistricting. The top eight Democratic votegetters advanced to the November general election, and Elliott came in ninth and was thus ousted from his seat. This was the same year as the Goldwater landslide, so some of the eight Democratic primary House nominees went on to lose to Republicans in November, but Eliott was already out.

Elliott then entered the governor's race in 1966. You could safely say that he was the most liberal of the ten candidates. The others in the field were Alabama Democrats; Elliott was a national Democrat. There were nine men and one woman in that race. Lurleen Wallace trounced the nine men without a runoff. Included in the carnage were two former governors, John Patterson and Jim Folsom, Agriculture Commissioner A. W. Todd, State Senator Bob Gilchrist, Charles Woods, and Attorney General Richmond Flowers. Flowers ran second because he received the bulk of the black vote. Elliott finished a distant third.

Elliott had a loyal following in his old congressional district, especially in Jasper and Walker County. He had two very loyal friends who worked tirelessly in his 1966 race for governor. Both were from Jasper. Mary Jolly had been Elliott's congressional chief of staff and was his most loyal and ardent ally. His other stalwart supporter was Jasper businessman Garve Ivey Sr., who had made and lost several fortunes and just recently had been wiped out again in the chicken business. Nevertheless, Mary Jolly and Garve Ivey were campaigning full-time for their friend, Carl Elliott.

They were riding down a desolate country road one day late in the campaign and Mary looked over at Ivey and says, "Garve, I believe we're going to win this race." Ivey, the older and wiser of the two and the ultimate pragmatist, replied, "No, Mary, we are not going to win."

A few moments later, Mary gets real serious and says to Ivey, very solemnly, "Garve, we are going to win. I've prayed about it and God is telling me we are going to win."

Garve replied, "Mary, I'm a lot older than you and I've been praying longer than you, and it is my experience that the Lord don't get involved in the chicken business or Alabama politics."

Senator Jim Allen

Jim Allen had an illustrious career in Alabama politics. He was born and raised in Gadsden. He served in the Alabama House and the Alabama Senate from his native county. He was elected to his first term as lieutenant governor of Alabama in 1950 and to a second term in 1962. He was lieutenant governor during George Wallace's first term as governor. He was also a very successful lawyer in Gadsden.

Jim Allen is known for being the most astute parliamentarian in Alabama political history. He developed this trademark early in his career and honed it during his terms as lieutenant governor. Most state senate observers, and most notably, McDowell Lee, the secretary of the Alabama Senate for 48 years, said that Allen had no peer when it came to knowing its parliamentary rules.

Allen went to the U.S. Senate in 1968. Many political experts expected Allen, the incumbent lieutenant governor, to run for governor in 1966 when George Wallace could not succeed himself and had failed to get the legislature to change the succession law. But Allen was a savvy politician who never lost a political race. He knew that Lurleen Wallace, as proxy for George, could not be beaten in 1966. He opted to lay low and take on the aging Lister Hill's seat.

As expected, Hill announced early that he would not run for reelection in 1968. However, he did the unexpected and endorsed Congressman Armistead Selden to become his replacement. Selden was an eight-term congressman from the Black Belt and Hill had grown fond of him.

Another obstacle arose for Jim Allen. Wallace also backed Selden, although not openly. Wallace and Allen had been friends and allies, but Wallace blamed Allen for not gaveling through his succession bill in 1965.

So Allen began the race with both Hill and Wallace on the other side. However, Allen had gotten to know a lot of the Wallace organization and wound up with at least half the Wallace crowd. Jere Beasley and Tom Coker were his chief campaign lieutenants. They ran the 1968 campaign out of Allen's Gadsden law office.

As the campaign began, there were riots in Washington. It was a time of civil unrest over the Vietnam War and the civil rights marches and landmark civil rights laws were fresh on people's minds. Alabamians were sick of Washington. Allen came up with the best campaign slogan of the last 60 years. He ran against the "Washington Crowd." He had a graphic photo of the riots and used the photo in his message of running against the Washington Crowd. Of course, the subliminal message was that Allen was against the liberal Washington establishment that had forced integration and civil rights on the South.

Jim Allen became the conservative, anti-civil rights, pro-South candidate with that slogan. He tied Armistead Selden to the Washington Crowd and won.

When Allen arrived in the U.S. Senate in 1969, the dean of its Southern delegation was the venerable Richard Russell of Georgia, a master of the rules and the filibuster. He led the powerful bloc of Southern U.S. Senators. Because of their seniority, they ruled the Senate. It had taken a massive movement to steamroll the civil rights legislation over this bloc.

Richard Russell, knowing of Allen's reputation as a parliamentarian brought him under his wing and made him his protégé. He told Allen from day one that the only way that he would be a power in Washington was to master the rules of the U.S. Senate. Allen took Russell's advice. Allen and Senate Parliamentarian Dr. Floyd Riddick became inseparable. They ate together and spent hours each day in Allen's pursuit at becoming expert at the rules.

The job of presiding over the Senate is sometimes perceived by outsiders as prestigious. However, it is a menial job that nobody wants. It is time-consuming and boring. Russell and Riddick convinced Allen that it was good training. He presided over the Senate more than all other 99 senators combined in his first two years in the Senate. He won the Golden Gavel Award for most hours in the chair presiding his first three years in the Senate. He learned the rules so well that he was considered the most able parliamentarian in the Senate during his first term.

Tom Coker was Allen's chief of staff during his entire nine-year tenure. Allen was a hard worker and taskmaster. He worked 10–12 hours per day, six days a week. He expected his staff to try to keep pace; they were the only Senate staffers at work on most Saturdays. Allen, like his predecessors Lister Hill and John Sparkman, was diligent in responding to constituents' mail and requests. Allen's chief lieutenants, Coker and Wendell Mitchell, would delve into the mail and constituent problems, but Jim Allen insisted on signing every letter personally.

Allen became the stalwart leader of the conservatives in the Senate during his years in Washington. His positions were very reflective of his Alabama constituency. He almost single-handedly led the charge to thwart what he considered the giving away of the Panama Canal by President Jimmy Carter.

He had been fighting this battle for several months. He also had to fight diabetes. He came home to Alabama very tired one weekend during this fight and succumbed to a massive heart attack at his Gulf Shores condominium.

Even though he was considered one of the most conservative members of the Senate, at his death he was eulogized and idolized by the most liberal members of that body including Jacob Javits of New York and Abe Ribicoff of Connecticut. He was worlds apart from them philosophically, but they admired and respected him as the most astute parliamentarian in the body. Because of his skill, he was an enemy to be feared. Richard Russell's advice and counsel had been wise and well taken.

Jim Allen was a great Alabamian.

Senator Jeremiah Denton

Those who have followed politics closely in Alabama for five or more decades are still slackjawed over the short, enigmatic career of Jeremiah Denton, our one-term junior U.S. Senator from 1980 to 1986. During that one six-year term, he wrote the book on how to lose a U.S. Senate race.

Denton was swept into office in 1980 in the Ronald Reagan conservative landslide. Denton was a military hero. He was a Rear Admiral in the Navy. During the Vietnam War he was shot down, captured, and held prisoner by the North Vietnamese for seven years and seven months. He never aspired to go into politics. He only wanted to be a good soldier. After his released from captivity, he came back to a hero's welcome.

Alabama had an open seat for the Senate in 1980. Denton called Mobile home but he was basically living in the Washington area when he ran for the seat. The fact that a Catholic Republican from Mobile could be elected to a U.S. Senate seat from Alabama was an enigma in itself.

Denton's record and exploits during his one-term career provides a classic textbook of what not to do in politics.

He began his career by announcing that he was a United States Senator and not the Junior Senator from Alabama. He said his role was bigger than just taking care of mundane senatorial duties. He saw his role as being the top moralist in the country. He made it clear that his job was to rid the nation of pornography and abortions. As a devout Catholic, he perceived it his duty to be the country's top abortion abolitionist. Thus, he immediately forewarned Alabamians that for the next six years we would only have one U.S. senator—the country would be blessed with our other Senate seat.

Most people have driven through Conecuh County on their way to Mobile or the beach. Undoubtedly, Denton had been in the State of Alabama so seldom during his life that he mispronounced the name of the county and called it *konekee*.

Most senators visit each county every year to at least give lip service to ascertaining what their constituents are interested in. They also are asked to help with bureaucratic federal problems. Denton never once visited his home state. Remember, he was a "national senator."

He further illuminated this national senator status by declaring that he didn't have time to come home and "kiss babies' butts." This statement really resonated and came back to bite his own butt in his 1986 reelection campaign.

A cardinal rule of any U.S. senator is to always acknowledge and answer a constituent's letter. Our two greatest U.S. senators, John Sparkman and Lister Hill, would respond to all letters from Alabamians practically by return mail, even though each was one of the ten most powerful members of the august U.S. Senate. Jeremiah Denton, who was considered a nut by all of Washington, was ranked the least influential and least effective member of the U.S. Senate. Yet as far as most people can tell, he hardly answered any constituent letters despite the fact that by this time each senator had such vast office resources that they could have three full-time staff members doing nothing but answering constituents' correspondence.

Instead, Denton lent his staff out to work on anti-abortion or other issues, which brings me to a prime example of his dereliction of duty. There was a lady in my community who was a pillar of the Baptist Church, a devout young mother and Sunday School teacher. She was a schoolteacher by profession, but she wanted to stay home while her children were young. She told me that we should have legislation that rewarded families tax-wise for staying home with their children. She was very sincere and felt strongly about this issue. I told her that it was of course a federal issue and that in fact Senator Denton had made family value issues his calling card and that she should write him about her beliefs. He, if anyone in Washington, would be sympathetic to this issue. She sat down and wrote Denton a six-page, handwritten, heart-wrenching, well-thought-out letter. She never got even an acknowledgment.

Ralph Adams was a very powerful man in state politics during this era. He was president of Troy State University and was George Wallace's best friend. He called Denton six times and asked him to return his call. Denton never called him back. Adams, who kept his cards close to his vest, told me, "I'm going to do what I can to beat that man when he runs for reelection."

The worst example in Denton's book on how to get beat for a U.S. Senate seat is the coup de grace.

The Alabama Farmers Federation leadership is made up of the most revered and respected men in their counties. These farmers have been lifetime residents of their communities. They are conservative family men and leaders in their churches. They are the epitome of Alabamians who voted to elect Jeremiah Denton to the U.S. Senate.

Those farmers make an annual trek to Washington to lobby their Congressional delegation on issues relating to Alabama farming. These gentlemen had overlooked the fact that Denton had turned down a seat on the Agriculture Committee in order to work on national anti-abortion issues. In contrast, our senior senator, Howell Heflin, chose to serve on the Agriculture Committee and had done yeoman's work to help the Alabama farmer.

Well, over 200 of the top leaders in the Alabama Farmers Federation set out on their annual pilgrimage to Washington. Heflin meets them personally at the airport at their arrival. He attends every one of their breakfasts and basically spends the entire three days with the Alabama delegation. He attends their barbeque and even gives them a personal tour of the Agriculture Department and gets them passes to visit the White House.

They have an appointment with Senator Denton for 2 p.m. on their last day in Washington. All 200 of them gather in the Capitol to meet with their phantom senator. They sit waiting. 2:30 p.m. arrives and they are still waiting. Finally at 3 p.m., Denton sends an aide out to tell the 200 farm leaders from Alabama that he doesn't have time to meet with them today. He has to go to a meeting about abortion. The appointment with Denton had been made one month in advance.

It is only proper and fitting that Denton, the most inept politician to serve in office in Alabama, was replaced by one of the best politicians in our lifetime, Richard Shelby.

Shelby in the 1986 race made Alabamians aware of the fact that Jeremiah Denton and his wife drove matching Mercedes cars and that Denton paid for his membership in an exclusive country club with campaign money. Jeremiah Denton truly wrote the book on how to get beat for a Senate seat.

Representative Bill Dickinson

As the leaves changed colors along the Potomac in the fall of 1964, all eight Alabama congressmen were Democrats (and white males). By Thanksgiving that year, five of the eight were wiped out by Goldwater Republicans. Along with those five washed away into the waters of the Potomac went over 100 years of congressional seniority.

The prototypical loser that year was Congressman George Grant. He had represented the Second Congressional District since 1938, having succeeded Lister Hill when Hill went to the U.S. Senate. In fact, Grant had been endorsed by the Hill Family machine. Montgomery was and still is the largest city in the Second District. At that time two of Montgomery's prominent political families, the Hills and Gunters, were like political machines. Grant was a Troy lawyer and got the Hill family blessing. He served with distinction for 26 years.

Grant was related to my mother. I recall as a young boy attending a

With friend and mentor Congressman Bill Dickinson who represented south Alabama's Second District in Washington for 28 years.

large Grant family reunion and Mama politely saying to George Grant she was sorry he lost. He very humbly thanked her and said, "Gloria, I will be okay." Soon after, I read in the paper that a large paper company had retained former Congressman George Grant, at a princely salary of $100,000 a year, to be their lobbyist. This was at a time when congressmen made $25,000 a year. Therefore, I learned at a young age that there was more money in being a lobbyist than in actually being in the arena. Some would argue that it is also more prestigious and powerful.

William L. "Bill" Dickinson was the Goldwater Republican who took out George Grant and his 26 years of seniority. Bill was tall, handsome, and articulate. He had been a circuit judge in Opelika where he was born in 1925. He had served in the Navy during World War II. After the war he graduated from the University of Alabama law school and soon thereafter he was elected to the state bench in Lee County as a Democrat. At that time Alabama judges made a paltry salary. Dickinson had a growing family and needed to make more money so he took a job as an executive and in-house counsel with Southern Railway in Montgomery

The Republican Party came to him and asked him to run for Congress. He signed up with probably no expectation of defeating the 14-term George Grant. At that time none of the district's living residents had been represented by a Republican. However, when President Lyndon Johnson signed the Civil Rights Act of 1964, it was a new deal. The South changed parties overnight as white Democrats switched to the Republican Party. Dickinson was the beneficiary of some long GOP coattails with Barry Goldwater on top of the ticket. Goldwater carried the second district of Alabama by a 75–25 margin. Dickinson beat Grant by 25 points.

Even though Dickinson and the other GOP nominees won by default, they were all excellent candidates. Dickinson and Jack Edwards of Mobile went on to become outstanding congressmen.

I had become very interested and involved in politics by the time Dickinson won in 1964 and was reelected in 1966. I also fancied myself a young Republican. I got to know my new congressman. My dentist, Dr. Allen Jones, had been a fraternity brother of Bill's at Alabama and Dr. Jones knew of my affinity for politics and made me acquainted with the congressman. We hit it off and became friends. In 1968, Dr. Jones and I were the Pike County coordinators for Dickinson's reelection campaign. I went on to work for Bill in all of his subsequent races. He asked me to work in his Washington and Montgomery offices during my years at the University of Alabama.

He had a challenge in 1972 when redistricting combined the second and third districts and Bill picked up Dothan and the Wiregrass. I worked as a coordinator in that campaign and drove him around the district. He prevailed and never had a serious challenge again except for a surprise in 1976. He went on to serve for 26 years and was on the Armed Services Committee the entire 26 years. The congressman for the second district needed to be on that committee—the largest employers and most important economic engines in that part of the state are the military bases of Maxwell and Gunter in Montgomery and Fort Rucker in the Wiregrass.

Bill worked diligently to protect these bases. He was the primary reason that these military plants prospered and expanded through the 1970s and 1980s. He was instrumental in other military/aircraft companies like Sikorsky and Lockheed-Martin locating in the Montgomery-Wiregrass region.

He rose to become the ranking Republican on the House Armed Forces Services Committee and was without doubt the most influential and important congressman the second district has ever had.

He died in Montgomery in 2008 at age 83.

With, from left, Senator Jeff Sessions and Congressmen Spencer Bachus and Jo Bonner.

Representative Spencer Bachus

Spencer Bachus represented Alabama's 6th Congressional District with distinction and effectiveness for 22 years. The district encompasses the suburbs of Jefferson and Shelby counties and is consistently ranked as one of the most Republican districts in the country.

When Bachus went to Congress in 1993, Birmingham had three major bank holding companies. To better represent his district, Bachus went on the Financial Services (the old banking) Committee. Over the years he rose to the chairmanship of the House Financial Services Committee.

Bachus was born and raised in the Birmingham area. He graduated from Auburn and earned his law degree from the University of Alabama. He practiced law in Birmingham before going to Congress. We served together one term in the House of Representatives. He represented the Vestavia area in the legislature for a term.

Bachus was always a Republican and voted with the GOP leadership during his tenure in Congress. He was never really challenged for reelection after his initial victory. He retired from Congress in January 2015.

Senator Jeff Sessions

As of 2015, Jefferson Beauregard Sessions III, Alabama's junior U.S. senator, may very well be Alabama's most popular political figure among conservative whites.

President Ronald Reagan appointed Sessions as the U.S. Attorney for the Southern District of Alabama in 1981 and tried to nominate him to a judgeship in that district in 1986, but the Senate did not confirm him. Then he was elected Attorney General of Alabama in 1994, serving only two years before being first elected to the U.S. Senate in 1996. He has been one of the most ardent conservatives in the U.S. Senate since his first day. The *National Journal* ranked him as the fifth-most conservative of the 100 members.

In keeping with his prosecutorial background, Sessions has served on the Judiciary Committee his entire 18 years in the Senate. He is also a ranking member of the Appropriations Committee.

Sessions was born in 1946 in Selma and grew up in Camden. He attended Huntingdon College where he was active in the young Republicans and was student body president. His law degree is from the University of Alabama.

Representative Jo Bonner

The First District congressional seat (primarily Mobile and Baldwin counties) has had a long line of outstanding congressmen. Jo Bonner represented the district for 10 years with distinction (Jack Edwards held the seat 1965–85, then Sonny Callahan 1985–2003).

Bonner could have stayed in the seat for life. He was not only popular in his district but was very well liked in Washington. He left to be the head of political and economic affairs at the University of Alabama.

He is a graduate of the University of Alabama. Like Sessions, he was born in Selma and grew up in Camden. He is a graduate of UA's prestigious journalism school.

11

Howell Heflin

Alabama's most colorful and notorious U.S. Senator may have been "Cotton Tom" Heflin in the 1920s. Fifty years later his nephew, Howell Heflin, took that same seat in the Senate and served with distinction, motivated in part by a desire to redeem the family name. Unlike his uncle, who was a renowned racist demagogue, Howell Heflin was considered a moderate in Washington and even a progressive by Alabama standards. Senator Howell Heflin's 18-year Senate career and record mirror those of our two greatest U.S. Senators, Lister Hill and John Sparkman. These two giants served in the Senate twice as long as Heflin.

Heflin got to the Senate later in life as he practiced law in Tuscumbia until he was 50 years old and then served one six-year term as chief justice of the Alabama Supreme Court. He campaigned for and won statewide voter approval for a constitutional revamping of the Alabama Judiciary known as the Judicial Article. After finishing his term as chief justice in 1976, he turned his attention to the U.S. Senate, winning the open seat of the retiring John Sparkman in 1978. Sparkman and Heflin were cut from the same cloth. Sparkman urged Heflin to run and endorsed him. They were both progressives from north Alabama who worked hard to give Alabama a good image and also bring home the bacon.

Howell Heflin graduated from Birmingham-Southern College and then from the University of Alabama law school. During World War II, he served as a U.S. Marine Corps officer in the Pacific, winning the Silver Star for bravery and two Purple Hearts for injuries sustained during combat on Bougainville and Guam.

Heflin was one of the last of the Roosevelt-style Southern progressives to serve in the United State Senate. A large, folksy man, his engaging personality masked a keen mind and political cunning that served him well in

Washington and made him friends on both sides of the aisle. He is one of the few politicians in recent history to have spent a career in the public eye and retired with his integrity intact.

In fact, he was held in such esteem by his colleagues that when he arrived in the Senate in 1978, his sterling reputation for integrity had preceded him and he was asked as a freshman to serve on the Ethics Committee. He rose to become chairman.

He also chose unselfishly the Senate Agriculture Committee, which is not a glamorous or high-profile committee for fundraising. However, it was his work on the Agriculture C ommittee that he should be remembered for by the Alabama and Southern farmer as the greatest friend they ever had in Washington. His work on the Agriculture Committee single handedly saved the peanut program and many other Southern mainstays for two decades. Many an Alabama farmer owes a large debt of gratitude to Howell Heflin. He was also a giant on the Senate Judiciary Committee. He was a natural leader of this important committee because of his brilliant legal mind and background.

Heflin's fellow Colbert Countian, Representative Marcel Black, successfully got the State Judicial Building named after Heflin. It is fitting and proper acknowledgment for the man known affectionately throughout Alabama and even to his colleagues in the U.S. Senate as Judge Heflin.

The Son of a Methodist Minister

Howell Heflin was a loyal family man, a loyal Marine, and a loyal Methodist. Heflin loved his family and his roots. He could tell you who he was kin to in every corner of the state. He revered his mother and his wife. Once the *National Enquirer*, that pillar of journalistic accuracy, included Heflin on a list of ten members of Congress who were "space aliens." A reporter asked the Judge for his comment, and he responded, "I always knew my mother was heaven-sent."

Heflin's father, the Reverend Marvin Heflin, was a Methodist minister. Having grown up in the Methodist Church, Heflin was an active layman in the church. He even enjoyed, in his own words, "The sacred bird of the Methodist, fried chicken."

The Methodists insist on periodically moving their ministers around. Heflin often used his father as the reason for his being born in Georgia, a potential problem for an Alabama politician. He would say, "Well, you know, my father was a Methodist preacher, and he was over in Georgia doing missionary work among the heathen."

Hoot with the Owls

John and Clara Ruth Hayman wrote Heflin's biography, *A Judge in the Senate* (NewSouth Books, 2001). They depicted a man whose life had been lived above reproach. He will be remembered as a great senator and judge. By all historical measures, he overshadowed his uncle, "Cotton Tom" Heflin, as a U.S. Senator.

He also had no peer in Alabama politics as a storyteller. He was spellbinding and unequaled on the political banquet circuit. Because I knew him well, he was my favorite politician. My nickname is Tree. He would get a gleam in his eye when he saw me because I had a nickname, and he would gleefully and loudly say, "Well, there's old Tray."

Heflin was a natural story teller. He loved stories and had a magnificent repertoire of jokes. It was not just the jokes that were good, but how he told them. He had a brilliant quick wit. He used this gift of wit to not only entertain but many times to make a point or to defuse tension.

Howell Heflin's humor is part of political folklore.

On occasion as state legislators we would go to Washington to seek federal funding for a project or a legislative conference—you would probably call it a junket. Heflin would oftentimes take time out of his busy Senate schedule to have dinner with us. He loved to eat. He would insist on going to the famous Monacle Restaurant just down from his Senate office for dinner. The waiters and maître d' knew him well and loved him like we did in Alabama. Only Texas Senator John Tower frequented the Monacle more than Heflin.

Heflin would regale us with jokes and anecdotes and funny political stories. Some of the legislators would enjoy the Monacle libations more than others.

Heflin himself was a teetotaler. He was not judgmental of his guests' overindulgence. He would just look their way with a twinkle in his eye and admonish them with one of his succinct sayings. He would simply say, "You can't hoot with the owls all night and expect to soar with the eagles the next day."

Howell Heflin Faces a Mountain Brook Republican

By 1980 Heflin had become our senior U.S. Senator, a rank he held until he retired in 1996. In 1990, he had been in the Senate for 12 years and was running for a third six-year term. He drew as his Republican opponent State Senator Bill Cabaniss of Birmingham. Bill was one of the finest men I ever served with in the legislature. He was honest, forthright, smart, and his word was as good as gold. He was a successful businessman who owned a manufacturing business. He served on several prominent bank and insurance boards in Birmingham and was a well-respected gentleman.

Bill Cabaniss was a Republican when it wasn't cool. He was born a Republican. If there are any old money families in Birmingham—and of course Mobile and Montgomery old-money families will argue that Birmingham is too new a city to have any old money—the Cabaniss family would be on top of the list. Cabaniss was born in Mountain Brook, the richest suburb in Alabama and second only to a suburb in Dallas as the richest enclave in the South. The Cabaniss family had homes all over the world, besides their Mountain Brook residence. One of their summer homes was in Kennebunkport, Maine, and they were next-door neighbors to another old Republican Connecticut family known as the Bushes. So Bill Cabaniss and George W. Bush are lifelong friends; President Bush later appointed Cabaniss as ambassador to the Czech Republic.

Alabamians have always resented the wealth and privilege of Mountain Brook people. Due to our archaic constitution, local measures are on a statewide ballot. Mountain Brook would try to enact tax increases on themselves to raise funds for their own schools and the rest of the state would vote them down just because it had Mountain Brook on the ballot.

In 1990, Senator Heflin had access to the best media consultants in Washington. As the incumbent, he had plenty of campaign money and a tremendous head start on the wealthy Cabaniss in name identification. Cabaniss was completely unknown to 90 percent of Alabamians. Given that advantage, Heflin's consultants decided that they needed to define Cabaniss to Alabama voters in a negative way before he could define himself. Heflin's consultants were studying sophisticated methods to stop Cabaniss before he could get out of the gate. Heflin guffawed and off the top of his head said, "I'll tell you how we will define him. We'll just tell folks all over Alabama that Cabaniss is one of those Gucci shoe-wearing, Rolex watch-wearing, Grey Poupon mustard-dipping, Kennebunkport, Maine-vacationing, Mercedes-driving Mountain Brook Republicans." He used that phrase all during the fall campaign and he won reelection, overwhelmingly.

Howell Heflin and Gays in the Military

During most of Heflin's 18 years in the Senate, he was blessed with a brilliant chief of staff named Steve Raby. Raby was young, but everybody respected him and the Judge relied on him heavily. Raby was like a son to Heflin, but Heflin also took orders from Raby on where he should be in reference to his schedule and votes. Raby went a lot of places with Heflin and reminded him about important matters. Most folks knew you had to keep Raby attuned and abreast of important projects or votes they were interested in.

Early in President Bill Clinton's first term, he was promoting his gays in the military initiative. He was gung-ho to pass the measure. The Senate Democratic Caucus met for a lunch once a month. It was a very rare occasion when the president would ask to come to the luncheon. The group acquiesced and invited the young Democratic president to speak.

Raby told Heflin early that morning when they got into the office, "Judge, you remember the president is coming to y'all's caucus and it starts at noon." It got to be close to noon and Heflin wasn't heading that way. Raby came by his office and asked Heflin's secretary if he was ready yet. Heflin seemed in no hurry to get to the caucus meeting. He finally ambled over there around 12:30 p.m. while Clinton was up talking to the Democratic senators and Heflin quietly took a seat in the back of the room and seemed to want to blend into the crowd. He had not missed catching the attention of the president. On his way out, President Clinton came over to buttonhole and lobby Heflin. Clinton's habit was to effusively charm folks by grabbing their arm and slapping them on the back. He cajoled Heflin in this way and said, "Judge, I hope you will consider supporting me on this measure." Heflin politely told him, "Mr. President, I can't help you on that matter." Clinton persisted and grabbed Heflin closer and slapped him on the back and said, "Well, Judge, don't close the door. Why don't you go home and pray about it?"

Heflin pushed the president back and looked him straight in the eye and said, "Son, I have done prayed about it and I've read my Bible about it, and I can't help you on that issue."

Heflin had made it clear to the president where he stood on gays in the military. This episode was not well known or publicized like other Heflin stories. Raby shared this one privately with me. Even though Heflin was considered a moderate Southerner in Washington, his background made that issue tough for the Judge. Heflin was a very highly decorated Marine. He had been wounded in a major battle of World War II. He was also the son of a Methodist minister.

Howell Heflin and His Handkerchief

One of the most famous stories surrounding the Judge was his infamous handkerchief.

Heflin was a somewhat frugal man. When he got to the Senate, he and his wife rented a modest apartment near the Capitol. These apartments were once the home for retired Methodist ministers. However, they had become quite desirable because they were very close to the Capitol. They were basically on the Capitol grounds. Their proximity had made them exclusive, but they were small.

Heflin and his wife, Elizabeth Anne, whom the Judge called Mike, were happy with their accommodations. As always, Steve Raby, Heflin's chief of staff, went most places with Heflin. On that particular day, Heflin's and Raby's day began early. They had several breakfasts to attend on the Hill, but they also had a high-profile luncheon with the top NBC News producer. She and her lead reporter were to have an exclusive luncheon with Heflin and Raby with the understanding that their meeting and discussions were off the record.

Heflin had a habit of blowing his nose after eating. Mrs. Heflin had worked hard to break the Judge of this habit. He had done pretty well through the breakfast meeting, however, when he finished eating lunch with the two female NBC producers, he pulled out his handkerchief to blow his nose. He pulls it out full four corners and holds it up to his face. There sitting on his nose was his wife's underwear. The two female reporters could hardly contain their laughter. Raby said he had seen the Judge do everything under the sun and even fall off a stage and not get embarrassed, but at this situation, he was so humiliated and embarrassed he turned red. He apologized profusely to the ladies.

As many couples did who have been together for a long time like the Judge and Mike, they kept their clothes together. Especially since they lived in a small apartment. He and his wife apparently used the same drawer for his handkerchief and her underwear. He had gotten up early that day for his breakfast meeting and hadn't turned the lights on as he didn't want to wake Mike. He had just reached into the drawer to get his handkerchief and mistakenly gotten his wife's panties.

The NBC women, true to their word did not tell the story, but it somehow made the Capitol Hill paper, *Roll Call.* After the story was told, it became national news and will live in infamy as part of Howell Heflin's legacy.

Howell Heflin and John Warner

While in the Senate, Heflin became good friends with Republican Senator John Warner of Virginia. He and Warner were attending a defense-related gathering in Europe. Heflin followed Warner as the Speaker at one session and he flavored his remarks with the knowledge that the Republican had once been married to actress Elizabeth Taylor.

"I wanted you to know," Heflin told the audience, "that I'm going to do like Elizabeth Taylor told John Warner after they got married—I'm not going to keep you very long."

Howell Heflin and Ted Kennedy

One of the best stories that illustrates Heflin's wit and wisdom is a little risque. However, it is in the *Congressional Record* so it is appropriate to include.

Heflin had developed a friendship with Ted Kennedy. They served together on the Senate Judiciary Committee. Kennedy respected Heflin for his keen legal mind and admired the Judge for being a progressive Southerner. Heflin did not broadcast in Alabama the fact that he was friends with the liberal Kennedy.

At the time of this story, Kennedy was between marriages. He was leading quite the bachelor life. One day he had a date with a beautiful young brunette. He took her sailing on his sailboat off Hyannis Port, Massachusetts, where the famous Kennedy compound is. The mainstream media was following Kennedy constantly and taking pictures of his romances. The *Boston Globe* and *New York Times* were especially interested in Kennedy's social life. This particular day they were using a telescopic lens camera to scope out Kennedy's sailboat. Well, they got an eyeful. They caught Kennedy and his date in a very compromising position and put the pictures in their Sunday papers.

Early Monday morning Heflin ambled onto the floor of the U.S. Senate. He immediately asked for recognition. The presiding officer quickly recognized him and said, "The senior Senator from Alabama has the floor." Heflin said, with a straight face, "I only want to say that I'm glad to see that the senior Senator from Massachusetts has changed his position on offshore drilling."

HEFLIN AND THE NUNS

One Senate committee meeting was late into the night and it was tense. Debate was hot and tempers were surfacing when Judge Heflin sought recognition. When Heflin sought recognition he would lean into the microphone and raise his finger and intone, "Mr. Chaaairmaan . . ." After being recognized, he continued, "Mr. Chairman, I'm reminded of a story back home an old friend of mine, Brother Ham Benderson, told. Now Brother Ham was a great observer of people and a sage philosopher. One day he happened upon a very unusual sight. A car was on the side of the road and there were two Catholic nuns walking around the car with a bedpan. What Brother Ham didn't know was that these two sisters had run out of gas, walked down to the next farm and asked for some gas. The farmer said they could have some gas but the only spare container he had was a bedpan. It was at this time Brother Ham pulled up and watched these two nuns pour out of a bedpan into the gas tank. Brother Ham was awestruck by this sight and said to his boy, "I'll tell you right now, if them sisters get that old Dodge to crank, me and you are a trading cars and switching churches. Now, Mr. Chairman, the solution to a problem is not always what it appears to be . . ."

"Is the Senator from Alabama suggesting we use a bed pan?"

"Weeelllll, you could, but the real issue is knowing what you are pouring out of it."

A Few Concluding Heflin Stories . . .

. . . transcribed as he told them at various times:

I'll Now Take Any Questions from the Floor

A certain Congressman was prone to indulge in alcohol. He would come home late, a little inebriated. His wife was getting tired of his late-night antics.

He came home late one night about 3 a.m. really drunk. He was trying to get the key in the door and the wife heard him and came down to open the door. When she opened the door he tumbled in and fell on the floor

Standing over him, his wife said, "What do you have to say for yourself?"

"Well," he said, "I don't have any opening statements, but I'll take questions from the floor."

"What do you mean coming home half drunk?"

"Well, I ran out of money."

"You're so sorry, I ought to leave you."

"You can't do that," he said. "I've already lost you."

"What do you mean you lost me?"

"I lost you in a poker game."

"What are you talking about?"

"It wasn't easy, I folded with four aces."

You're Gonna Die

An old man was not feeling well. So his wife took him to the doctor.

After running one round of tests and then another the doctor asked to see the wife in private.

"He's got some problems," the doctor said of the old man, "but nothing that's not curable. He just needs three home-cooked meals a day and sex three times a day."

When the woman came out of the meeting, her husband nervously and anxiously asked the wife, "Honey, what did the doctor say?"

"Honey," the woman replied, "he says you're gonna die."

You and Me Are the Only Ones for It

This old guy who was a real rounder. He would partake of too much alcohol, especially on the weekends. His wife was a saint and a real churchgoer. He would generally be hungover on Sunday morning, but his wife would nag him and make him go to church. He had an especially rough weekend, and she insisted that he go to church with her. So he was situated in church and fell asleep. The preacher saw him dead asleep and thought he would try to wake him up. So he thundered out, loud as he could, "Everybody who wants to go to Hell stand up!" It woke the old guy up from his sleep and he jumped to his feet. Well, everybody in the church just stared at him. The preacher looked at him and said, "Brother, have you got something to tell us?" The old guy stammered and said, "Preacher, I don't know what we're voting on, but it looks like you and me are the only ones for it!"

Congressman Bob

A fellow was elected to Congress from south Georgia. Old Bob got to Washington. He got busy with committees, etc. He told his wife the life of a congressman was hard. Since he was so busy, his wife said that she and the rest of the family would go back to south Georgia until things in Washington settled down. He would write numerous times and say the life of a congressman was hard. Finally, his wife decided to go to Washington and check on old Bob. He said he would take her out to an exclusive restaurant. When they went in, the hat check girl said, "Hi, Congressman Bob." His wife asked, "How do you know her?' Bob said, "I represented her in a lawsuit one time." Then the maître d' said, "Where would you like to sit, Congressman Bob?" His wife said, "I thought you were always busy working, so how do you know him?" He answered, "Oh, everyone knows you in Washington when you're in Congress."

After dinner, the floor show began. Dancing girls yelled, "Hi, Congressman Bob." At that, his wife said, "I've had enough!" She storms out of the restaurant and jumps in a cab to leave. Congressman Bob follows after her, hastily jumps into the cab, and says, "I can explain everything." She says, "I don't want to hear anything and I don't want to have anything to do with you." At that point, the cab driver looks around and says, "You've got a tough one tonight, haven't you, Congressman Bob?"

Part III

Legislators

12

South Alabama Legislators

My First Campaign

My first race for the legislature was in 1982 when I was 30; I would turn 31 about the day I was elected. I subsequently served five terms in the Alabama House of Representatives. That first race was my most memorable. I only had an opponent one other time.

My true mentors were Probate Judge Ben Reeves and State Representative Gardner Bassett. They had been grooming me for the job of state representative since I was a boy. Mr. Gardner was my primary mentor and best friend. He had been waiting for me to get old enough to take his seat.

Judge Reeves and Mr. Gardner had forged a formidable political machine in the county. It was made up of about 20 veteran political icons who were in charge of their boxes or precincts in the county. They would actually be the chief clerks of the polling place, appointed by the probate judge. Judge Reeves and Mr. Gardner's man in each precinct oversaw all the voting and delivered the boxes to the sheriff for counting.

Judge Reeves and Mr. Gardner took me to see each man a good year before I was to run and before it was even known that Mr. Gardner's seat would be vacant. All 20 pledged their allegiance to my succeeding Mr. Gardner. You might say that I became the heir apparent to the Reeves/Bassett machine.

I got 82 percent of the vote in that 1982 race against two opponents. Our vote total was the most ever cast for any candidate for any race in Pike County history. It still stands today, thanks in no small part to the unified support of that machine.

Mr. Gardner was getting really old but he insisted on riding with me to campaign. We started in the rural areas. Our first foray together was to the Needmore Community in north Pike County. We began on a dirt road.

He would slowly get out of the car and we would walk together to the door of the farm house to solicit votes. The old couple who met us at the door would embrace Mr. Gardner like he was their uncle or grandfather. You could see the love for him in their eyes. Mr. Gardner would not rush things. We would sit in their living room. They would serve us ice tea. Mr. Gardner would ask about their family members, the weather, their garden, and then finally he would look at them and say "I want y'all to vote for Steve Flowers for my House seat." They would pause for a moment and give him their word—you could take it to the bank. I knew we had two votes. We would thank them and head back to the car. I would look over and say, "Mr. Gardner, those folks are going to vote for me because of you. Why do they like you so much?" He would say, "I got their son a job with the state and got their roof fixed."

We would go to the next house and it would be almost the same scenario. They would firmly commit and I would again say to Mr. Gardner, "They are going to vote for me because of you. Why?" His response would be, "I got their brother out of jail." The next house, "I helped them buy Christmas gifts for all their children when they were out of work." He had personally helped literally every person on that road and he was transferring over three decades of political favors to his protégé, Steve Flowers.

When the votes were counted, 114 votes were cast in the Needmore box. We got 111 of these votes. We knew where we lost two—the son of my opponent had married a Needmore couple's daughter and they told us that they wanted to vote for us but felt obligated to vote for their son-in-law's mother. We told them we understood. We never knew who the other person that didn't vote for us in Needmore was.

That lost vote always seemed to bother Mr. Gardner. He wanted to round up every single vote.

There was an old guy who lived way back in the woods in north Pike County. Mr. Gardner told me to go see him early in the campaign. The old fellow was aging and was quite a character. He didn't even have a road to his house. It stopped about a mile away from his cabin. His house looked more like a shed. It amazed me that a person could actually live in his abode. At Mr. Gardner's request, I sought out this man. I know he made his living making moonshine whiskey. I missed him the first time I went to ask for his support. However, I found him the second time.

He was like a character out of *Deliverance*. He had very few teeth. He carried an axe and looked at me menacingly. I kept my distance and asked him for his vote. He only had one eye and one of the suspenders on his overalls was missing. He gave me no answer regarding my request for his vote. He only grunted as he swung his axe toward a piece of wood he was chopping. I backed away, walked back to my car. Later that night I went by Mr. Gardner's to report on my day. He asked about this guy. I told him my journey had been unproductive. I only received a grunt. He looked thoughtful for a minute and said quietly, "Don't worry I will take care of him." It occurred to me that the old guy was a money vote. He wanted to be paid for his vote. Mr. Gardner was embarrassed to tell me that earlier in their career they had bought votes. Later in the campaign, Mr. Gardner told me that the old guy was going to vote for me.

With my friend and mentor Representative Gardner Bassett, who represented Pike County in the Legislature for 24 years.

Even though we won in a landslide, Mr. Gardner had taught me to pursue every vote. Every vote counted.

MR. GARDNER BASSETT

Gardner Bassett served as Pike County's representative for 24 years (1950–74). He only quit then because his wife, Mrs. Gennie, became real sick and had to go to the nursing home. He felt like he needed to take care of her and stay close by her side.

State Representative Gardner Bassett and Probate Judge Ben Reeves had been adversaries in the 1958 probate race. After that epic battle they became loyal allies and organized their formidable and legendary Ben Reeves and Gardner Bassett political machine.

The two men were very different. Judge Reeves was tough and crusty and all business. Mr. Gardner had a soft, sweet, caring spirit. He loved to help folks. He was always giving people his money, corn from his garden, or political favors.

I would spend hours sitting in his kitchen with him and Mrs. Gennie. She would ask me to stay for supper. I would call my mama and ask her if it was okay to stay. She said, "Be sure and tell Mrs. Bassett you enjoyed your supper." She taught me to say that to whoever cooked a meal whether I liked it or not. Of course, Mrs. Gennie was a great cook. She always topped dinner off with a fresh apple pie. My favorite meal was white lady peas and cornbread in the summer.

Mr. Gardner was about 70 and I was 12 at this time. We were more like buddies rather than a grandfather and grandson relationship. He decided early that I was going to be his protégé. He would tell everybody that I was going to follow him in his House seat when he retired—and that's what happened.

He started teaching me the ropes early. I became his perennial page. He would appoint other young boys to serve two-week terms but I stayed with him the entire session. We would ride to Montgomery in his big black Chrysler New Yorker. He had a good parking spot right in front of the Capitol. We would get out and walk right up the back steps to Mr. Gardner's desk. I got to know all the representatives because I stayed all summer. A good many of the other pages would just play. I liked to run errands and watch what was going on in the house chamber.

I would meander over to Mr. Gardner's desk and he would tell me why he was voting the way he was on a certain bill. It was generally because it was good for Pike County, but mostly he voted with the governor. He advised me, "Always vote with the governor when you can." That was not a bad admonition. At that time the governor had immense power over everything, especially roads.

Mr. Gardner was a little embarrassed for me to see some of the foibles and exploits of some of his legislative colleagues. He was especially embarrassed when one day the gentleman from Washington County got so drunk that he got his foot stuck in a garbage can. He got excited about a mundane local bill and walked all the way down to the microphone to slur his objection with the garbage can attached to his boot. Some of my page buddies and I had watched the old guy sipping from his bottle on his desk all afternoon. His foot-in-the-garbage-can escapade was hilarious.

Mr. Gardner and I would walk down the steps and ride home to Troy at the end of the day. He would talk to me about certain bills and people. He was really close to the young Speaker of the House, Albert Brewer.

When the legislature wasn't in session, he would drive to Montgomery on Wednesdays to look after constituent concerns. He would make the usual hour-long trip from Troy to Montgomery in 45 minutes. He would take me with him. Some days we would go to the Agriculture Department and see the Agriculture Commissioner about a problem a Pike County farmer was having. He would usually get it resolved. One day we might go to the Highway Department to see about a road.

Mr. Gardner and I lived on adjoining streets in Troy. I was the paperboy for the *Troy Messenger* in our area. One afternoon I was delivering my papers and Mr. Gardner was waiting in his front yard. He said, "Hurry up and finish your route, I got a trip for us to Montgomery." I hurriedly finished my paper route and hightailed it back to Mr. Gardner's. We got in his big black Chrysler and headed for Montgomery. He was going faster than usual which was pretty fast. The speed limit on the two-way highway was 50 and Mr. Gardner was easily doing 75 mph. We sped by our only trooper assigned to our county, "Curly" Long. Mr. Gardner simply waved at Curly as he sped by and Curly smiled and waved back. I said, "Mr. Gardner, why didn't Curly stop you?" He said, "I got him his job." Mr. Gardner had gotten a lot of Pike Countians jobs with the state. Legislators, especially those with some seniority, had a lot of power to get folks jobs with the state.

I finally asked him what our mission was that day. He smiled at me and said, "Steve, you're going to meet the governor." George Wallace was in his first term.

We got to Montgomery, parked in our spot in front of the Capitol, and walked straight to the governor's office. The secretary whisked us back to see Governor George Wallace. I proudly got introduced to the governor as Mr. Gardner's best friend and protégé. He said, "Governor, Steve is going to follow me in my House seat when I retire and he is old enough." Wallace never forgot that first meeting. Amazingly, 20 years later I indeed followed Mr. Gardner and became Pike County's representative. I represented a portion of Barbour County that encompassed Wallace's hometown of Clayton. Wallace was governor for his fourth and final term in 1983–87 and I was his representative. He loved to tell everyone that I was his representative. He vividly remembered that day in June 1963 when I first met him and Mr. Gardner told Wallace I was going to follow him into his House seat. Wallace made me a floor leader and would call me down to his office regularly to just visit. He would begin every conversation with, "Steve, remember when you were a page boy and Mr. Bassett brought you by to meet me?" It was a fun and memorable four years with Wallace as governor and me as his representative.

My first day in the legislature I walked up the back steps of the old Capitol to the old house chamber where I had spent my youth as Mr. Gardner's page. I walked the same steps that Mr. Gardner and I had walked. I walked into the house chamber and awaiting me was the longtime house clerk, John Pemberton. He said, "The other freshmen are going to have to draw straws for their seats. Don't tell anyone, but you are not going to have to do that; we've got your seat picked out for you." He led me to Mr. Gardner's seat. I said, "Thank you," and I took Mr. Gardner's seat.

U. L. Miller

Alabama politics was built around the "friends and neighbors" theory. Historically, Alabama voters have wanted to vote for their friend, neighbor, or relative. Country people used to say they liked to "tie" you to someone.

This was especially true in my first political race in 1982. I was fortunate to have been born and raised in my home county of Pike. Both sides of my family had been there for generations. My mama's people had been in Pike County since 1837, prior to the Civil War. So you might say I had the advantage of having some roots in the county.

My maternal great-grandfather was a tall, lanky man named Urban L. Miller. He went by U. L. He died the year I was born, so I never knew him, but I had heard about him all of my life. I could tell that my mama revered him. In fact, everybody in my family worshiped the legend and stories about U. L. Miller. It transcended family. Growing up I would hear about his humble demeanor, kindness, and generosity. He had lived his life in the northern part of my county near the Montgomery County line. He was a cattle farmer and ran a dairy.

When I started my campaign, I started early. I was fortunate to have as my mentor the two most prominent politicians in my county, Mr. Gardner Bassett and Probate Judge Ben Reeves. They both coached me and campaigned for me.

Early on it became apparent to them and me that U. L. Miller was helping me from the grave in the northern part of our county. The folks all over that end of the county were tying me to old U. L. It was evident that they thought a lot of my great-grandfather.

My mentors pulled me aside one day and said, "We need to send you on down to the southern part of the county. We believe you're going to get all the votes up there in Orion, besides, there are more votes in the southern part of the county."

I moved on, however, there was one man I needed to contact up there. He was an elderly black gentleman. He was a very respected man in his community. He was the patriarch of a large family and the leader of his church. It was well known that he controlled about 30 or 40 votes because his family and church all voted with him.

I kept going back to see him but kept missing him. Finally, I caught him at home about eight days before the election. He was back in his barn shoeing an old mule. I shook his hand and told him my name and that I was running for the legislature and that I knew he had a lot of influence and that I would like his vote and support.

He was slow to answer me. After a long pause, he looked me squarely in the eye and said, "Boy, I do control about 37 votes up here. Most of them vote with me. Some of them are going to vote against me on a few races. But I've made it clear to them that on one race I want every one of them to vote with me, and all 37 of them are going to vote for you."

I was pleased to hear this. At this time I had learned that if a country person, especially a prominent, respected person, told you something, that their word was their bond. Therefore, I knew I had those 37 votes. So I could let my guard down. I had to ask the old gentleman, "Mr. _____, I appreciate your vote and support more than you know, but I've got to ask you, you've never met me before, why are you so much for me?"

He said, "Boy, let me tell you a story. Back during the depression I was a little boy. There were six of us children and we had one milk cow. That milk cow was our salvation. She provided milk for our whole family. One cold March night, there come a bad storm, our cow got out and got trapped in a gully. Your great-granddaddy got out of his bed and spent the whole night getting our cow out of that ditch and brought her home. On top of that he brought us fresh milk from his dairy every morning for two weeks and left it on our porch and also made sure we had enough to eat. I've been waiting 50 years to pay back that debt."

Old U. L. Miller got me 37 votes from the grave in my first election.

PETE TURNHAM

I had a distinguished seatmate during my tenure in the legislature. Mr. Pete Turnham and I sat beside each other for 16 years. Mr. Pete was a legend. He served in the House of Representatives from 1958 through 1998, the record for legislative longevity. He saw and made a lot of history. He was Lee County and Auburn's representative during those four decades. He was truly a representative and advocate for Auburn and for Auburn University.

With my friend Pete Turnham; we were House seatmates for 16 years.

Like most folks of his generation, Pete grew up on a farm. He was born and raised in Chambers County, which adjoins Lee County and Auburn. He graduated from Auburn with a degree in agriculture. Shortly after, World War II began. Pete joined the Army. He won every honor for his valor. He was in the Battle of the Bulge and received the Bronze Star. He fought with Patton all over Europe. Most men who fought in World War II lost their hearing from the constant bombing. Governor George Wallace was also an enlisted man and his hearing was badly impaired like Pete's.

One day Wallace called me and Pete to come down to the governor's office to discuss some legislation with Governor Wallace. You would have to have been there to see the scene. Both men were getting up in age. I was the only one of the three of us who knew what was being said. Wallace and Pete were talking to each other and neither knew what the other was saying. They were both on different subjects yet they would nod to each other in agreement periodically. It was quite a show.

Mr. Pete's personal mission was to look out for Auburn University. I watched him year after year get additional appropriations placed into Auburn's budget. He served on the Ways and Means Committee and knew where money was hidden in the budget. Because of Mr. Pete, Auburn got their fair share. Mr. Pete never got the recognition he deserved for his efforts on behalf of his university. There should be a building or something named for Pete Turnham at Auburn. I dare say that no man in history has meant more to Auburn.

You build lasting friendships when you sit beside someone for that long a time. I truly love Mr. Pete. He is a class gentleman.

Mr. Pete retired from the legislature in 1998. The current Speaker of the House, Mike Hubbard, took his place.

Mr. Pete is now more than 90 years old. He and Mrs. Kay, his wife of 65 years, live in their same house in Auburn. He enjoys his Baptist Church and his garden. Mr. Pete is still referred to as the "Dean of the Legislature." He is the only person to have served in the legislature during all of George and Lurleen Wallace's terms as governor.

Jimmy Holley

Jimmy Holley was born and raised in Coffee County. He has represented his county in the legislature for 36 years. He has been a fierce and steadfast stalwart for his home county and surrounding area. He was a loyal Democrat for most of his legislative career. He switched to the Republican Party in recent years, more as a reflection of his district than his own change in philosophy.

Senator Holley is currently serving his fourth term in the State Senate after serving 20 years in the Alabama House of Representatives. Jimmy Holley has been one of the most thoroughly prepared and effective legislators I have seen over the past three decades.

Jimmy was my other legislative mate. He sat to my left and Mr. Pete Turnham to my right. Jimmy was known as a pork master. He knew where the pork was in the budget and how to get a slice for his folks back home.

During the session I would drive home to Troy because it was only a 45-minute drive from the Capitol to my home in Troy. Jimmy lived only about 30 minutes further away, but he chose to stay in Montgomery in a modest hotel room.

It occurred to me on more than one occasion that Jimmy was more fastidious than I or many of my other House colleagues. Many of them stayed in Montgomery and enjoyed the night life.

State Senator Jimmy Holley as a guest on my television show, "Alabama Politics," 2015.

One day we were sitting at our desks working on a lengthy list of bills. The Rules Committee had decided that we were going to work hard that day and pass some legislation. I looked down the calendar and was unfamiliar with a looming bill about three bills down on the calendar. Contrary to what one might think or assume, every legislator does not read every bill. Many times, I had to rely on the synopsis or listen to debate about a bill to determine how to vote.

I asked Jimmy about that certain piece of legislation. He calmly told me all of the details of the bill and told me I probably was not going to vote for it since it was a trial lawyer bill. He knew my pro-business propensity. It occurred to me that he had read the bill in entirety as well as all the bills on the calendar the night before in his hotel room. He must have read legislation most of the night while holed up in his hotel room.

On another occasion I watched Holley get the legislature to fund and build an entire new school system for Elba after the city was flooded.

A few years later he returned to get a new state-of-the art high school for Enterprise after a tornado destroyed the earlier school.

Jimmy Holley is one of the ablest and effective legislators I've ever been around. The people of Coffee, Covington, Dale, and Pike counties are fortunate to have him as their senator. Jimmy and his wife, Mary, have two sons. Both have done well.

13

North Alabama Legislators

Bedford, Fine, and Fite

Slings and arrows were hurled at Russellville State Senator Roger Bedford for decades because of his legendary ability to get extra state dollars for his northwest Alabama district. As chairman of the Senate Finance Committee he had immense power appropriating and distributing taxpayers' money to his constituents. It is because of the largesse of political bacon brought home to his area that he was dubbed by the state media as the Pork King of Goat Hill.

Although Bedford was tarred and feathered by the state press for getting pork for the folks in the northwest corner of the state, the home folks love him. He is a hero in his home county and area. The state press hated the fact that they could not affect his popularity in his district.

Bedford's prowess as a power in the legislature seemed to be inherent in his corner of northwest Alabama. The area has bred powerful legislators for several generations. Prior to Bedford, Joe Fine was a native of Russellville and a practicing lawyer in his hometown. Both men are strikingly similar. Besides both being from Russellville and both being lawyers, both went to the Senate at a young age and quickly became effective. In addition, both are smart, articulate, and quick studies on the art of parliamentary procedure. Both became among the most effective and influential senators almost immediately. Both ran unsuccessful campaigns for attorney general. Fine went on to become arguably the most prominent contract lobbyist in Montgomery and Bedford was easily one of the most powerful members of the State Senate.

Even though Bedford and Fine made their marks wielding immense clout for their northwest Alabama districts, neither can hold a candle to their predecessor, the legendary Rankin Fite, the House Speaker from Hamilton in Marion County. Now, you talk about a pork king . . . if you think the press has had a field day with Bedford, today's media would have gone berserk with Fite.

Ol' Rankin Fite was one of a kind. Mr. Fite served one term in the Senate during the Folsom era and was a Big Jim man. However, he moved to the House of Representatives in 1951 and served five terms, including two stints as Speaker.

Modern-day Speakers run a fairly tight ship. There is order and decorum. Not so during Fite's days. He had an open-door policy. Anybody could just walk onto the floor of the House for any reason. There was no protocol. He liked the confusion. It gave him more power.

If you crossed Fite you better watch out. He had a memory like an elephant and believed in rewarding his friends and punishing his enemies. Governor Folsom wanted Fite in the Speaker's chair. After Folsom left, Fite landed on his feet and got in with Wallace. Wallace supported Fite and kept him as Speaker of the House during his first term 1963–67 and during Lurleen's term. In his second term 1971–75, he stabbed ol' Rankin in the back and made Sage Lyons, a silk-stocking closet Republican from Mobile, Speaker.

Rankin never got used to being put back on the floor like a common House member after being Speaker for so long. He decided after that term to go home. He had moved most of the Capitol up to his hometown anyway, so he felt at home in either place. He had practically rebuilt his hometown of Hamilton with new streets and sewer systems. Fite had made a fortune as a divorce lawyer in the quickie divorce system Alabama had created in the 1960s. He got state funds to build an airport for Hamilton that would rival any airport of cities ten times its size so he could fly his plane to and from the Capitol and would not have to drive. It was simply unbelievable how much pork he brought home to northwest Alabama.

As a boy in the 1960s I was a House page and I would watch Fite carefully. Although he was beginning to suffer from palsy and his hand would shake uncontrollably with the gavel, it had not affected his mind. As a youngster, I was learning the legislative process and my mentor Representative Gardner Bassett would patiently answer all of my questions. There was this young loquacious representative from Birmingham who was always ranting and introducing bills. Nobody seemed to like him much, especially Fite. He would ignore the young whippersnapper until everybody else had been recognized.

One day the fellow had a real buzz on. He had a bill that was going to change Alabama's entire tax system. Fite, one of the crustiest and craftiest in the history of the legislature, automatically sent the young fellow's bill to the Highway Safety Committee. This confused me because I had learned that all revenue bills go to the Ways and Means Committee. So I asked my mentor, when and where does the Highway Safety Committee meet? He said it doesn't. It was Rankin's private graveyard committee. He was chairman and they never met. So if he did not like you and your legislation, your agenda met a quick and permanent death in the Highway Safety Committee.

Ethics Law Not Tough Enough

Campaign finance laws and ethics disclosure forms for political campaigns and officeholders were enacted throughout the country in the 1970s, mostly in reaction to the public outcry for ethics reform after the Watergate corruption. Practically every state passed an ethics law. There was even a model ethics law from which states could create their own acts, along with campaign finance disclosure laws. This model act was a very tough law, so in most cases the state legislatures chose to deviate from this strict model when drafting their own ethics laws.

In the 1970s, Alabama had a lot of veteran and crafty and crusty legislators who simply ignored the national trend and had no intentions of passing an ethics law. That did not keep the Alabama media from constantly harping on the need for such legislation. The press would hammer the need for ethics in the legislature daily from the front pages to the editorials.

George Wallace was governor and he had pretty much dismissed ethics reform as an issue. He did not want to put his friends in the legislature on the spot. He had a harmonious working relationship with the legislature and did not want to step on toes and create a hornet's nest.

However, one day late in the legislative session Wallace decided to get a little good press. He called his legislative leadership team in and said there are only a few more legislative days left in the session and it's too late for anything to pass, much less an ethics bill, so let's throw the press a bone by introducing one.

They not only put in an ethics bill, they used the toughest model act in the country. The bill was introduced in both chambers with an agreement that each body would kill the other's bill. The House would pass the House bill and all the representatives would get credit for voting for an ethics law, knowing full well that the Senate would kill it. The Senators would then do the same so they could get credit knowing the House would kill their bill. They went about with their plan and gleefully passed the strongest ethics law in the country. They and Wallace enjoyed their day in the sun for being tough on ethics reform, although hardly any Senators or House members were for the package.

The press put a spotlight on the measures like never before and focused on the need for final passage. Things got out of hand and the House succumbed to public opinion and the bill got to the floor of the House. Once it got to a vote, the representatives were hard pressed to vote against it. What began as a charade by Wallace ended up with Alabama having one of the toughest ethics laws in America.

"Just Don't Mess with Dog Hunting"

Only a handful of House members had the nerve to vote against the ethics law. One who did was Fite, who had done pretty well for himself and his county before any ethics law. A horde of House members and reporters gathered around Fite's desk and asked why he voted against it. He looked them squarely in the eye and said it wasn't tough enough. He also said, "I voted for every tax. Voting for taxes won't beat you. I just voted against the ethics bill. Voting against ethics won't beat you. The issues you need to avoid are voting on daylight-saving time, trout fishing, or hunting deer with dogs."

Roger Bedford

When the Republicans took control of the Alabama State Senate in the 2014 election, they wiped out almost the last vestige of Democratic lore.

The 60-vote loss of State Senator Roger Bedford was the end of an era in Alabama politics.

If Daniel Webster and Teddy Kennedy were called the lions of the U.S. Senate then Roger Bedford would be called the legendary lion of the Alabama State Senate.

Bedford was the best retail politician of my generation. He had some close rivals in Don Siegelman and Jim Folsom Jr., but I believe that Bedford was the best. He simply loved it.

Bedford served in the state senate for 30 years. He was an integral part of running that body most of those years.

For close to three decades he represented the northwest Alabama counties of Colbert, Franklin, Fayette, Lamar, Lawrence, Marion, and Winston. He represented them well. That area has had some legendary political power players. Names like Rankin Fite, Fuller Kimbrell, and Joe Fine preceded Bedford from their neck of the woods. These giants were adept at bringing home the bacon from Montgomery. Bedford probably eclipsed them in longevity and largesse.

Senator Bedford was first elected in 1982 at the age of 25. He actually qualified when he was 24. He is the youngest person ever elected to the Alabama State Senate.

He was born July 7, 1956, in Russellville, the county seat of Franklin County. He still resides in and practices law there. He earned his undergraduate degree at the University of Alabama and his law degree from Cumberland School of Law at Samford University. He is married to the former Maudie Darby from Florence and they are the parents of one son, Roger III, "Roge."

Bedford lost two statewide races, for attorney general and for the U.S. Senate—he was the Democratic nominee to replace Howell Heflin in 1996, but lost to Republican Jeff Sessions.

He didn't lose those two state races because he got outworked—nobody outworked Bedford. He was a tireless, relentless campaigner. Nobody worked their constituency better. My column appears in virtually every newspaper in his northwest Alabama district. As a courtesy they send me a copy so that I can see how they placed the column and what headline they gave it. As I perused the papers in his district, hardly a week went by without Roger's picture in every paper. He was either handing out a check, attending a county commission meeting or judging a 4-H contest, or eating supper with some sweet little old ladies. He truly loved to politick and he loved his people.

Bedford was a born politician. He was a politico at the University of Alabama, a senator, member of the Jasons, and an active machine member. He was on a fast track to be governor. George Wallace recognized Bedford's potential immediately. He asked Roger to introduce him at most of his rallies throughout the state in his last race for governor in 1982. Wallace's kickoff rally at the Jefferson County Convention Center that year drew thousands of Wallaceites. They packed the municipal auditorium. Headlining the event was none other than Tammy Wynette. The crowd went wild when she sang her famous ballad, "Stand by Your Man."

It was only fitting that a 25-year-old state senator-elect from Franklin County introduced Wallace and the famous Tammy Wynette who hailed from his county—she was born and raised in Red Bay in Franklin County.

Bedford served as chairman of the State Finance Committee in three of his seven terms. He was able to do a lot for his people over the years.

Bedford is a legend in Alabama politics.

He is a real Democrat. The white male Democrat is now a dinosaur in the Alabama State Senate. It is a different day. When I was a boy paging in the Senate, all 35 members were white male Democrats. Today there is only one—Billy Beasley of Clayton, who represents the 28th District (Russell, Macon, Lee, Bullock, Barbour, Henry, and Houston counties) and is coincidentally the brother of former Lieutenant Governor Jere Beasley.

Mac and Roger

One of Bedford's best friends is Mac McArthur, who has had a long career in Alabama politics. He has been around Goat Hill all of his adult life. He began as a 24-year-old chief of staff to Lieutenant Governor Bill Baxley. Then he was head of the State Ethics Commission for a while and has been head of the State Employees Association for close to two decades.

Mac's primary job as the lead lobbyist for state employees is to get them pay raises. The fact that Bedford sat as chairman of the Senate Finance Committee and Mac was head of the ASEA didn't hurt Mac.

About 2000, two years into Don Siegelman's administration as governor, Siegelman's finance director was a serious young man named Henry Mabry, nicknamed "Dr. No." He liked to turn down every financial request.

The Education Budget was flush with money. So the teachers were going to get a pay increase. Even the judges were going to get a raise. It appeared there would not be enough money to give the rank and file state employees a pay raise. Dr. No had declared so publicly. Mac and Bedford went over to see Henry about the dilemma and to urge Dr. No to reconsider his and the governor's position and to find some money somewhere for the state employees.

Henry would not budge, saying that the state could just not afford the raise. Bedford calmly said, "Henry, I understand. However, Henry, I hope you understand that if the state employees don't get a pay raise, nobody else is going to get one, either."

They got up and left. As Roger and Mac left the office, Roger looked at Mac and said assuringly, "I wonder how long it will take before my cell phone will ring?" Sure enough, before Mac and Bedford got across the street to the Statehouse, his cell phone rang. It was Siegelman and Henry calling Bedford to say they "had reconsidered and the state employees would be getting a raise."

Pete Mathews and *The Jamelle*

Pete Mathews of Clay County was one of the most colorful characters in Alabama political history over the past six decades. He knew more Alabama political stories than any man who ever lived. I only wish Mr. Pete was still alive as I was writing this book. If he had shared half the stories he knew with me it would be one heckuva book. He lived a lot of the old stories and he could relate them better than anyone. He was a great after-dinner speaker.

He was friends with both Big Jim and Wallace. Big Jim had bought himself and the state a yacht while he was governor. Folsom named it after his wife, Jamelle.

Pete was a floor leader for George Wallace and chairman of the Senate Finance and Taxation Committee, which the news media always calls "the powerful" F&T committee.

Pete got famous later, but not for being George's floor leader. He wound up in a page-one expose by a Montgomery newspaper on which legislators used the state yacht the most. It seems *The Jamelle* had been checked out just about every weekend the sun shined by Pete Mathews.

Pete, the only bachelor in the legislature at that time, never did tell the newspaper that he hadn't been on *The Jamelle* in his life. He would have gotten a lot of his friends in trouble if he had.

Jabo Waggoner

Jabo Waggoner has served over 40 years in the Alabama legislature, 17 years in the House and 24 years in the Senate. He may add some more to his record. He was first elected to the House in 1966 at 29 years of age. He was able to parlay his father's name into a House seat at an early age from the state's most populous county. His father was a legendary, fiery, racist politician from Jefferson County who served on the Birmingham city comission with Bull Connor and later was state public service commissioner.

Like most white veteran state legislators of our era, Waggoner was first elected and served most of his years in the House as a Democrat. His district then became very Republican and he has served his Senate years as a Republican.

He has been the ultimate conciliator in the tumultuous State Senate. He is respected by both party stalwarts, although there is no mistaking the fact that he is a real Republican. He represents one of the most Republican districts in the state, encompassing the silk-stocking suburbs of Hoover, Homewood, and Vestavia.

Waggoner is one of the most amiable men to have ever served in the legislature. He has reached a pinnacle of prestige and power. Yet he remains humble and the ultimate gentleman. He is one of my favorite friends in the legislature.

Waggoner is currently the Senate Majority Leader and Rules Chairman and has served over four decades in the Alabama legislature. He has the longest record of service of any legislator from Jefferson County in Alabama history. He has become a legend in Alabama political and legislative lore.

Jabo and his wife, Marilyn, are the parents of four children.

Fuller Kimbrell

Fuller Kimbrell was a legendary figure in Alabama politics. He wrote three books on his life and times. He was born and raised in Fayette County. He was a successful businessman besides being a prominent political figure during his time. He lived to be 102 years old and to almost the end was sharp and full of wit and wisdom.

He shared this story with me one day. Kimbrell was a Big Jim man. He stayed loyal to Folsom throughout his and Big Jim's careers. He never strayed from Big Jim. Big Jim rewarded Kimbrell's loyalty by making him his chief Senate lieutenant and floor leader. He later made Kimbrell his finance director. It didn't hurt Fayette County and the surrounding northwest Alabama area that Kimbrell represented in the State Senate that he and Big Jim were thick.

Folsom didn't have that many loyal friends in the Senate. That didn't deter him from promoting an ambitious agenda. His programs and initiations were big, just like the man.

There were only five Senators out of the 35 that Big Jim could count on. Two were from northwest Alabama—Fuller Kimbrell from Fayette and Rankin Fite from Marion County. Kimbrell and Fite would ride to Montgomery together. They would plan their strategy on the way. One day Kimbrell looked over at Fite and said, "Rankin, I believe it would be better for you and me and our people up here in northwest Alabama if we divided the goods from the state treasury five ways rather than 35." Rankin looked over at Fuller and winked and said, "You're right."

Fite and Kimbrell stayed loyal to Folsom and it paid off handsomely for their folks in northwest Alabama.

Kimbrell shared another episode from his days in the State Senate. There was a senator from the Anniston area who was also a veterinarian. This gentleman brought a large briefcase onto the floor every day. Inside his satchel was a large fruit jar full of moonshine whiskey. The Doc would partake of his brew from his mason jar all day. By mid-afternoon he was oblivious to the fussing and fighting and filibustering going on in the Senate. He could care less about the tensions and tempers rising around him.

However, seated right next to the old veterinarian was a hard-shell Primitive Baptist minister from the northeast corner of the state. This preacher was caught up in the spirit of the debates. He would never participate in the arguments and acrimony. He would, however, periodically look up and close his eyes and appear to be obviously praying. He would grimace and appear to be talking to the Lord and praying for his fellow senators.

The Doc would constantly reach into his satchel and pull out his fruit jar and take a sip and shout over to his neighbor, "Say a little prayer for me, Preacher. I need guidance on how to vote on this issue, too."

The Write-In Candidate

Lowell Barron was a powerful state senator from northeast Alabama for close to three decades. A pharmacist, he was first elected to the Senate in 1982 after previously serving as mayor of Fyffe in DeKalb County.

In a special legislative election in 1983, Barron pulled off a write-in campaign to keep his Senate seat. To the best of my knowledge it is the only successful legislative write-in campaign in the history of Alabama. It is a fascinating story of strategy, timing, and political savvy that always comes up when Alabama politics is discussed. .

The year was 1983. A federal court had ruled that the legislative reapportionment plan the legislature passed in the wake of the 1980 census and used in the 1992 election unfairly discriminated against blacks.

So the court installed its own plan and, in those days of Democratic hegemony, ordered new elections for November.

Since there weren't really any Republicans to worry about, the State Democratic Executive Committee (SDEC) decided not to hold new primaries. It would just appoint general election candidates for the 105 House and 35 Senate districts.

But the SDEC, mostly controlled then (as now) by the Alabama Education Association, organized labor, trial lawyers, and Joe Reed's mostly black Alabama Democratic Conference, also used the appointment process for a little payback, purging itself of some of the previous winners its powers-that-were did not think toed the party line closely enough.

Among those were Representatives Rick Manley of Demopolis and Jack Biddle of Gardendale and Senator Gerald Dial of Lineville, all of whom simply sat out three years and then got reelected in 1986.

But the party also excluded Senator Lowell Barron of Fyffe, replacing him with Representative David Stout of Fort Payne.

Although Barron had been in the Senate only 11 months and through one legislative session, he decided not to take his expulsion lying down. With the help of Jackson County Sheriff Bob Collins and Glen Browder, then a Jacksonville State University political science professor, Barron devised a stealth write-in campaign that was stunningly successful.

Barron, who subsequently was elected six times from his northeast Alabama district that includes Jackson and portions of DeKalb and Madison counties, said he came home from the SDEC meeting in Birmingham in October—a month away from the general election—"very dejected."

"It was real frustrating that they had taken away a seat that people had just elected me to," he said. "But when I got home, I found people very upset and calling asking me to run as a write-in."

"I had never heard of a write-in and I don't think many other people had," Barron said. "But I went to talk to Sheriff Collins, who was the most popular and best politician in the biggest county in the district, and he told me he thought I had enough support to pull it off."

Barron asked Circuit Judge Loy Campbell, whom he describes as "along with Bob Collins, the two political gurus" of northeast Alabama, for his advice and support.

"From there the fire started," Barron said. "It was one of those uprisings by people who thought their vote had been taken away from them and our job was to remind them that their vote had been snatched away by an undemocratic Democratic Party."

Barron said Browder, who later served in Congress from Alabama's 3rd District from 1989 to 1997, was his chief political advisor and laughed when he first mentioned running a write-in campaign, especially with only about three weeks to go before the election.

"But he called me back the next day and said he had thought it over and although it had never been done, in that environment, you maybe could win that thing," Barron said. "But he said it could only be done by surprise. He said if I let the AEA and the trial lawyers know what I was up to too soon, they could bring in money and manpower and overpower me."

Browder advised announcing the write-in candidacy via hastily recorded television spots beginning on a Monday eight days before the election.

"It was a daunting task, especially for novices like us," Barron said. "But [Browder] wrote me a commercial that consisted of four different people in a smoke-filled room—one each representing AEA, trial lawyers, labor, and blacks. He wrote out each person's script and had them talking about me and how bad I was while the announcer said this is what went on in the Democratic Party and how they stole your vote."

A friend in Chattanooga who used the University of Chattanooga drama department to cast the commercial cut the spot. It featured unflattering stereotypes in each role.

"We put two guys under the table with cigars so that it would really look like a smoke-filled room," Barron remembers.

In a stroke of political genius, Browder had the stereotypes bring up the fact that Barron was considering a write-in campaign, to which the potbellied union guy says, "That bunch of dumb hicks up there in Jackson and Dekalb and Madison County can't spell their own names, much less Lowell Barron."

Much hilarity and backslapping followed on the commercial.

"What we had to do was ridicule the voters to get them so pissed off that they would support a write-in," Barron said. "It was absolutely brilliant what Browder came up with."

Although the commercial ran numerous times in the Huntsville and Chattanooga markets, it created some confusion. Barron said his mother-in-law reported she saw on television about how a bunch of men were out to get him and advised carrying a gun. However, for the most part, the message got across.

"We also did radio spots and talked to the newspapers to explain what we were doing," Barron said. "But by this time there were only a few days to go until Election Day."

Barron, who later made his peace with AEA Executive Director Paul Hubbert, said Hubbert told him he thought at first the write-in campaign was a joke.

"But by Wednesday they ran some polls and found we were winning. So they pulled all their resources from all over the state and rushed up here. But we already had that ball rolling and it was gaining speed," Barron said. "They did some radio and newspaper ads, but it was too late for television and we beat them. I got something like 7,500 votes to 5,100 votes in a district that normally would have voted only about 10,000 total."

Barron also said he had to do a little acting in the crucial final days. "I chose the path of acting pitiful," he said. "When I'd go to meetings, I'd stand around in an undertaker's pose and look dejected . . . I wanted the voters to get mad, not me get mad. I'd just say, 'I'm helpless. It's all in your hands, if you want to get out and get people to write my name in we may be able to win this thing.' The election couldn't be about me . . . it had to be about them and having their votes stolen."

And it worked.

SENATORS DEAL WITH LIQUOR PROBLEM

Bob Ingram told a great story about a north Alabama legislator that occurred one day in the State Senate in the late 1950s.

Senator Harlan G. "Mutt" Allen, a wee man from Cullman who was seldom seen without a foot-long cigar in his mouth, was at the mike making an impassioned speech about the evils of strong drink. Pending was a bill relating to the sale of alcoholic beverages. As he was waving his arms passionately denouncing Demon Rum, Allen inadvertently knocked some of his notes off the podium.

As he stooped to pick them up a half-pint bottle of booze—I think it was Early Times—slipped out of his inside coat pocket and fell noisily to the floor. The crowded Senate chamber exploded in laughter.

To his credit, Allen didn't miss a beat in his speech, but in a move that would have done justice to a World Cup soccer player, he deftly kicked the bottle across the floor to where Senator Broughton Lamberth of Alex City was seated, waiting his turn to speak.

Lamberth wanted no part of the bottle. Displaying footwork I never would have dreamed he had, he expertly kicked the bottle toward Senator E. L. Roberts of Gadsden who was seated nearby.

Lamberth's footwork generated a roar from the crowded gallery that rattled the rafters of the Senate chamber. Senator Roberts, who had never seen a bottle of Early Times he didn't like, wasn't about to kick the bottle to anybody. As nonchalantly as he could, he picked the bottle up and put it in his pocket. Meanwhile, Allen, seemingly oblivious to the whiskey bottle soccer game being played kept right on speaking.

Ingram later asked Allen if he ever got his liquor back, and he replied with a straight face, "What liquor?"

Legislator Votes to Abolish His Own County

Our Alabama Constitution is very antiquated and one of the flaws inherent in the document is that it does not allow local county governments very much authority or power.

Therefore, the county governments have to channel most changes or actions into local acts that have to be advertised in their local paper for four weeks and then taken to the State legislature to be enacted. Thus, the entire state legislature has to act on a local bill for Fayette County that might involve something as mundane as whether to pave a road or buy a tractor.

As a legislator, I dreaded this procedure because it took most of every legislative day. We would sit for hours every morning and vote on these local bills from all over the state which had nothing to do with state government.

In addition, these local acts were not noncontroversial, either for those of us from rural counties or from urban areas of Jefferson, Mobile, or Madison. In fact the Jefferson County delegation could be embroiled for hours if not days on local issues that should have been determined back home in Birmingham City Hall or among Jefferson County commissioners.

Those of us from rural counties were often the only resident legislators from our county. In essence, if you wanted the power, you could become the czar of your local county government. If you didn't want some act to pass, all you had to do was not sign it out of committee, because you were the committee. Legislators, out of what is known as local courtesy, would not vote on another county's local legislation. So in essence a legislator from a rural county often could thwart road paving or whatever local matter they objected to. Invariably a disgruntled county commissioner who was not getting his way would come to me to kill his rival county commissioner's bill to get a new road. However, early in my legislative career I made an ironclad policy that I would not be involved in local county business. I insisted that all local bills be voted on in public by all the county commissioners in their open meetings before being presented for passage. The recorded vote would have to be attached to the bill when I got it. Therefore, my only participation would be as a perfunctory messenger or conduit for the local issue.

A legendary dirty trick played on a legislator by a fellow legislator still reverberates 60 years later. It occurred during the second Folsom administration in the late 1950s. Legislators Emmett Oden of Franklin County and Jack Huddleston of Colbert County despised each other. These two counties adjoin each other in northwest Alabama. These two men were constantly at adds.

Oden introduced a local bill for Franklin County that repealed another local bill passed in December of 1869. His brief explanation to the House of Representatives when the measure came up for a vote was that it was simply a "housekeeping bill . . . It corrects an error made when the original bill was passed."

Through the custom of local courtesy, the local bill passed unanimously. Even Representative Jack Huddleston voted for the bill. After the passage of the measure, Representative Oden told the Press what his bill actually did. The 1869 law which he was repealing was the law that had created Colbert County out of part of Franklin County. Representative Huddleston had just voted to abolish his own county. That one vote ended Huddleston's political career. His constituents in Colbert County could not forgive that he had voted to abolish his own county.

Part IV

Other Stories

14

Alabama Political Lore

Two More Well-Known Chief Justices

Judge Perry O. Hooper Sr.

Perry Hooper Sr. was the first Republican Chief Justice of Alabama's Supreme Court since Reconstruction. His election not only marked the partisan change in Alabama's Supreme Court, but also its philosophical tent.

Alabama had become a haven for gigantic, almost comical large plaintiff cases. We became a trial lawyer's paradise throughout the 1970s and 1980s. By 1990, *Time* magazine had labeled us "Tort Hell."

The business community finally got busy trying to resolve this crisis. They brought political guru Karl Rove out of Texas to advise and plan their strategy. It has worked. Twenty years later, we have an all-Republican pro-business court.

The business community chose a longtime Montgomery Republican judge named Perry Hooper to lead them out of the wilderness.

The trial lawyers didn't go down without a fight. In 1994, Hooper defeated trial lawyer Chief Justice Sonny Hornsby by a narrow margin—262 votes to be exact. After a protracted legal battle, Judge Hooper was sworn in as Alabama's 27th chief justice.

Hooper and Winton M. "Red" Blount were the mainstays of the early modern-day Republican party in Alabama. Hooper was for Eisenhower in the 1950s and was a delegate for Richard Nixon in 1960. He was the state's national committeeman. He campaigned for Jim Martin for the U.S. Senate in 1962 and was the Republican nominee for the U.S. Senate in 1968.

Hooper was elected probate judge of Montgomery County in the 1964 Goldwater landslide. He served in that capacity for ten years, then moved to a circuit judgeship in 1974. He then was elected chief justice of the Alabama Supreme Court in 1994. However, he was not sworn in until October 1995 due to recounts and challenges related to his very narrow victory. He remained chief justice until his retirement in 2001.

Hooper is a Methodist, a Marine veteran of World War II, and an Alabama football fan. Hooper is enjoying his retirement years in Montgomery. He just turned 90. His lovely wife of 65 years, Marilyn, takes care of him. He enjoys the company of his three sons, Walter, John, and Perry Jr. He especially enjoys his nine grandchildren.

Perry Hooper Jr. has also enjoyed a successful political career. He served 20 years as a state representative in Montgomery. He built a stellar record as a pro-business legislator. He is now a successful businessman and a leader in the state Republican party like his father.

Judge Roy Moore

Roy Moore succeeded Perry Hooper Sr. as chief justice of the Supreme Court. Moore was elected as Alabama's 28th chief justice in 2000.

Moore was born and raised in rural Etowah County. Gadsden and Etowah County was a solidly Democratic area during Moore's formative years. Goodyear Tire had one of its largest American plants there. Gadsden was a bedrock blue-collar, organized-labor city.

Moore won an appointment to West Point and graduated with a B.S. in 1969. After serving in Vietnam he went to law school at the University of Alabama. He came back home to Gadsden and practiced law. He was elected to a circuit judgeship on his second attempt. Within a couple of years on the bench, he became known as a law-and-order judge and also as a very religious man. He eventually began to display a Ten Commandments plaque in his courtroom. This attracted a lot of publicity and the notoriety propelled him to election as Alabama's chief justice. Soon after becoming chief justice, he installed a 5,300-pound Ten Commandments monument in the rotunda of the state judicial building. His fellow justices and federal courts directed him to remove his monument from the rotunda and he refused. He was eventually removed from office for defying the edict.

This made him a hero of evangelicals not only in Alabama but throughout the nation. He became known nationwide as the Ten Commandments Judge. He began a foundation and preached all over the country.

He run unsuccessfully twice for governor, but in 2012 support from evangelicals and Tea Partiers boosted him to the Republican nomination for chief justice and he then rode the Republican wave in the general election back to another term on Alabama's Supreme Court. If he can keep his job this time, he will serve through 2018. However, that is not a foregone conclusion, since in 2015 he returned to national news with a new defiance of the federal courts, this time over the issue of same-sex marriages.

Alabama is one of, if not the, most fundamentalist states in America. This hardcore, Bible-belt philosophy prevalent in Alabama makes Roy Moore one of its most popular political figures with some people and one of its most despised by others.

Other Offices and Stories

The Probate Judge

As late as 50 years ago the office of probate judge in Alabama was the most powerful and prestigious position in Alabama politics. In every county in Alabama, especially in rural Alabama, the probate judge was essentially the king of the county. He was not only the judge, he appointed all county positions, hired all county employees, and presided over the county commission.

Not only was he the most powerful political figure in the county, he also became one of the wealthiest people in the county through his judgeship. There were no ethics laws in that era. Therefore, it was common practice for someone aspiring to sell equipment, gas, supplies or to build roads for the county to grease the palms of the probate judge. However, this pay-to-play practice was not the most lucrative remuneration for the probate judge. By law he was on the fee system. That means that he essentially owned the highest office in the county. He received a fee off of all transactions made in the office. He got a cut off of every car tag or license sold in the county.

It was estimated that the salary of a probate judge in 1962 was around $100,000 per year even in small counties. That, my friend, would equate to about $360,000 or more today. He was not only king of the county, but he made a kingly salary. The probate judge term is for six years. With that kind of reward, you can image the competition to capture that perch in that era.

The best politician in the county essentially emerged victorious. He knew where the votes were and how to count votes. There were quite a few votes that could be bought at that time with a pint of whiskey and a $5 bill. The probate judge knew who those folks were and where to find them. Thus, the economic saying that you have to spend money to make money applies to politics in this case. To the victor went the spoils. The rewards of victory were quite lucrative and powerful.

The famous Southern political historian and scholar, Dr. V. O. Key, said in 1950 that without a doubt the most powerful figure in Alabama politics is the probate judge. In the days before television the best way to campaign for governor was to garner the support and endorsement of the probate judge in each county. Aspiring gubernatorial candidates would begin their statewide journey for the brass ring of Alabama politics by kissing the ring of the king of each county, its probate judge.

The probate judge of my county while I was a boy was the prototypical probate judge of that bygone era. Ben Reeves was the king of Pike County. The Reeves family owned the sheriff's office in our county. A Reeves had been sheriff since the county's inception. Judge Reeves's mama had even served a while as sheriff. His relative Burr Reeves was legendary and tough to say the least. Therefore, it fell to be Judge Reeves's fate to become the high sheriff at a young age. However, Judge Reeves had higher aspirations, after a while as sheriff he got elected state senator. He served one tumultuous term at the Capitol. Then the kingship of Pike County became available. Long-term Probate Judge Alex Brantley retired and a lengthy battle ensued to take the throne. After an arduous and costly contest, Ben Reeves emerged victorious. His runoff opponent in that epic 1958 race was State Representative Gardner Bassett. After the dust settled, the two shook hands and became a powerful duo. They were thereafter a team and built what was known as the Ben Reeves and Gardner Bassett machine. Neither was ever defeated. Bassett served 24 years in the legislature and Reeves served 24 years as probate judge. Their machine was not only used to keep them in office but to help other anointed office holders. Their benevolence was usually extended to aspiring young state senators. They needed that seat to be beholden to them since legislators have omnipotent power over local county governments under our state constitution.

As I described in Chapter 12, Reeves and Bassett became my mentors early on. By the time I was ten years old I had developed a love and obsession with politics. My passion was evident to the two old men. They would smile fondly when I came to see them. They would ask me to recite quotes and vote counts from every governor's race. It was my hobby to memorize these facts. Indeed they would show me off to their coffee-drinking buddies at the downtown political hangout. The Riverside Café on the square was the favorite gathering spot of all the older guys. They would ask me to name all the counties in the state in alphabetical order and say who carried each county and by what margin. I might add why I thought they won that county. Usually it was because of the "friends and neighbors" effect. Folks generally ran strong in their neck of the woods in Alabama in that era. The two men were also my neighbors. I lived around the corner from them. My folks lived on Maple Street in Troy. Reeves and Bassett both lived on the next street over, Orange Street. I was also their paper boy as I carried the *Troy Messenger* on our two streets.

Both would take time to teach me about Pike County politics. They would go over the great local races, especially that 1958 probate race which they ran against each other. Judge Reeves especially enjoyed relishing his victory. It was not taboo but expected that you bought votes at that time in rural Alabama politics. Usually the price was five dollars and a bottle of whiskey.

One day I was sitting in Judge Reeves's office with him and he began to reminisce about his 1958 conquest. Now, you've got to picture me about 12 years old and at that time and still somewhat naive and innocent to the wiles of real dirt-road, rural, hardball politics. Ben Reeves had a map on his wall with all of the precincts of the county. He looked at the map and told me how many votes were in each box and how many he got in that box in the '58 race. Then to my amazement he began to tell me how many of the votes were money votes. He winked at me and asked me if I knew what money votes were. I thought I knew and he confirmed that these folks sold their vote. He then proceeded to point to the boxes and said that box had 367 votes and 193 were money votes. He would point to the next rural box and he would say that box had 314 votes and 129 were money votes. He stopped at that box and got a nostalgic and satisfying look on his face and revealed to me an act of chicanery he had employed against his then-nemesis, Gardner Bassett. He told this little 12-year-old understudy that Mr. Gardner had bought those votes on Friday and he had slyly slipped up there and paid them a little more on Sunday night. He grinned and said you should have seen the look on old Mr. Gardner's face when the Josie beat votes came in Tuesday night. Judge Reeves was a lot prouder that he had bought those votes out from under Mr. Gardner than he would have been if the voters in question had really liked him.

Listening to Judge Reeves's story awakened me to the fact that politics was not a popularity contest. It was a business and it definitely was Judge Ben Reeves's business. He knew how to count votes. It didn't matter how you got those votes, you just needed 50 percent plus one to win.

If I hadn't learned that lesson that day, it was hammered home by Judge Reeves about a year later. His custom was to sit in a chair in the lobby of the courthouse for three to five hours a day. He smoked one cigarette after the other. He ultimately died of cancer from his chain-smoking.

One day we were sitting in the lobby and chatting about political history. An old farmer came walking into the courthouse and gave Judge Reeves a glare of obvious dislike. Judge Reeves observed that I had seen the farmer's disdain for him. He looked over at me and said, "I don't care what anybody thinks about me as long as I get 51 percent of the vote." You could tell he meant it. It was his business, not a game. He knew where his votes were and he knew how to get them by whatever means necessary. He was a tough and crusty old fellow. He was the King of the County and he knew how to rule.

Tell Your Sister Hello

Colonel Floyd Mann was one of the most beloved political figures in Alabama lore. He served as public safety director in both the John Patterson and Albert Brewer administrations. He was an administrator at the University of Alabama when I met him as a young, aspiring student politician. We became good friends and remained good friends until he passed away. He would share old Alabama political stories with me.

One of the best stories he ever told me was during his time as police chief in Opelika. One of his officers came to him one day with a look of consternation on his face.

"I think we have a problem, Chief," the officer said.

"Tell me about it," Mann responded.

"You know Officer ____, 'Big Un,' we call him," the officer said. "Well, every Saturday night about midnight he comes into the station with some little scrawny hobo he has arrested down at the depot. Always they are beaten up something terrible. Big Un weighs about 280 pounds, and I just don't believe these men are fool enough to give him any resistance. What I think is happening is that he is beating up on them just because he enjoys it."

Mann agreed that if that was happening that it was indeed a problem. He said he would handle it. The following Saturday night, about 30 minutes before the freight train was due in, Mann drove down near the railroad station, parked his car some distance away, and then hid in the shadows of the building. Sure enough, minutes before the train was to arrive a police car pulled up and out stepped Big Un with billy club in hand.

When the train came to a stop, the policeman began walking alongside the freight cars, sliding the doors open, looking for hoboes. He opened a door, and lying right in front of him was a man. Big Un slapped him across the head and ordered him out of the car.

The hobo turned over ever so slowly, and as he did he laid the barrel of a pistol between the eyes of Big Un. The policeman froze in terror.

"Mr. Police," the hobo said ever so slowly, "I've got a Momma in heaven, a Papa in hell, and a sick sister in Columbus, Georgia. I aim to see one of them tonight."

Big Un swallowed hard, trying to get the words out of his mouth, and finally responded.

"You tell your sister I said hello, you hear."

Jere Beasley Story

Jere Beasley tells a great story that illustrates how fleeting political fame and notoriety can be for a politician.

Beasley was elected lieutenant governor in 1970. A young Bill Baxley was elected attorney general that same year. Albert Brewer lost a very close race to Wallace that same year. All three were primed to run for governor in 1978 as Wallace could not succeed himself. State Senator Sid McDonald and Fob James also joined the Three B's in the race. As was common at that time, there were political rallies and candidate forums all over the state. Most political pros will tell you that these forums get you very few votes. The reason that you don't gain any new voters is that almost all of the people who come to attend are committed followers of the other candidate. However, if you don't attend one, it gives you a black eye in that county for shunning that particular community.

The folks in north Alabama are especially sensitive about your not attending their county gathering. Each gubernatorial candidate has his most loyal supporters there, adorned head-to-toe in their campaign paraphernalia. They congregate early to hear their candidate. Wallace used to even have professional yellers follow him all over the state. One particular one looked like he belonged in a circus but he could cut a rebel yell like you've never heard.

Each candidate is given 30 minutes to speak, but very few confine themselves to that time limit once they get cranked up.

At an event up on Sand Mountain, all five gubernatorial candidates appeared. As was the protocol, they drew straws to see who would go first. As luck would have it, Beasley ended up as the last speaker, which meant he would have to sit on the stage dutifully and politely for three hours or more listening to his enemies extol their virtues and occasionally lambast him or his fellow candidates, depending on who the speaker thought was his primary opponent. The speeches dragged on and, as was customary, after each candidate spoke they would excuse themselves and head on to the next campaign event in an adjoining county or elsewhere in the state. Likewise, when the candidate left the scene and stage, so did his supporters.

By the time Beasley got up to speak, there were only a handful of people left in the audience. Beasley dutifully began to give them his best speech. As he droned on, he noticed an overalls-wearing farmer standing right in front with rapt attention.

When Beasley finished he came down off the flat-bed truck and shook the old farmer's hand vigorously and hugged him and looked him squarely in the eye and said, "You don't know how much I appreciate you. You have to be the best Beasley supporter I've got in Alabama."

The farmer looked at Beasley apologetically and with a little sympathy and said, "Boy, I ain't never heard of you. That flat bed truck y'all been shouting from is mine. I was just waiting for you to get off my truck so that we can both go home."

GEORGE WALLACE JR.

George Corley Wallace III, often called George Wallace Jr., was born October 17, 1951, in Eufaula.

In 1970, Wallace graduated from Sidney Lanier High School in Montgomery, Alabama. He then completed a bachelor's degree in history from Huntington College in Montgomery in 1976.

In 1986, Wallace was elected as Alabama state treasurer and was reelected in 1990. Early in his second term, he won the Democratic nomination for Alabama's 2nd congressional district, his father's home district. He was an early favorite, however, he lost to Terry Everett by 3,500 votes. After his second term as state treasurer, he worked at the Center for Government and Public Affairs at Auburn University Montgomery.

Wallace became a Republican sometime in the mid-1990s, and was elected to the Alabama Public Service Commission in 1998. He served two terms and stepped down in 2006.

George Jr. is nothing like his father. He readily admits his differences. He is more like his mother. He has a kind and genuinely caring persona. He has a retrospective and sensitive demeanor, very much unlike his famous father's fiery and gregarious nature.

He is very much enjoying his life out of politics. He seems happy and content.

AN ACT OF CONGRESS

A good many people wonder why simple, straightforward, no-nonsense, good-government legislation fails to pass even though it appears to have universal and overwhelming support and appeal for many voters and legislators.

You will remember old sayings that you heard from your elders when you were young. Old bits of wisdom spouted from the lips of your grandparents and older folks, which went in one ear and out the other. Sayings like, "If you've got your health you've got everything"; "If it ain't broke then don't fix it"; and if you are a golfer, there is no truer aphorism than, "You drive for show and putt for dough," or "it ain't how you drive, it's how you arrive." The older you get, it occurs to you how wise these old sayings are in actual life. They are golden facts.

One of the sage morsels pertains to getting something accomplished. You say "it takes an act of Congress" to get something done. In politics, there is no clearer truism. It is really hard to pass a piece of legislation through Congress and it is equally difficult to channel a bill through the labyrinth of legislative approval in Alabama.

Ask any successful lobbyist or legislator which side they would rather be on in legislative wars. They much prefer to be against something than to be trying to pass a bill. It is probably 100 times harder to steer a bill through legislative approval than it is to kill a bill. The Alabama Senate rules are such that if a handful of the 35 Senators are adamantly opposed to something then they can kill the bill. And, if the right Senator is against it, if for example he is chairman of the Rules Committee and he wants it killed, it is dead.

It doesn't matter if the proposed legislation is as all-American as saying the legislature is in favor of apple pie and motherhood. The bill has to go before both House and Senate committees, win approval, and not get an amendment put on it. If it gets an amendment attached, it has to basically start all over. It then has to get placed on the special order calendar set by the Rules Committee, and there are hundreds of bills waiting to get on this calendar and only a few get on each day, and there are only 30 legislative days in the session. If a bill gets on the calendar, it then has to pass both houses, and hopefully the governor is also for apple pie and motherhood, because if he vetoes the bill, it has to start all over again.

Let me give you an example of a piece of apple pie and motherhood legislation I was asked to sponsor when I was a freshman legislator. There was a quirk in Alabama criminal law that allowed the family of a criminal defendant to be in the courtroom in a criminal trial and sit behind the criminal and observe and cry on behalf of their relative. However, unbelievably, the family of the crime victim could not be in the courtroom. The Victims of Crime and Leniency (VOCAL) sought to correct this injustice. VOCAL asked me to sponsor its bill and work for its passage. I worked diligently on the bill. The press gave me and the bill glowing editorials for its fairness. We got the bill out of the House. It passed overwhelmingly. However, when it got to the Senate it was rightfully assigned to the Senate Judiciary Committee, chaired by Senator Earl Hilliard from Jefferson County. He was opposed to the bill and as chairman of the committee, he deep-sixed it and would not let it out. No amount of haranguing from the VOCAL people or bad press would budge Earl. However, one day I was on the floor of the House and the VOCAL leader, Miriam Shehane, called me out to the lobby. She said Earl was sick and would not be in Montgomery today and the Senate Judiciary Committee was meeting and the vice chairman would bring our bill up out of order. We quickly went to the 6th floor and whisked our bill out of the Judiciary Committee and it won final approval in the Senate a few weeks later and became law.

Remember that truisms like "it will take an act of Congress to get something done" are very accurate, especially in politics.

One Vote Can Make a Difference

Having served your county in the legislature a long time, you are considered by many to always be their legislator. A good many of my former constituents still call me with questions or problems.

Some ask how to get in touch with their congressman or senator about a certain issue so that they can express their opinion. They invariably ask me will their letter or e-mail make a difference. My response is, "Yes, it will."

As a young legislator.

Jeremiah Denton excepted, all legislators or congressmen want to know what their constituents are thinking. They generally want to vote like their districts feel. When I was a legislator, I would cherish this input and actually solicit it.

One year, I received a nice note from one of my favorite retired teachers. I loved her. She had not only taught me but had also taught my mom and dad. She was as fine a lady as I had ever known. Her note simply asked me to vote for some issue. I was not even cognizant of the issue until she made me aware of it. She even referred to it by bill number. It did not pertain to education and I didn't perceive it to have much opposition or controversy. I don't even remember now what the issue was. However, I revered this lady, and she was asking me to vote yes on a matter I had no position on anyway. So I called her and told her that due to her interest I would vote for the measure. I kept her note on my desk with the bill number referenced. Lo and behold, about halfway through the legislative session, I saw the bill on the special order calendar for the day. I got primed for the vote. I voted for the bill simply because that lady had asked me to. To my amazement, when I looked up at the large electronic vote tally machine, the bill had passed by one vote.

Decibel Level

Those of us who served a long time in the legislature have a lot of stories. I served 16 years from 1982 to 1998 from my home county of Pike. I chose not to run again in 1998 in order to devote more time to the business of making a living as I had two daughters approaching college age.

However, I missed the camaraderie and friendships of the legislators. You make lifetime friends. It's like being in the war together.

It was apparent that those of us who hailed from smaller towns and rural counties knew our constituents better and were better known by our constituents than those from urban areas.

Our name identification would be astronomical compared to our big-city colleagues for obvious reasons. Our folks usually knew us. They knew everything about us. They knew when you went to work, when you walked, when you ate, what time you got up, and what ball game you attended. In essence they knew how to find you. It was a full-time job for a small-town legislator. The big-city boys could simply come to Montgomery and vote and go home to anonymity. We small-town legislators were expected to go to every fish fry, barbeque, dinner on the ground, homecoming, and ball game in our county.

My own notoriety was exacerbated by the fact that my mama's and daddy's families had been residents of my county for a long time. Mama's people had been some of the earliest settlers of Pike County prior to the Civil War. I had also had an early attraction toward politics. I had started paging for my mentor, the local legislator, when I was 12 and had basically been running to succeed him since then. I was elected at age 30 when he retired.

My phone started ringing and it never stopped the entire 16 years. I still get constituent calls today after being out of office 14 years. We had no resident congressman, so I got all his calls. If a pressing matter was being discussed on the national scene people called me because they didn't distinguish a difference between a state legislator or a national legislator. In fact, they would see me on the street and ask me why I was not in Washington. Most of the congressional calls I got, however, were for lost Social Security checks. In fact, most of the calls I got were not related to my job as a state legislator. There were calls that pertained to why someone's garbage hadn't been picked up, a neighbor's dog was barking all night, a road needed paving, roadside litter was not being picked up enough, or state workers are lazy and don't work. In my first few years, a trend set in that was especially irritating—some folks thought that since you were a state politician you could wave some magical political wand and solve all their crises and problems.

As you know, Saturday night is a honky-tonking, drinking night. Every drunk that got put in jail for drunken behavior would invariably call my house and ask me to bail him out. I finally refused to answer the phone after 8 p.m. on Saturday night. Years later I was so glad to vote for the legislation that mandated that every drunk driver has to stay in jail for 24 hours.

However, prior to that decision I got an interesting call one Saturday night about 7 or 8 p.m. It was from a gentleman my parents' age who was from a large family in the northern part of my county. I could tell he was in a bar because I could hear music in the background. I thought, here we go, he's wanting to get either bailed out or his garbage had not been picked up on time. He began slowly; he wasn't quite drunk but he was on his way because he was slurring his words. He began, "You know, Steve, I've known you all your life and we all voted for you up here, and I've known your mama and daddy all my life, we all went to school together . . . Well, Steve, I'm out here at the Holiday Inn bar trying to enjoy a quiet drink and all these young people out here are playing this music too loud . . . When you get back to Montgomery will you pass a bill requiring bars to lower the decibel level for music?"

Bless his heart, at least he was asking me for something that pertained to my job.

SHELBY COUNTY

Shelby County sits in the geographic center of Alabama. Because of his seniority and longevity in Washington, some people probably think that the county is named for our senior U.S. Senator, Richard Shelby.

However, it is the birthplace and childhood home of Governor Robert Bentley. It is also renowned for being the fastest-growing county in Alabama for the past four decades; it is now one of the most populous counties in Alabama.

Although it has become a Mecca for upscale suburbanites in the Birmingham metropolitan area, it has not always been a suburban enclave of Jefferson County. While Governor Bentley was growing up it was a rural county much like most of the counties in the state. It is part of a four-county — Shelby, St. Clair, Chilton, and Bibb—that was home to the original white Republicans in the state. These folks epitomized the Alabamians who were not inclined to leave the Union at the onset of the Civil War. They were yeoman farmers who worked their own land and lived off their own labors. They owned few if any slaves. They simply wanted to be left alone to raise their crops and their children and go to church. They were Protestant and went to church three times a week. Their life revolved around their church and their Bible. Even today these counties are probably the most religious in Alabama. There is a church on almost every corner in Chilton County. If Alabama is the Bible belt, this area is the buckle.

Shelby County was the home of Progressive Republicans. In fact they more closely resembled New England Republicans in their political philosophy. They were frugal yet they might be willing to pay more in taxes to the government, especially if it went to education. They believed that education was the route for a better future for their children. Even though they lived off the land and were proud of their 40 acres, they aspired for their children to move past the life of seeing the rear end of a mule for 12 hours a day. They felt that with a good education their children could grow up to be a doctor in Tuscaloosa.

That is precisely what happened with Robert Bentley. He grew up in rural Shelby County, the son of hard-working Shelby County people. His father had little formal education and had a sawmill. Lots of us native Alabamians called it pulpwooding.

Bentley went to school in Columbiana, the county seat and the largest town in the county. The only other town in the county of any size was Montevallo, home of Alabama College, which was an all-girl school at that time.

During those years, the Shelby County school superintendent was Dr. Elvin Hill, the father of longtime Shelby County State Representative Mike Hill. Mike has served close to three decades in the legislature and is one of the most likeable and popular members of the House of Representatives. He and Bentley are close friends. Their families go back as Shelby County friends for generations.

Several old Shelby County political families have been around Alabama politics for quite a while. I recall walking down Dexter Avenue toward my perch as a commentator for one of the Montgomery television stations at Governor Bentley's first inauguration in 2011. I stopped to speak to Governor Bentley and then ran into a host of Shelby County folks. I knew these people as the scions of original Shelby County political leaders. I saw Mike Hill and his pretty wife Carol. Then I saw Conrad Fowler Jr., who practices law in Columbiana. He was a stellar tight end for Bear Bryant at Alabama. Bear won a couple of national championships with Conrad as his big end. He was 6 feet 5 inches and tough to cover.

Conrad Jr.'s daddy was Conrad "Bully" Fowler. He was a distinguished and longtime probate judge of Shelby County. Bully Fowler holds the distinction of being one of the few who ever beat George Wallace in a political race. Bully Fowler and Wallace were contemporaries at the University of Alabama. Bully beat Wallace for the presidency of the Cotillion Club.

Conrad Jr.'s partner for more than four decades in the most prominent law firm in Columbiana and Shelby County has been Butch Ellis, who served a couple of terms in the State Senate with distinction. He was one of the most honest, friendliest, and popular men to have ever served in the Alabama Senate. Butch's daddy, Handy Ellis, was also a state senator as well as lieutenant governor. He ran second to Big Jim Folsom in the 1946 governor's race. Butch Ellis and Governor Bentley are related by marriage.

As Kathyrn Tucker Windham told us, "Alabama is really just one big front porch."

MISS MITTIE

As a youngster I spent my summers working as a page in the legislature. It was an invaluable learning experience and a glimpse into the world of politics, but it was a lot simpler time. When I observe today's legislature the most striking difference is computerization. In the 1960s the telephone was our most advanced technology. However, I fondly remember a little lady named Miss Mittie who was far superior to any computer.

The legislature then met in the Capitol. The second floor housed both chambers. The circular rotunda between the two bodies was total chaos while the legislature was in session. Lobbyists, legislators, and everybody who thought they had some interest in legislation were shoulder to shoulder. Grand Central Station in New York could not have been more hectic.

Sitting quietly on a corner bench next to the door was Miss Mittie, wearing a floor-length black dress and black hat. She sat in her same place every day, knitting and seemingly never looking up. Some people said she had been coming to her spot in the Capitol for over 25 years. It was not certain who paid her, or if she was even paid, but she was more knowledgeable than anyone about what was going on at the Capitol. For you see, Miss Mittie knew where everybody was at any time day or night. She was the first one there in the morning and the last to leave at night. She never left her perch. It did not matter what legislator was needed, she could tell you exactly where they were. As a permanent page you can bet I got to know Miss Mittie. If a veteran lobbyist who Miss Mittie trusted and liked asked her about a House bill, she used to tell him without looking up from her knitting, "It's in Ways and Means, but it ain't going nowhere. Rankin Fite don't like it. It's dead." When asked about a Senate bill she might say, "It's pending in the Rules Committee and Senator Walter Givhan can't get it out because the governor ain't for it."

As I got older, Lieutenant Governor Albert Brewer made me head of the Senate pages. When other pages would come in for their two-week appointments I would introduce them to Miss Mittie. They were amazed at her knowledge of each legislator's whereabouts. If we needed a senator for a vote and nobody knew where he was, I would maneuver through the maze of people in the rotunda and ask Miss Mittie. Without looking up she would say, "He's down at the Elite eating supper." I would ask about a House member and without missing a stitch she would whisper, "He's down at his room at the old Exchange Hotel taking a nap." Or, "He's down in the governor's office. Wallace is trying to change his vote." She knew if there was a poker game going on, who was in it, and where it was being held. She probably knew how much money each legislator had lost.

Although Miss Mittie knew everything that went on under the Capitol dome, she would hardly look at you, much less talk to you, unless you had won her trust. She knew that as head of the pages I needed to know where somebody was for a reason. I did not care why they were there or what they

Miss Mittie, with, from left, Bob Ingram, a lobbyist, and Tom Brassell.

were doing, but I had to report back to the lieutenant governor or Speaker when to expect the legislator back because their vote might be important.

Miss Mittie was an institution. Casual observers would see her in her 1940s garb, knitting in the corner of the crowded Capitol rotunda and looking like a grandmother going to a funeral, and think to themselves, "What is that odd lady doing here?" However, you can rest assured veterans of Goat Hill knew who Miss Mittie was, and if they were smart they got to know her well.

I never knew Miss Mittie's last name. I do not know when she died. But I guarantee you no computer today could do what Miss Mittie did at the Capitol for several decades. Her prowess as the oracle of Goat Hill was legendary. Miss Mittie

She almost whispered when telling you where a legislator was or what was going on in each legislative chamber. However, if you got to know Miss Mittie you knew she was very opinionated. She would tell you in a heartbeat if she liked or disliked a certain politician. She definitely had her favorites.

As a youngster I often thought to myself how I sure would not want to be on Miss Mittie's bad side. I quietly wondered if she was some kind of witch, because no ordinary human could know what she knew without some sort of magical power.

Alabamians Love the Governor's Race

When talk turns to politics in Alabama, it usually leads to the governor's race. It does not matter if the governor's race is four years away, political gossip starts early as to who will run for governor. In Alabama politics, the governor's race is *the* race. As each new race approaches it is talked about more than ever around the coffee clubs and kitchen tables from Sand Mountain to the Wiregrass. It is comparable to college football being the king of all sports in Alabama.

This infatuation is borne out in voting history. In most states the presidential race sees the largest voter turnout, but that is not the case in Alabama where historically we have voted heavier in gubernatorial years. However, the turnout has gotten closer in the last few decades since Alabama became a two-party state. The emergence of the Republican Party in Alabama since 1964 has caused us to be more like the national norm. In the 40 years prior the largest turnout in Alabama was in the Democratic primary for the governor's race.

Gubernatorial years have most of the important local offices up for grabs which may account for part of the large turnout. Former U.S. House Speaker Tip O'Neill popularized the saying that "all politics is local." Also, in gubernatorial years all probate judges and sheriffs are on the ballot, as are all 105 House members and 35 state senators along with the other constitutional offices such as lieutenant governor, attorney general, secretary of state, state auditor, treasurer, and agriculture commissioner.

The book on Alabama politics, according to George Wallace, is that more people will vote against someone or something than for someone or something. Wallace ran against the big money interests and corporations. "Big Jim" Folsom ran against the same big mules. Sadly, polling reveals that negative attack ads are effective. Wallace and Folsom knew this instinctively and used it effectively.

The Get-Acquainted Race

Alabama had a somewhat peculiar law until 1968 which prohibited the governor from serving more than one consecutive term. However, you could come back and run again after waiting out four years. Big Jim Folsom did this. Bibb Graves also did it earlier in the century. After the succession law was changed, we had two more two-term governors, Fob James and Guy Hunt. Fob won in 1978 and came back to win again in 1994. Hunt won back-to-back races in 1986 and 1990 (he left office before finishing the second term). Therefore, the only men to be elected to two terms as governor of Alabama in the twentieth century were Bibb Graves, James E. "Big Jim" Folsom, Forrest "Fob" James, and Guy Hunt. George Wallace was elected governor four times.

As a result of the constitutional prohibition against a governor succeeding himself before 1968, a recurrent theme developed called the "get-acquainted race." Political theory in Alabama was that you ran your first race to get acquainted with the voters. If you ran strong that first race but finished second then you became the front-runner for the race four years later because there would be no incumbent standing in your way. This theory made sense because there was no television, so you could not buy instant name identification. In the get-acquainted race, you got to know people and build a statewide organization. If you were serious about winning and loved politicking as George Wallace did, then you would run your campaign for four full years. You were simply getting acquainted in your first race so there was no stigma in losing, but you did need to finish second.

This practice started early in the century. William "Plain Bill" Brandon made his first run for governor in 1918. He ran a close second to the winner, Thomas Kilby. Brandon continued to campaign vigorously for four years and was elected governor in 1922 by a margin of three to one over Bibb Graves. Graves, having run second, campaigned for four years and won his first term for governor in 1926 and came back to win a second term in 1934. Frank Dixon ran against Bibb Graves in the 1934 election and lost badly. However, he had run a get-acquainted race and won in 1938, defeating Chauncey Sparks of Barbour County in the primary. So when Frank Dixon left office in 1942 you can guess who won the governor's race that year: Chauncey Sparks. Guess who ran against Sparks in 1942, none other than Big Jim Folsom. Big Jim ran a good get-acquainted race that year, so as was the practice Big Jim won the 1946 governor's race. Gordon Persons and John Patterson were one-term wonders in 1950 and 1958. Big Jim won his second term sandwiched in between the two, but guess who ran second to John Patterson in 1958. You guessed it, George Wallace, "the fightin' judge." After his loss to Patterson, Wallace began running for 1962 and he won and the rest is history.

So if you ever hear an old timer refer to the "get-acquainted race" while discussing Alabama political history you will know what he is talking about.

Legislative Experience Would Be Good Training

Alabamians have had a history of electing governors who have basically had no governmental experience, much less legislative experience.

I might be somewhat prejudiced since I served 16 years in the House, but I believe it might stand a governor in good stead if he or she had legislative experience. I understand that most Alabamians believe that the average legislator is a no-good scoundrel, but there are some pretty good quality people serving as your legislators. Even though statewide polls will show that the legislature as a body and legislators in general are held in low esteem, the same polls will show that in their home county a legislator is one of the most popular elected officials. Legislators, especially if they have served for a decade or two, have learned a few things about state government. In fact, if they are moderately active and attuned, they have gotten a feel for how state government operates. They understand the budget process. A good argument could be made that if you were hiring someone to run your business, you would hire someone who had worked in your line of business from the ground up for many years before hiring someone off the street with no experience.

Furthermore, a legislator-turned-governor not only understands state government and how it works, but he or she knows the members of the legislature on a personal, friendly basis. These relationships are invaluable in getting your program approved or at least addressed. Lasting lifetime friendships and bonds are developed by legislative colleagues. They know each other, what they believe in, how they operate, and what makes them tick, and whose word is good.

However, we have had a penchant for electing governors who are basically outsiders. Big Jim had never been elected to anything before becoming governor in 1946. Gordon Persons came in 1950. He had served one term on the Public Service Commission but had no legislative experience. John Patterson became governor in 1958. He had served one term as attorney general and had no legislative experience. Fob James became governor in 1978 and had no political experience at all. He was a dismal failure with the legislature. Guy Hunt won in 1986. His only experience was as probate judge of Cullman County. He actually worked hard to cultivate the legislature but failed. Little Jim Folsom followed Hunt for two years and his only prior political experience was being on the Pubic Service Commission. Fob came back again and was as ineffective his second time as he was his first. He was basically ignored by the legislature and was irrelevant in the scheme of things on Goat Hill. Bob Riley had come to the governor's office from Congress and was in the same boat as Fob. Basically, he was irrelevant in the legislative halls.

You might have noticed that I skipped the 1970s and the 1980s. George Wallace had served in the legislature and was one of the most effective and powerful governors in history. He understood the legislature and legislative process. He knew every member by name and he cultivated their votes and friendship. He was in a league of his own.

The second most effective governor in the past 66 years would be Albert Brewer, who was governor only two years, 1968 to 1970, but he was loved by members of the legislature, and they wanted him to succeed. He, like Wallace, had grown up in the legislature. Both men came to the House at a young age and became tireless workers and spent long hours learning the rules and process as well as cultivating lasting relationships with their colleagues. They were very effective and knowledgeable legislators. Brewer went on to become Speaker of the House.

On the other hand . . .

Legislature Is Not a Good Steppingstone to Governor

Alabama legislators live under the delusion that they are well known politically. It is a trap that has befallen state senators and representatives forever. In the course of state politics, only one legislator has ascended directly from the legislature to governor, and only a handful of governors have ever served in the House or Senate. The legislature is basically a dead-end street in Alabama politics. Our current governor, Robert Bentley, is the only person in state history to ascend to governor directly from the legislature.

Let me take you back 100 years and give you the prior experience of our governors and prove that legislative experience is not a stepping stone. Starting in 1906, Braxton Bragg Comer was an industrialist, a very successful businessman, and his only political experience had been as president of the Public Service Commission. Emmet O'Neal was a lawyer and president of the Alabama Bar Association with no elected office experience. Charles Henderson was governor 1915–19. He was one of the most successful businessmen in Alabama history, mayor of Troy, and had been elected to the Public Service Commission prior to being governor. Thomas Kilby became governor in 1919. He was also a successful businessman. He did serve one term in the Senate, but he was also mayor of Anniston and lieutenant governor of Alabama. William "Plain Bill" Brandon was probate judge of Tuscaloosa and state auditor before becoming governor in 1923. Bibb Graves served two terms as governor between 1927 and 1939. He was a lawyer in Montgomery and a war veteran as well as active in Alabama Democratic party politics. He served one two-year term in the House 25 years before he was elected governor. B. M. Miller was governor 1931–35. He was a judge prior to being elected governor. Frank Dixon was governor 1939 to 1943. He was a Birmingham corporate lawyer. Chauncey Sparks was governor from 1943–47. Chauncey Sparks and George Wallace served more than one term in the legislature, but neither rose to the governor's chair directly from the legislature.

A legislator only has name recognition in his home county and that would only apply to rural legislators. Urban legislators would not register on a name-identification radar in their home county. Less than 2 percent of the voters in a suburban Birmingham district could name their own representative. When Seth Hammett was Speaker the majority of voters of Covington County could name Seth Hammett as their House member, but very few people outside of Andalusia knew who Seth was and he was the most powerful member of the legislature. He got daily mention in the media for four months out of the year as Speaker. Yet, when he launched a trial balloon for governor, a few years back, his statewide name identification registered 3 percent, while his potential rival, Lucy Baxley, had 80 percent. This was an insurmountable hill to climb. That's why he opted to run for Speaker of the House again after the 2006 election. Speaker is now the second most powerful position in state government, second only to governor since the lieutenant governor's office has been stripped of its power. Seth made a wise decision. His dilemma only accentuated the tremendous hurdle that legislators must conquer to move up the political ladder.

They have to vote on dozens of controversial bills every year for four years and thus have a record that any opponent can shoot at from every angle. They go to the floor and debate a bill and then see their names mentioned in the big city dailies, but undoubtably people do not remember their names.

If Seth Hammett had only a 3 percent name recognition, then what do you think the average backbencher from Jefferson County has? He would be better off to go rob a bank. He would become much better known and probably more popular.

The bottom line is, the legislature is not a good stepping stone to higher elective office in Alabama politics.

Paths to Governor: 100 Year History

Suppose you are some young person keenly interested in being governor of Alabama one day. If that young person approached me and asked what would be the best course to take to capture that brass ring, my response would be that many times the best way to look into the future would be to study the past.

Therefore, I will share with you the historical paths taken to the governor's office over the past 100 years. There have been 19 governors over the last century. There could have been 25, but George Wallace took four terms and Big Jim Folsom took two terms. Eighteen of the 19 have been men. Eight have been lawyers. Seven have been businessmen (five were very successful in business). We've had one farmer and one housewife and mother and now one doctor.

The proven route to governor has been to run for governor, lose that race but come in second to the winner, and start running for the next race four years away, building on the name identification you received in your first losing race. This was the way it was done from 1922 through 1962. During this 40-year period, only nine different governors were elected and six ran the get-acquainted race and came back four years later to win. This worked repeatedly for the entire 20th century, however, that route has cooled since a governor could succeed himself and run for a second consecutive term. Also, the advent of television has created the mechanism to achieve instant statewide name identification.

In the 100-year history, 6 of 19 were out of office and did not ascend to governor directly from political office.

Only 8 of 19 have ascended directly from another political office. Over the last century, the best stepping stone has been the Public Service Commission. Three men have gone from the PSC to the governor's office. This is somewhat misleading in that two of those men were two of the earliest governors in the survey. Braxton Bragg Comer and Charles Henderson were governors from 1907 to 1911 and 1915 to 1919. Comer and Henderson were also two of the richest men ever to serve as governor and they served on the PSC when it was called the Railroad Commission; they were more interested in regulating the railroad and utilities to protect their business interests than striving for political acclaim. This was also true for their interest in being governor. They looked upon being governor as a civic tour of duty while amassing their vast business empires. Montgomery businessman Gordon Persons moved from the PSC to governor in 1950.

The second most popular stepping stone has been lieutenant governor, however, only 2 of 19 have moved up from that post: Thomas Kilby in 1918 and Don Siegelman in 1998.

There has been one attorney general, John Patterson in 1958, and only one congressman, Bob Riley in 2002.

Of the eight lawyers, four were known primarily as politicians who had law degrees. However, four were prominent and skilled attorneys. Two came out of the blue to be elected governor with only their prominence in the law as a resume.

In recent history, only three men have bolted out of the blue to be elected governor with no state political experience: Big Jim Folsom and Fob James had never been elected to any office prior to running for governor. Guy Hunt had only been a probate judge. Two of the three, Folsom and Hunt, came from Cullman County.

So there you have it. If you are a young aspiring politician, take these historical facts and run with them and good luck!

THE MACHINE

There has been a political organization called the Machine on the University of Alabama campus for close to a century. The Machine is a well-organized political entity that has produced many influential leaders in Alabama politics. The secretive coalition of fraternities and sororities has completely dominated campus political life because of the cohesiveness and commitment to the Greek system within the University of Alabama. The student newspaper, the *Crimson and White*, has exposed the Machine periodically since the 1920s.

The Machine has been the training ground for Alabama politicians. Our two legendary senators, Lister Hill and John Sparkman, were products of the Machine as well as our current senior senator, Richard Shelby. Over the years, a good many of Alabama's Supreme Court justices and legislators were members of the Machine. At one time eight of the nine members of our congressional delegation were Machine alumni.

Over the years, the University of Alabama has been the spawning ground for Alabama political leaders. Alabama's forte is business, political science, and law, whereas Auburn excels in agriculture, engineering, and architecture. So it is only natural that the University of Alabama would attract young Alabamians interested in politics.

The list of Machine alumni is long and prestigious. In addition to Hill and Sparkman, several of our legendary Washington solons like John Bankhead, Jack Edwards, Walter Flowers, Carl Elliott, Albert Rains, and

William Dickinson were all Machine members. Birmingham politician Albert Boutwell was a Machine man. Bill Baxley and former governor Don Siegelman were also Machine members.

Baxley and his closest ally, Julian Butler, now a prominent lawyer in Huntsville, met secretly one night to decide which office they would run for since they would not run against each other. Butler chose president of the student body, which was the most prestigious, and Baxley craftily preferred Cotillion president, because at that time the Cotillion president got a cut of all the entertainment brought to campus. It was rumored that Baxley made about $30,000 that year as a college senior, which was more than most of the professors on campus made at that time. Butler became SGA president and made nothing. Butler and Baxley remained friends and Butler ran all of Baxley's campaigns for attorney general, lieutenant governor, and governor.

Many Machine members continued on the political stage but most moved on to be powers behind the throne as lawyers and businessmen. Many of the most prestigious law firms in Birmingham are laden with Machine members. Tommy Wells, a prominent Birmingham attorney, and president of the American Bar Association was president of the SGA and a Machine member. CEOs Don Jones of Vulcan Materials and Johnny Johns of Protective Life were active Machine members at Alabama.

Longtime state senator Roger Bedford from Russellville was a very active member while at the University of Alabama. He had been out of campus political training only a few years when he arrived as a state senator.

Machine members Jack Edwards, Joe Espy, Don Stewart, Bill Blount, Don Siegelman, and Lister Hill were presidents of the Student Government Association at Alabama; Hill founded the UA SGA and of course went on to become the most prominent U.S. senator in Alabama history.

But the most prominent political figure in University of Alabama history, George Wallace, chose not to be a member of the fraternity club machine organization. He felt it would be a long-term plus in Alabama politics to be a "common man" independent. He lost as an independent in the Greek-dominated university politics, but his tactic paid off in the long run. However, my bet is that George Wallace would have succeeded in Alabama politics regardless of whether he chose to be a Greek Machine member or an independent at the University of Alabama.

ALABAMA GOVERNORS' HOME COUNTY

Barbour County is known as the "Home of Alabama Governors." Indeed, six Barbour countians have become governor, more than from any other county.

The best source on the history of our governors is Samuel Webb and Margaret Armbruster's book entitled *Alabama Governors*. They give a brief biographical sketch of every Alabama governor beginning with William Wyatt Bibb, in 1819. Throughout the first 75 years, it is difficult to determine what was really home to some of our governors. With Alabama being a new state and even an undeveloped territory, all of the men elected governor for the first 50 years were born in another state. Many had held political positions in their native states. Many were from Virginia or Georgia. Most were from wealthy, planter backgrounds.

Furthermore, after they got here, they tended to move around. They might start a law practice in Huntsville then move to the Black Belt to start a plantation. In determining where their home was, do you look at where they were born and grew up, where they lived during their adult working years, or where they died? If you follow Southern etiquette and say that where someone is born is their home, you put a completely different slant on our former governors. Close to one-third of them would call some county out of Alabama their home county. Two of our Reconstruction governors were not only born in New York, but were residents of New York while they were our governor.

Let's take, for example, the six governors that Barbour County claims. There could be dispute about whether several were from Barbour County.

Barbour's first governor was John Gill Shorter. He was elected governor of Alabama in 1861 just as the Civil War broke out. Shorter was born in Monticello, Georgia. His family moved to Barbour County in the early 1830s and became one of Eufaula's wealthiest families. The Shorter Mansion is one of the highlights of the annual Eufaula pilgrimage tour of antebellum mansions. Shorter was a prominent lawyer as well as governor.

The second Barbour County governor was William Jelks. He was born in neighboring Macon County in 1855. His father was a Confederate captain who died a Civil War hero. His mother was widowed with four children and married a Confederate major from Union Springs. So young Jelks was born in Macon County but grew up in Union Springs in Bullock County. He grew up to be a newspaper man and owned the *Union Springs Herald* and only later bought the *Eufaula Tribune* and moved to Eufaula after he had made the *Eufaula Daily Times* the dominant paper in southeast Alabama. Jelks was an ardent white supremacist. He was elected governor of Alabama in 1900 and served through 1907. He was a Bourbon governor.

Barbour's third governor was another conservative Bourbon, Braxton Bragg Comer, 1907–11, who was one of the most successful businessmen in Alabama history. Comer was indeed born in Barbour County, but he left Barbour County as a young man, never to return. Comer made a fortune as the largest owner of textile mills in Alabama, and perhaps in the South. He lived near his mills in Calhoun County but also had a home in Birmingham where he owned banks and other interests. After serving as governor, he lived out his life in Birmingham and died there in 1927.

Barbour County's fourth governor was Chauncey Sparks. Sparks was born in Barbour County, practiced law in Barbour County, served as governor during World War II, 1943–47, and died in Barbour County.

Sparks's term ended an era from 1900 to 1947 when all of Alabama's governors were wealthy Black Belters or Birmingham Big Mules. It was a 50-year span where most of the governors such as Braxton Bragg Comer and Charles Henderson not only served a term as governor but were also the richest men in the state. The industrial interests of Birmingham would team up with the large agricultural interests of the Black Belt and select a governor in a boardroom. It was like a civic commitment for four years for a wealthy businessman to take the job. However, they mainly made sure that the interests of the Big Mules and Big Planters were protected. Comer stood in the way of moves to prohibit child labor; he used them in his textile mills. It was not uncommon for children ages 12–14 to work alongside their parents in the mills for 60–70 hours a week. Some people refer to this era as the Bourbon/Progressive era. Whatever you call it, there were no paupers serving as governor from 1900 to 1947. Big Jim Folsom broke the stranglehold of Bourbon governors as World War II ended.

Barbour County native George Wallace became the county's fifth governor in 1962. He served four terms. His wife, Lurleen, was elected governor in 1966. She is Barbour County's sixth governor. Both of them could be questionable. Wallace was born in Barbour County and was elected to the legislature and a judgeship from Barbour, but after losing the 1958 governor's race, he and Lurleen moved to Montgomery to run for governor in 1962. He was living in Montgomery when he was elected governor and finished his life in Montgomery after leaving office in 1986. And of course Lurleen also lived out the rest of her life in Montgomery.

Tuscaloosa County could certainly claim Lurleen; she was born and raised in Northport.

The point is not to dispute Barbour County's claim as the home of governors, but to point out that it can be hard to determine a governor's home. Even going back to our first governor, William Wyatt Bibb, it is hard to decide if he was a resident of Madison or Limestone County. Even our more recent governors are confusing. Fob James was born and raised in Chambers, built his business and got elected governor from Lee, and now calls Baldwin County home. Governor Big Jim Folsom was born and raised in Elba in Coffee County, lived his early adult life there, then moved to Cullman County from where he was elected as governor twice. Jim Folsom Jr. was born in the Governor's Mansion in Montgomery while his daddy was governor, but also called Cullman home. Speaking of Cullman, in the modern post-World War II era, they have had three: Jim Folsom Sr., Jim Folsom Jr., and Guy Hunt.

The toughest one to pin down would be Don Siegelman. He was born and raised in Mobile, went to school in Tuscaloosa and Oxford, England, settled in Birmingham, was quickly elected secretary of state and moved to Montgomery, and lived there for more than 20 years while he held public office. Let's call him from Mobile so they will at least have one governor.

After Barbour's six, there is a second-place tie with Montgomery and Lauderdale having four each. All of Lauderdale's four were in the early years, including one Reconstruction governor. Montgomery has also had four. Their four legitimately were born and raised and lived their lives and died in

Montgomery. They are truly second in number to Barbour and under more strict rules may be first. Monroe has had three, Cullman has had three, and now with the election of Robert Bentley, Tuscaloosa has three.

Madison and Jefferson have had two, and guess what, because of Reconstruction the state of New York has had two.

The Bogeyman

The new political professionals who run campaigns today are highly paid hired guns. They go from state to state running U.S. senate and governors' races all over the country. Much like the gunslingers of the Wild West, they build a reputation. Just like the gunslingers who would swagger into a bar of a new town and haughtily soak in their deference and respect or fear, these modern-day political hired guns waltz into a state demanding huge fees to elect the candidate who has hired them for that year's campaign.

They bring with them their team of pollsters, speech writers, and ad men, and of course their reputation for success and meanness. They must be mean in today's political world. The hired gun must be feared not only for his success and number of victories, but he also must have a collection of scalps. He must be renowned for negative ads and attacking and destroying the opposition. Negative ads and success usually go hand in hand because they generally work.

These hired guns will usually find somebody or some entity to create fear and hatred against. In political terms it is called finding a bogeyman and running against him. Before the days of these political handlers, our greatest Alabama politicians knew this theory instinctively.

George Wallace created the greatest Southern bogeyman, the race issue. He ran against integration and then when that issue subsided, and more importantly after African Americans began voting, he made pointy-headed liberals his bogeyman. He proudly proclaimed that if one of those long-haired pointy-headed liberals lay down in front of his car he would run over them. Wallace's followers nationwide ate it up when he said that those liberal intellectual elitists at Berkeley could not even park their bicycles straight.

Big Jim Folsom used the "soak the rich" philosophy the same way that Huey Long did in Louisiana. Big Jim ran against the Big Mules of Birmingham, declaring that he was the little man's big friend and he would defend them against the giant greedy corporate "gotrocks."

For decades, Republicans have played the liberal card as though the word generically captures everything evil and corrupt in politics and threatens the Southern way of life. In the 2006 governor's race, Bob Riley's handlers' initial ad attacked Lucy Baxley as being a liberal and likened her to Hillary Clinton.

Hillary Rodham Clinton was the biggest bogeyman, or should we say bogeywoman, used in the 2006 races by Republican candidates. She overtook Ted Kennedy as the most liberal and hated Democrat in Washington by most Republicans. Over the past few years, fiery Democratic Leader Nancy Pelosi has been a lightning rod for Republicans to bash. Of course, Obama is the most vilified of all modern Republican targets.

In Alabama it has been safe to jump on the illegal immigration issue because most of the illegal Hispanics here do not vote. Just as it was easy to demagogue the race issue in the early 1960s because African Americans did not vote. However, nationwide, because of the tremendous importance of the Hispanic vote in crucial swing states, it is tricky for Republican handlers to exploit this issue.

The political gunslingers think they are geniuses by creating bogeymen for voters to hate, but smart politicians like George Wallace and Big Jim Folsom knew inherently how to create a bogeyman 60 years ago.

Buck's Pocket

For decades, losing political candidates in Alabama have been exiled to Buck's Pocket. It is uncertain when or how the colloquialism began, but political insiders have used this terminology for at least 50 years. Alabama author Winston Groom wrote a colorful allegorical novel about Alabama politics in the 1960s, and he referred to a defeated gubernatorial candidate having to go to Buck's Pocket. Most observers credit Big Jim Folsom with creating the term. He would refer to the pilgrimage and ultimate arrival of his opponents to the political purgatory reserved for losing gubernatorial candidates.

Which brings me to another contention surrounding Buck's Pocket.

Many argue that Buck's Pocket is reserved for losing candidates in the governor's race. Others say Buck's Pocket is the proverbial graveyard for all losing candidates in Alabama.

One thing that all insiders agree on is that once you are sent to Buck's Pocket, you eat poke salad for every meal. It is not certain whether Big Jim or Groom began the poke salad myth. Once you are sent to Buck's Pocket, Groom suggested you were relegated to the rural resting place forever. However, history has proven that a good many defeated Alabama politicians have risen from the grave and left Buck's Pocket to live another day.

Most folks don't know that there really is a Buck's Pocket. Big Jim was the first gubernatorial aspirant to hail from north Alabama in the twentieth century. He was the first to campaign extensively in rural north Alabama, often one-on-one on country roads. One day while stumping in the remote Sand Mountain area of Dekalb County, he wound up in an area he referred to as Buck's Pocket. It was a beautiful and pristine area, but it was sure enough back in the woods. Big Jim, who loved the country and loved country folk, was said to say that, "I love the country but I sure wouldn't want to be sent to Buck's Pocket to live."

Buck's Pocket is not a mythical place. If you are traveling up the Interstate past Gadsden, on the way to Chattanooga, you will see it. There is a Buck's Pocket State Park in Dekalb County, thanks to Big Jim.

So the next time you hear an old-timer refer to a defeated candidate as going to Buck's Pocket, you will know what they are talking about.

Small-Town Boys Succeed

While a student at the University of Alabama I had the opportunity to intern with the dean of students, Dr. Joab Thomas. A few years later Dr. Thomas became president of the University and I was elected to the legislature. He invited my wife and me to sit with him at an Alabama game. We had just had our first daughter and she seemed to us quite precocious. Dr. Thomas and I were discussing my newborn and the topic of her early education came up. I lamented that she might not be able to compete on an even footing academically in college because she would be raised in a small town without the advantages or competition that a larger city school might offer.

Dr. Thomas, who himself was from the small town of Russellville, was a Harvard-educated botanist and had done quite well academically. However, he shed an interesting light on the difference in growing up in a small city as opposed to a large one. He said a person from a small place who has leadership talents can develop them better than someone from a large place. It is much easier in a small town to be class president, captain of the football team, homecoming queen, or otherwise the big fish. It allows someone to develop confidence and leadership abilities that may far exceed the slight disadvantage of their academic development. That small town person grows up expecting to be the leader. They expect to be governor or president.

Dr. Thomas suggested that I do some research on the success of small town folk. Since I knew politics, I looked into the Alabama political arena and found, much to my amazement, that Dr. Thomas was right. Small-town boys dominated Alabama politics and the governor's office.

Our current governor, Robert Bentley, was born and raised in Columbiana in Shelby County. Looking back over the past 66 years really tells the story. Big Jim Folsom grew up in Elba and lived his adult life in Cullman. George Wallace was from the small hamlet of Clio in Barbour County and his wife Lurleen was from the small town of Northport in Tuscaloosa County. Albert Brewer is from the midsize city of Decatur, still no metropolis. John Patterson's home was Phenix City but he was born in a Tallapoosa County crossroads. Fob James is from the small east Alabama town of Lanett. Guy Hunt was from the village of Holly Pond in Cullman County. Jim Folsom Jr. is from the city of Cullman like his father. Bob Riley is from the small Clay County town of Ashland.

Incidentally, another small-town boy from Ashland who made his mark on Alabama and national politics was Hugo Black, who served in the U.S. Senate and then was appointed to the Supreme Court by FDR. Black is one of the most influential Alabamians ever on the national stage.

The only city governor of Alabama in the last 66 years was Don Siegelman, who is from Mobile. Therefore, during the last 66 years that is 9-to-1 small-town governors over big-city governors, but if you count Wallace's 4 terms, Big Jim's 2, and Fob James's 2, that would make it 14-to-1.

This small-town dominance does not end with Alabama governors. A cursory look at the presidents over the past 60 years reveals that our U.S. presidents were small-town boys. Harry Truman was from Independence, Missouri. Dwight Eisenhower was from a small town in Kansas. Lyndon Johnson was from a small town in east Texas. Richard Nixon was from a small town in California. Jimmy Carter is from the small hamlet of Plains, Georgia. Ronald Reagan was from a small town in Illinois. George Bush Sr. is from a small place in Connecticut and his son, George W. Bush, calls Crawford, Texas, home. Bill Clinton is from the small town of Hope, Arkansas. John F. Kennedy was from a big city, Boston, Massachusetts, and Barack Obama was born in Honolulu, Hawaii. That is nine small-town presidents and two from cities. If you include in the count those who were elected two times, it is 14 to 2.

Dr. Thomas was right in his assessment of success inherent in politics and growing up in a small town. He said if you think it is true in politics, you should read the almanac of success in business, because it is just as dominated by small-town boys.

LABOR WAS IMPORTANT IN POST-WAR ALABAMA

Alabama experienced the wrenching throes of the Great Depression like the rest of the nation. There were tragic stories of devastation that paralleled those illuminated in the classic novel, *The Grapes of Wrath*. On the other hand, I have heard many old timers who lived during the Depression say we never knew there was a depression in Alabama. We were poor before so there was no marked difference to our standard of living. We had plenty to eat. There were people jumping out of buildings in New York City committing suicide because they were millionaires one day and penniless the next. We didn't have much of that in Alabama.

These Depression-era rumblings resonate pretty accurately because most Alabamians lived off the land. Most of our ancestors were farmers and most had modest farms where they grew all their staples and food. Therefore, the Depression probably did not change their standard of living. In fact, it could have helped them buy their Sunday suit and pair of shoes for the year at a reduced price.

The South was an agrarian region. There was little industry in Alabama.

Eight out of ten Alabamians, black or white, made their living on the farm. Although they had enough to eat they were very poor compared to the rest of the nation. It was a hard life with little discretionary income.

World War II brought America out of the Great Depression. The country had to become industrialized in a hurry. Most of Alabama's young yeomen farmers were drafted or enlisted in the military. They saw the world and were exposed to a vast new world of glamour and opportunity. They came home aspiring to more than their fathers had experienced. They wanted out of their poverty but they also loved their native Alabama roots. The best of both worlds was about to occur. Industry came to Alabama.

The post-World War II economy expanded into the Heart of Dixie. Birmingham became one of the South's largest cities. Franklin Delano Roosevelt's New Deal programs transformed the Tennessee Valley from an impoverished Appalachian region to a vibrant industrial area that would later attract Werner Von Braun and the Redstone Arsenal. The northern part of Alabama became the largest population base in the state due to this industrial expansion. Today it is still home to the majority of Alabamians.

A new generation of Alabamians moved from the farm to the factory. They also went a stage further than the rest of the South and joined labor unions. Alabama became the most unionized state in the South.

Every major industry in Alabama was served by a unionized workforce. The steel mills of Birmingham were Alabama's largest employers. The steel workers' union ruled supreme. The state docks in Mobile boomed with the economic expansion. The dock workers were all unionized. The explosion of new automobiles desired by Americans created the need for tires. Tire makers looked to Alabama and built major plants here. B. F. Goodrich landed in Tuscaloosa. Goodyear settled in Gadsden and Opelika. These tire plants became the largest employers in these three cities. They were all unionized. The paper mills in Tuscaloosa were unionized. Reynolds Aluminum built their largest plant in the world in Sheffield. It became the premier employer in the Tri-Cities. The workers were all union. The massive Tennessee Valley Authority, which harnessed the vast natural water of the Tennessee Valley, gave employment to an array of north Alabamians. These TVA workers were union members.

The Black Belt planters were like ostriches with their heads buried in the sand when they wrote Big Jim Folsom off as a buffoon in the 1946 governor's race. They dismissed that Big Jim had won the overwhelming endorsement of the AFL-CIO. However, they quickly realized that their Alabama had changed when Big Jim crushed their candidate and became governor because of the endorsement of organized labor.

However, over the past half-century, the American and world economy has changed and labor union strength has diminished almost to the point of insignificance.

The Terry Family Reunion

The Terry Family Reunion in the northwest corner of Alabama is the largest such event in the state. Serious Alabama politicians know about this annual event that has been going on for many years. There are political speeches and lots of one-on-one campaigning. There are Labor Day barbeques from one end of the state to the other. However, none are more political than the Terry Family Reunion.

It has become a must-do event for aspiring statewide and definitely local candidates. Every candidate for sheriff, probate judge, legislature, or constable will be at the Terry Reunion just south of Tuscumbia and just north of Moulton and Russellville in Lawrence County. It is an event for all politicians running for statewide office and in the counties of Colbert, Lauderdale, Franklin, Lawrence, and Morgan.

The actual location is in the Loosier Community of Lawrence County. That's where the large Terry family originated. Actually, a good many of the folks who attend have kinship or ties to the Terry family.

It is now officially called the Terry Club Family Reunion. It has a carnival atmosphere. They have lots of camp stew, barbequed pork and chicken, hamburgers, hot dogs, catfish, and fried pies. You name it. The barbecue is not just barbeque, but mighty fine barbeque. They cook the chicken and camp stew all night the night before.

A regular at the Terry Club Family Reunion was Howell Heflin, who of course hailed from nearby Tuscumbia. No politician ever loved barbeque, or food, for that matter, more than the Judge.

Every candidate for any office is allowed to speak, but of course, deference is given to the gubernatorial candidates. I remember attending the event in 1978. Jere Beasley's caravan was arriving just as Bill Baxley's was leaving. Albert Brewer and Sid McDonald arrived later and Judge Heflin meandered around most of the day, eating most of the time.

Besides everybody being kin to each other up in this corner of the state, a well-known fact politically was that it was almost a requirement to be a member of the Church of Christ denomination. They were almost clannish and very loyal and devoted to voting for someone from their church.

Also, at one time, the Terrys claimed that by marriage or blood, they were about half the population of Lawrence County. Whether that's accurate or not, the Terry Family Reunion was and still is a must event for an aspiring state politician.

WALTER JOHNSEY

Walter Johnsey was one of the most powerful behind-the-scenes political brokers in Alabama history. It was common knowledge in political circles that he controlled the Alabama Senate during the 1960s.

George Wallace was jealous of his political hold on the Senate and he became Johnsey's nemesis. Johnsey was the only thing that kept Wallace from having omnipotent power over state government during the tumultuous 1960s.

Johnsey was one of the most influential men in Alabama politics for close to three decades. He was a power behind the throne in Montgomery. He did it from his perch above the fray in Birmingham. Many an aspiring politician for statewide office came calling on Mr. Walter to kiss the ring of the king-maker. If Johnsey liked their pitch, they left with a healthy contribution to their war chest.

There is an old saying that "money is the mother's milk of politics." Johnsey supplied a lot of milk to Alabama politicians over the years. He garnered some power from his generosity but what he enjoyed more was the game of politics. He understood Alabama politics and could size up an aspiring politico almost instantly. He had a grasp of what makes Alabama politics tick better than anyone in the state. He conducted polls monthly to find out how each politician fared and what the issues were, and he would share his data with his favorites. He lived by the political golden rule that you stay loyal to your friends come rain or shine. If one of his friends got barraged by negative events, Johnsey was the first to stand by their side. If Walter Johnsey was your friend, you had a true friend for life.

Johnsey was born August 22, 1924, in the coal mining community of Jasper in Walker County. He was born into a large and poor family. He had to go to work in the mines as a young boy to survive. He lost the sight in his left eye in a coal mining accident as a youngster. However, it did not deter Walter.

He was accepted to Auburn University and worked his way through and finished in the top of his class in engineering. He applied for a job with the power company and they hired him as a pole climber. However, he climbed that pole all the way to the top of the company. He rose through the ranks of Alabama Power at a meteoric pace, outshining all his engineering peers. He earned a law degree at night. He became CFO of Alabama Power by age 50. He was successful in other business interests as well. I remember one of our first meetings in his palatial office overlooking Birmingham. It was 1974, and I was a 22-year-old aspiring politician just getting to know Mr. Walter. I read in the papers that Johnsey made $150,000 a year at Alabama Power, a kingly salary at that time. Somehow the subject of his salary came up and he quietly stated that his salary from the power company wouldn't pay his taxes.

Johnsey was the epitome of the Horatio Alger story. He also loved the game of politics. Walter was one of my favorite friends in Alabama politics.

He died in Birmingham in 2008.

Monroeville

The city of Monroeville rests at the edge of the Black Belt in southern Alabama. Its closest major city is Mobile. It prides itself on being the literary city of Alabama. Indeed, given its size, it boasts numerous literary successes. However, the primary reason for its claim to fame is that it is the home of Harper Lee, author of *To Kill a Mockingbird*. To say that the novel is the most famous book written by an Alabamian would be an understatement.

Harper Lee published the book in 1959. It was made into a movie in 1962. The book is considered one of the most influential novels ever written, and it is printed in more than 30 different languages. The royalties from the book and the movie have made Miss Lee wealthy. Her book is just as famous as Margaret Mitchell's *Gone with the Wind.* Both authors are very similar. Both wrote about their Southern hometowns. Both disliked the limelight.

Miss Lee probably never realized how successful or famous her book would become when she penned it. She simply wrote an allegory about her childhood growing up in Monroeville. She undoubtedly adored her father. She freely admits that her main character in the book, Atticus Finch, is based on her father.

Old-timers who grew up with Miss Lee in Monroeville can easily identify all of the characters in the book including Boo Radley. Harper Lee is known by her friends in Monroeville as Nelle. She was the youngest of four children. There were three girls and one boy. At this writing, Nelle Harper Lee is 88 and in failing health, and living in an assisted living facility. Her oldest sister, Alice, practiced law in Monroeville up until her death last year at age 100. She still went to her law office every day. Both of these girls, Alice and Nelle Harper, never married. They were old maids who obviously worshiped their father.

Their father was a small-town Monroeville lawyer. He was quiet and reserved but much respected for his integrity, honesty, and resolve, much like the Atticus Finch from the novel, portrayed brilliantly by Gregory Peck in the movie.

Not many people are aware that A. C. "Coley" Lee served 12 years in the Alabama legislature. Old folks who remember him say he played golf once a week in his suit.

This reserved and private trait was definitely passed on to his daughter Nelle Harper. Soon after her book became popular and she became known worldwide, she seemed to withdraw into her privacy. It became even more pronounced as she got older. She has basically been a recluse for the past 30 years. She seldom grants interviews and signs very few books. She is not rude to her fellow Monroevillians but lets them know that she does not like to be engaged. While she was younger, she divided her time between her residence in Monroeville and an apartment in New York. Neither residence was pretentious. She lived and dressed modestly. Her modesty, frugalness and reclusiveness have given her a reputation for being somewhat eccentric. The more accurate picture is that she is probably just shy.

While she was in good health, she would walk from her small modest home in Monroeville to get the local paper, the *Monroe Journal*. The award-winning paper was read religiously by Nelle Harper. Her father was the editor for 18 years from 1927 to 1949 in conjunction with his law practice and legislative service.

There was a real-life case very similar to the case in the novel. Mr. Lee was asked to defend a black man accused of raping a white woman behind an old factory in Monroeville. The black man was convicted and most people in the town suspected that he was innocent. After he was convicted, some of the leading citizens of Monroeville went to see Governor B. M. Miller to ask for leniency for the convicted man. Miller, who was from Camden, refused to commute the sentence and castigated the petitioners for not coming forward during the trial to speak up for the black man.

To Kill a Mockingbird was simply Nelle Harper Lee's story about her childhood and her father, even Truman Capote as the little boy who would visit from New Orleans.

Nelle and Truman Capote remained lifelong friends. The New York media loved the flamboyant Capote and some even insinuated that Truman Capote had written *To Kill a Mockingbird* for Miss Lee. This is far from the truth. In fact it is probably more likely that she helped the troubled alcoholic Capote write his famous book, *In Cold Blood,* a lot more than he helped her with her book.

Miss Lee resented the New York media accusation and many say that is why she vigorously avoided the media and any interviews. She was asked many times, just like Margaret Mitchell was, why she wrote just one book. Finely, she told them simply, "Why should I. I have nowhere to go but down."

However, in 2015, it was revealed that her publisher would issue a novel she had written before she published *To Kill a Mockingbird*. In any case, she and Margaret Mitchell will go down in history as among the greatest Southern writers. Mitchell and Lee can each lay claim to writing one of the ten best-known and most-read novels in history. *Gone with the Wind* and *To Kill a Mockingbird* are legendary novels.

Nelle Harper Lee put Monroeville on the map. A visit reveals that the town has been made into a testament to the book. The old courthouse seen in the movie has been preserved to replicate the courthouse scene in the movie. There are hotels and restaurants named Mockingbird and Boo Radley.

Old-timers still reminisce about Gregory Peck's time in Monroeville.

A visit to Monroeville to see the Old Courthouse Museum is a must for anyone interested in Alabama literary history.

My Boys State Experience

Every June, the American Legion and the American Legion Auxiliary sponsor one of finest programs for high school students in Alabama, Boys State and Girls State. Rising seniors in high schools all over the state are invited to these week-long leadership confabs held each year at a different state university. It is a lesson in civics and first-hand politics for these future leaders. The students are taught about government by practical experience. During their week at Girls or Boys State they build city, county, and state governments and then they run them. They form political parties and run for every office. They draft and pass mock legislation. They culminate their week by visiting the Capitol and running mock state government.

This program has been going strong for more than seven decades and many of Alabama's past and current state leaders have been participants. I had the opportunity to be a Boys Stater 47 years ago. It was a magnificent experience. I developed lifetime friendships from Boys State.

As a teenager I was already involved in several high school political endeavors. My high school principal told me earlier in the school year that I would be chosen to attend Boys State, so it gave me ample time to plan to run for state office. I decided to run for governor. As might be expected, with aspiring young high school politicos from all over the state, by the time that Boys State began there were 27 of us running for governor.

My best state political buddy was a fellow from Auburn. He and I had been to numerous political leadership meetings together. We were both running for governor and as young politicians we were already cutting backroom deals. We were both presumptuous enough to assume that one of us, if not both, would be in the runoff. We agreed we would endorse the other in the runoff against any third interloper who might make the runoff against either of us. Much to our chagrin, neither of us made the runoff. I finished third and he ran fifth.

I always blamed my loss on the infamous City 13. Each delegate is assigned to a "city" when they arrive. There were 14 cities with 30 boys in each city. As soon as the city's citizens were determined, all serious gubernatorial candidates started organizing a campaign plan for each city. You begin by getting a campaign manager in place for each city. I had determined that I needed only six votes in each city to make the runoff.

As is usually the case, the star football player is generally the most popular guy in his high school. By virtue of this they are considered leaders and they are picked to go to Boys State. These guys are usually more interested in lifting weights, talking to college football recruiters, or hanging out with their girlfriends than in playing politics for a week. Most of them got bored early in the week and treated all the protocol with disdain. Toward the end of the week they were only participating in the sporting events. For some unknown reason every high school football star in the state had been assigned to City 13.

Being an athlete myself, I knew quite a few of the citizens of City 13. I told my friend and campaign manager in City 13, who was a star split end and destined to sign with Alabama, that I only need six votes in his city. As I said, by the end of the week when it was time to vote they had grown disinterested in politics and were ready to go home. When the votes for governor came in, I got zero votes in City 13. In fact, only six of the 30 had even bothered to vote.

The sordid and comical story of City 13 and their arrogant lack of interest in participation became legendary. In later years I asked the director of Boys State if they had intentionally put all of the state's top athletes in City 13. He said it was totally unintentional but they vowed it would never happen again.

I had the opportunity to speak to Boys State in June 2012 on the occasion of the 75th Anniversary of this magnificent program. The legendary

Judge Pete Johnson has been directing the program for three decades and has been involved for 50 years. He is a beloved institution. He served with distinction as a Jefferson County judge for several decades and is now retired.

Pete's introduction of me prior to my speech included his memory of my donkey. It brought howls of laughter from the current Boys Staters. They were quite an impressive group.

Our donkey was named Gregory. He was about 15 at the time. He was the pet of one of my best buddies, Jere Colley, who is now a prominent Opelika veterinarian.

THE ALABAMA–AUBURN GAME

The only sport that Alabamians enjoy more than Alabama politics is college football. We especially love the Alabama–Auburn football game, one of the fiercest of college football rivalries. It is the game of the year. It is a state civil war that divides friends and even families. It is bragging rights for the entire year. The loser has to live with his boasting next-door neighbor for 364 days. You must choose a side even if you despise college football and could not care less who wins. Newcomers to our state are bewildered on this fall day each year. They cannot comprehend the madness that surrounds this epic war.

Young boys all over Alabama grow up playing football in their front yards and dream of playing in this big game. It is often said that when these two rivals meet one can throw out the record books, however, this is not true. In fact, in 90 percent of the meetings, the favorite has won, although a lot of SEC championships and bowl games have been decided in the game. It has made many Alabamians' Thanksgiving holiday either joyous or sad.

I liked the rivalry better when it was played at Legion Field, but I'm an old-timer in heart and age.

The game was not played for 40 years between 1908 and 1948. Myth has it that the game was halted because of the intense rivalry. This is not the case. The history is that after the 1907 game, the schools could not agree on the terms of the contract. The dispute involved meal money, lodging, officials, and how many players each side could bring. Football was not the passion it is today so the two schools let the matter rest and the fans didn't seem to care. That began to change as college football grew to a major sport in the 1940s.

When the series resumed, a popular myth is that the Alabama legislature called a special meeting and forced the teams to play. That never happened.

The House of Representatives passed a resolution in 1947 to encourage, not force, the schools to meet in football, and officials at Alabama and Auburn agreed. The presidents of Auburn and Alabama simply talked with each other and decided it would be in the best interest of the schools to start playing again.

The contract was drawn up, papers were signed, and the rivals literally buried the hatchet. On the morning of December 4, 1948, the presidents of each school's student body dug a hole at Birmingham's Woodrow Wilson Park, tossed a hatchet in, and buried it.

The series resumed in 1948 with a 55-0 Alabama victory and the teams have squared off every season since.

THE MONTEVALLO MAFIA

On St. Patrick's Day night, March 17, 2010, about 500 people attended a gala event honoring and roasting Dr. Jack Hawkins, chancellor of Troy University. The event, organized by the board of trustees, was held at the elegant Renaissance Hotel in Montgomery. The purpose of the event was to honor Hawkins on his 21st anniversary as chancellor and pursue $100,000 for a scholarship in his name. The event garnered more than $200,000 to endow the Jack Hawkins Leadership Scholarship for deserving Troy students.

The patrons to the event were made aware of a unique fraternal bond. Some political observers in the state were aware of this interesting fraternal organization and have dubbed it the "Montevallo Mafia." These men were all fraternity members at the University of Montevallo in the early 1960s. The school was known as Alabama College at that time. It was not long removed from being an all-female college. The enrollment was still predominantly female when these gentlemen chose to attend this college in the heart of Alabama.

This group has an amazing track record of success.

Among the members of the Montevallo Mafia is of course Troy Chancellor Hawkins. Two became mayors, Todd Strange of Montgomery and Jay Jaxon of Eufaula. Bill Cobb and Fred Crawford are retired from serving as two of the most prominent lobbyists in the state. Danny Copper heads the Alabama Realtors Association. Andy McGinnis and Bobby Horton are two of the founding members of the well-known musical group, Three on a String.

All have maintained their friendship forged in the 1960s and affectionately refer to themselves as members of the Montevallo Mafia.

Shorty Price

Alabama has had its share of what I call "run for the fun of it" candidates. The most colorful of all these perennial also-ran candidates was William Ralph "Shorty" Price. Shorty was born and raised in Barbour County just like the successful Alabama politician George C. Wallace. They were not only from the same county but from the same town, and even briefly roomed together at the University of Alabama, and both were lawyers. Shorty had a tremendous enmity toward Governor Wallace, probably because Wallace was as successful as Shorty was unsuccessful. Shorty would run every four years. He was appropriately nicknamed since he was barely 5 feet tall. Shorty not only ran for governor perennially, but he ran for numerous other offices. He often used recycled campaign signs to save money but he rarely garnered 2 percent of the votes in any campaign. He was elected only once, as an alternate delegate to the Democratic National Convention.

Shorty loved Alabama football. Following the Crimson Tide was Shorty's prime passion in life. You could spot Shorty at every Crimson tide football game, always sporting a black suit with a black hat with a round top and sporting his Alabama tie and flag. I don't know if Shorty actually had a seat because he would parade around Denny Stadium or Legion Field posing as Alabama's head cheerleader. In fact he would consistently intersperse himself among the real Alabama cheerleaders and help them with their yells. There was never any question that Shorty was totally inebriated. In fact, I never saw Shorty when he was not drunk. Shorty worshiped Paul "Bear" Bryant. Indeed, Bryant, Wallace and Shorty were of the same era. All three thrived through the 1958–72 era. Like Bryant, Shorty hated Tennessee. Bryant and Shorty had rather beat Tennessee than anybody. This traditional rivalry goes back more than a hundred years and was highlighted during the Wallace Wade and General Neyland rivalry.

Speaking of Tennessee rivalry, I will share with you a personal Shorty story. Shorty was from Louisville in Barbour County, a short drive from my hometown of Troy. Since I had been in politics since a young boy I had become acquainted with Shorty early on in life. Therefore, on a clear, beautiful, third-Saturday fall afternoon in October, Alabama was playing Tennessee in Legion Field. As always Shorty was prancing up and down the field.

I was a freshman at the university. Shorty even in his drunken daze recognized me. I had a beautiful date whom I was trying to impress, and meeting Shorty did not impress her. He pranced up the aisle and sat by me. Shorty might not have bathed in two months. His daily black suit had not been changed in probably over a year. He reeked of alcohol and body odor and my date had to hold her nose. After about 20 minutes offending my date, Shorty then tried to impress the crowd by doing somersaults off the six-foot walls of Legion Field. He did at least three, mashing his head straight down on the pavement. On each dive, I thought Shorty had killed himself with his somersaults. His face and his head were bleeding profusely and he was developing a black eye. The alcohol must have saved Shorty that day. Fortunately, Shorty left my domain and proceeded to dance with Alabama cheerleaders, as bloody as he may have been.

Shorty was beloved by the fans and I guess that's why the police in Birmingham and Tuscaloosa ignored his antics. However, that was not the case in a classic Alabama game four years later in New Orleans. By this time I was a senior at the University. We were facing Notre Dame in an epic championship battle in the Sugar Bowl on New Year's eve. It was for the 1973 national championship. Bear Bryant and Ara Parseghian were pitted against each other. We were ranked #1 and #2.

One of the largest television audiences up to that time was focused on the 7:30 p.m. kickoff. It was electrifying. Those of us in the stands were awaiting the entrance of the football team as were the ABC cameras. Somehow or other, Shorty had journeyed to New Orleans, had gotten on the field and was poised to lead the Alabama team out on the field. As customary, Shorty was as drunk as Cooter Brown. He stared off by beating an Irish puppet with a club, and the next thing I knew, two burly New Orleans policemen, two of the biggest I had ever seen, picked up Shorty by his arms and escorted him off the field. They did not know who Shorty was and did not appreciate him. Sadly, Shorty, one of Alabama's greatest fans, missed one of Alabama's classic games because he was sitting in a New Orleans jail. I have always believed that Shorty's removal from the field was a bad omen for us that night. We lost 24–23 and Notre Dame won the National Championship.

Shorty died in a car crash between Troy and Montgomery about 30 years ago. He was probably sipping on a Budweiser when he had his accident. Shorty expressed disdain for Governor Albert Brewer and stated that the reason was that Brewer had enacted a levy of two cents on every can of beer. Shorty said, "I'm a Budweiser man."

His slogan was "Smoke Tampa Nugget cigars, drink Budweiser beer, and vote for Shorty Price." In one of his campaigns for governor his campaign speech contained this line, "If elected governor I will reduce the governor's tenure from four to two years. If you can't steal enough to last you the rest of your life in two years, you ain't got enough sense to have the office in the first place."

In the 1958 governor's race there were several also-ran, run-for-the-fun-of-it candidates. Shorty ran behind all of them. He took his last-place finish not as a slight but as a point of honor. When a newspaper reporter wrote some years later that Price ran next to last in 1958, Shorty replied in mock anger, "That's a blasphemous lie! There were 14 of us in that race and I finished last." Shorty was quite a colorful character .

Wilcox County Prominence

Wilcox County has enjoyed a remarkable history in recent years. This sparsely populated Black Belt county is home to an elite number of public figures in Alabama.

The county has produced U.S. Senator Jeff Sessions, one of Alabama's most popular political figures. He is an 18-year veteran of the U.S. Senate. Lieutenant Governor Kay Ivey hails from Wilcox County. Kay is beginning her second term as lieutenant governor.

University of Alabama President Judy Bonner was born and raised in Wilcox County, as was her younger brother, former 1st District Congressman Jo Bonner. Congressman Bonner served with distinction for more than a decade. The Bonners have a long lineage in the rich political history of this County. Their forefathers were probate judges and state senators. They have family ties to Governor Benjamin Miller (1931–35) of Wilcox County. They also have ties to one of Alabama's most famous and effective state senators, Roland Cooper, known in political folklore as the "Wily Fox from Wilcox."

They May as Well Move the Capitol Back to Tuscaloosa

Throughout Alabama history certain cities, counties, and enclaves have had an inordinate number of their citizenry serve in state politics. The most dominant example is the number of governors Barbour County has produced.

However, currently we have a remarkable occurrence that may have never happened before and will probably never happen again in Alabama politics. Tuscaloosa County's prominence and representation on the Alabama political stage in the year 2015 is unparalleled.

Tuscaloosa presently lays claim to Governor Robert Bentley and our senior U.S. Senator Richard Shelby. Laying claim to the two leading political figures in the state would be sufficient to make political history.

However, you may add to that coup that Tuscaloosa also has the chairman of the House Ways and Means Education Budget Committee, State Representative Bill Poole. He is joined in the House by another young, outstanding state representative, Chris England, whose father is former State Supreme Court Justice and current Tuscaloosa Circuit Judge John England. Representative England knows more about Alabama football than the sports information office. And speaking of Crimson Tide football, legendary Alabama linebacker Rich Wingo will be joining Poole and England in the House from Tuscaloosa.

Their state senate delegation is also remarkable. Gerald Allen is their resident senator. He is joined by veteran Senator Bobby Singleton from Greensboro and one of the brightest rising stars in Alabama politics, Senator Greg Reed of Jasper, is representing Tuscaloosa in the Alabama Senate. Very few counties this size have three state senators.

The Tuscaloosa delegation also pulled off a coup in reapportionment when it comes to Washington representation. They now have Congressman Robert Aderholt representing them in Congress. Aderholt is currently Alabama's most powerful and senior member of Congress. He got to Washington at a very young age and if he stays the course will be an even more prominent leader in Congress in years to come. And the southern portion of Tuscaloosa County is represented in Congress by Alabama's only Democrat in Washington, Congresswoman Terri Sewell. She has tremendous ties to the White House. She is a Harvard Law School graduate who was a successful Birmingham lawyer prior to going to Congress a few years ago. She is considered a bright rising star within the national Democratic ranks. Having two superstar, fast-moving U.S. representatives representing one county of this size is again unheard of in Alabama politics.

Finally, added to that mix is State Civil Court of Appeals Judge Scott Donaldson of Tuscaloosa, along with Tuscaloosa's John Merrill who has just been elected secretary of state.

INHERITED NAMES HELP IN POLITICS

Those who inherit businesses from their parents are fortunate, especially if they like and enjoy the work of that business or profession. The name and reputation of that inherited firm gives quite a head start to the beneficiary. The great book of Proverbs says in chapter 22, verse one, "A good name is rather to be chosen than great riches." The author of Proverbs, King Solomon, was indeed blessed by being the son of a great man. King David was his father. Solomon was wise and rich but he was given quite a leg up with such a famous father.

The political business is no different than any another. In fact it could be more beneficial to have a famous father in politics than in any other arena if you want to go into politics. You need look only at one of our most recent past presidents to see the advantage. The first George (H. W.) Bush made it easier for his son, George (W.) Bush.

We have seen as much of the family advantage in Alabama politics as any other state. The great 1962 race for governor saw three of the greatest names in Alabama politics in the race, George Wallace, Big Jim Folsom, and Ryan DeGraffenreid. Twenty years later, the three best-known young politicians in Alabama were Jim Folsom Jr., George Wallace Jr., and Ryan DeGraffenreid Jr.

Name identification is the most valuable asset a politician can acquire. These three inherited this precious commodity. George Wallace was elected governor four times and his wife once. His name was on the ballot for governor and president ten times. Big Jim Folsom was elected governor twice and was on the ballot ten times. Ryan DeGraffenreid ran second for governor in 1962 and was heavily favored to win in 1966 before he died in a plane crash. Their sons did not reach the pinnacle that their fathers achieved, but all benefited immensely from their names.

Jim Folsom Jr. has been elected to the Public Service Commission three times and lieutenant governor three times. His last victory in 2006 was so close that I'm convinced that Big Jim's reservoir of popularity in rural Alabama won that race from the grave for Little Jim.

Similarly, George Wallace Jr. parlayed his father's legendary name into a political career of his own and was elected state treasurer and to the Alabama Public Service Commission.

In the legislative ranks, the name identification inheritance factor enabled a young Jabo Waggoner to win a legislative seat from Jefferson County due to his father Jabo Waggoner Sr. being a fiery segregationist Birmingham politician who was allied with Bull Connor. Young Jabo is now 76 and has been in the legislature 40 years. Phil Poole won his first legislative seat at age 26 due to his famous father, Victor Poole. Likewise, Gadsden Representative Craig Ford followed his father Joe Ford in his House seat after the elder Ford passed away. Representative Earl Hilliard Jr. followed his father, Earl Hilliard, who had served in the State Senate and Congress.

Perry Hooper Jr. served 20 years in the House of Representatives with distinction. He won many accolades as one of Alabama's most pro-business legislators. His daddy was chief justice of the Alabama Supreme Court.

Wives can also benefit from this name identification transference. Vivian Figures took her husband's state senate seat upon his early death from a stroke. Her husband Michael was a powerful state senator from Mobile. He had served with distinction in that seat. No doubt Lucy Baxley was propelled into state politics by being the former wife of Bill Baxley who was a two-term attorney general and lieutenant governor. And of course there was Governor Lurleen Wallace, who won as her husband's proxy.

But the name transference does not always work. After U.S. Senator Jim Allen died of a heart attack in 1978, Govenor George Wallace appointed his widow, Maryon, to the vacant seat. Having the Allen name, however, did not help her in the subsequent special election, in which she lost in the Democratic primary to the eventual winner, Donald Stewart of Anniston.

CONSTITUTIONAL MALAPPORTIONMENT

Alabama's 1901 constitution is as archaic as any in the nation. It has contributed to the poor image that persists today regarding our racist past. However, much of the damage was done during the 1960s. It was a fascinating and tumultuous era. Alabama political history was being written every day. I was a page in the legislature during these years. It was a great learning experience. The older House and Senate members would visit with the pages and tutor us on the rules and nuances of parliamentary procedures.

One day I was looking around the House and it occurred to me that the urban areas were vastly underrepresented. I knew that the U.S. Constitution required that all people be represented equally and that the U.S. Constitution superseded our state constitution. Both constitutions clearly state that the U.S. House of Representatives and the Alabama House of Representatives must be reapportioned every ten years and the representation should be based on one-man, one-vote.

In other words, all districts should be apportioned equally, so that every person has the same and equal voice in their government. That is why the census is taken every ten years. You determine the number of people in a state and divide them into districts with the same number of people in each district. For example, currently Alabama has about 4.2 million people and our constitution calls for there to be 105 House districts. So each representative represents about 40,000 Alabamians.

As a boy, I knew that the Birmingham area was home to about 20 percent of the state's population but they certainly did not have a fifth of the

House members. The same was true of Huntsville and other large cities in north Alabama.

My county of Pike had 28,000 people and two representatives, while Madison County and the city of Huntsville had 186,000 people yet they also had two representatives. The most glaring malapportionment example would have to be in the late 1950s. Lowndes County with 2,057 voters had their own senator, while Jefferson County had one senator for 130,000 voters. Well, folks, that ain't quite fair.

The rural and Black Belt counties were enjoying the power that had been granted to them in 1901. The state was probably malapportioned at that time, but it had grown severely imbalanced over the years.

The legislature had simply ignored the constitutional mandate to reapportion itself every ten years. It was not until 1974 that the courts finally intervened and made the legislature reapportion itself. They still could not do it themselves. The federal courts not only mandated the reapportionment, but eventually also had to draw the lines and districts. This finally gave blacks representation in the legislature and today about 25 percent of the seats are held by African Americans. The reapportionment also gave fair and equitable representation to the urban areas and north Alabama.

As of 2015, apportionment is still being argued and litigated, with the U.S. Supreme Court agreeing with Democrats and blacks that the Republican-dominated legislature had wrongly redrawn district lines after the 2010 Census.

1948 Dixiecrats

Throughout the course of Alabama political history there have been two pervasive and prevailing issues, race and religion. The issue of religion was prevalent in the 1928 presidential race when the good Democrats of Alabama became Hoovercrats and almost 48 percent voted Republican for president that year over the issue of Prohibition. The Democratic candidate was Al Smith, who was rejected by many Protestant voters, especially in the South, because he was a Catholic. Herbert Hoover supported Prohibition, and Smith did not, which was another strike against him in Baptist Alabama.

The race issue had remained dormant in Alabama politics for most of the first half of the 20th century. The 1901 Constitution had disenfranchised blacks in Alabama. In 1900, there were 180,000 black voters. By 1905, there were fewer than 4,000. Therefore, blacks became irrelevant in the political process. In fact, during this period Alabama had essentially reverted back to the previous century when blacks were slaves. In the first half of the 20th century, many blacks were left in a subservient system of sharecropping on the same plantations that had held their grandparents in slavery. They were without political or economic power. The system was still intact in 1948 when the winds of civil rights began to blow.

FDR had given lip service to civil rights and had made some incremental changes in the North. But he had refused to rock the boat in the South, partly because he needed the votes of powerful Democrats from Southern states to support his New Deal programs. Alabama's feudalistic farm system was left in place in the Black Belt. The bulk of FDR's New Deal Programs had been bestowed on the white area of north Alabama.

This region had reaped the rewards of the New Deal. These folks had pulled themselves up by their bootstraps during the New Deal recovery. The Tennessee Valley became not only the most heavily populated area but also the most prosperous.

FDR let sleeping dogs lie with the Deep South traditions of segregation and disenfranchisement of blacks. However, when FDR died in April 1945, his successor, Vice President Harry Truman, had bolder plans. In October 1947 the president's committee on civil rights recommended a program for the protection of civil rights for Negroes. It was only three months later in January 1948 that Governor Fielding Wright of Mississippi called for a break with the Democratic Party over the civil rights issue. Undeterred, Harry Truman sent civil rights legislation to Congress. White Southern leaders immediately called conferences in March to determine their course of action. Mississippi and South Carolina threw down the gauntlet first and passed resolutions to bolt the party if they further pursued the civil rights issue.

Even though most white Alabama Democrats of this era were for segregation, they were not enamored with the idea of bolting the party. There were two distinct groups in the state politically in 1948. There was a strong progressive contingency that was emboldened by and loyal to the national

Democratic Party of Jefferson and Jackson and that had given us the New Deal. FDR was revered in Alabama. All nine of our congressmen were loyal Progressive New Deal Democrats. Our two senators, Lister Hill and John Sparkman, were the most powerful and respected duo in the U.S. Senate. Both were Progressive New Deal Democrats. Our young governor, Big Jim Folsom, was the most progressive and liberal of them all.

However, the Democratic Party machinery was controlled by the conservative Black Belters who were allied with what came to be called Dixiecrats. The Alabama Democratic Party chairman was the racist Gesser T. McCorvey. McCorvey and company enacted a policy that no Democratic elector from Alabama could support a candidate pledged to civil rights. It was enforced by a signed pledge.

In the primary of 1948, Alabamians selected a mixed bag of delegates to the Democratic National Convention. It seemed that they simply followed the "friends and neighbors" tradition of voting for the most popular and well-known candidates rather than for the Dixiecrat bolt-the-party slate versus the progressive slate. The biggest vote-getters for delegates were Senator Lister Hill, a progressive, and McCorvey, the Dixiecrat bolter and leader of the Democratic Party. So when the national convention nominated Truman and adopted the civil rights plank in the platform, about half the Alabama delegates got up and left and half stayed on the floor. It should be noted that a young George Wallace, who was a Barbour County legislator and delegate to the 1948 convention, was one of the progressives who did not walk out with the anti-civil rights states' righters.

The Dixiecrats nominated Strom Thurmond for president. Alabama, along with the other Deep South states of Mississippi, South Carolina, and Louisiana, cast its 1948 electoral votes for the Thurmond/Fielding Wright ticket.

It has been assumed for years that Alabamians were so consumed by the race issue that year that they abandoned the national Democratic party en masse and voted overwhelmingly for the Dixiecrat ticket. However, a major caveat should be put in that analysis.

The Alabama Democratic Party leadership, headed by the racist McCorvey, had enacted a state law that did not allow the names of the national candidates on the ballot. One could only vote for the party. The names of Harry Truman, Thomas Dewey, and Strom Thurmond were not on the ballot in Alabama. Your choice was either voting for the Republican Party or for the Democratic Party. Alabamians had been pulling the Rooster for the Democratic Party for close to 80 years. In addition, most Alabamians either wanted to vote for the Dixiecrat Party headed by Strom Thurmond or the national Democratic Party of the New Deal and Harry Truman. Who they actually voted for will never be known. The state Democratic party controlled by McCorvey's Dixiecrats had basically hijacked the party label. I suspect that more than a few rural Alabamians who were helped immensely by the New Deal felt like they were voting for the national ticket headed by Harry Truman. But the Alabama Democratic Party machine controlled by McCorvey voted the electors chosen in Alabama's 1948 Democratic Primary for Dixiecrat Strom Thurmond.

JIM MARTIN—1962 SENATE RACE

John Kennedy was president. Camelot was in full bloom. Forgotten was the fact that Kennedy's father, Joseph, who had vowed to buy the presidency for his son, had in fact done just that in collusion with Chicago Mayor Richard Daley. They had shifted just enough votes in Chicago wards to tilt the pivotal swing state of Illinois to Kennedy over Nixon. It was days before the final count was in. Daley had to make sure he had enough votes being counted to cast Nixon out.

The Congress was controlled by Democrats only because the South was solidly Democratic. The Southern bloc of senators and congressmen were all Democrats. Because of their enormous seniority, they controlled both houses of Congress, especially the Senate. The issue of civil rights was a tempest set to blow off the Capitol dome. Kennedy was under intense pressure to pass major civil rights legislation. However, he was up against a stone wall to get it past the powerful bloc of Southern senators.

Race was the only issue in the South, especially in Alabama. George Wallace was riding the race issue to the governor's office in his 1962 campaign. The white Southern voter was determined to stand firm against integration and was poised to vote for the most ardent segregationists on the ballot.

Our Congressional delegation was Democratic, all eight congressmen and both senators. All had all come to Washington during the Roosevelt New Deal Era and were somewhat progressive. They had been the authors of legislation to help poor Southern whites. All were instrumental in providing health care for the rural South and also federal aid for college educations and of course the Tennessee Valley Authority for north Alabama and the electric cooperatives for the rest of rural Alabama. Senators John Sparkman and Lister Hill had a combined 40 years of service.

Hill had gone to the U.S. Senate in 1938. He had served four six-year terms and had become a national celebrity in his 24 years in the Senate. He was up for election to a fifth six-year term. It was expected to be a coronation. He was reserved, aristocratic, and almost above campaigning. Hill was also soft on the race issue. He was a progressive who refused to race-bait.

Out of nowhere a handsome, articulate Gadsden businessman, Jim Martin, appeared on the scene. Martin was 42, born in Tarrant City, a decorated World War II officer who fought with Patton's 3rd Army in Europe. He entered as a private and became an integral part of Patton's team, serving as an intelligence officer in the Army of Occupation, and rising to the rank of major. After the war he went to work for Amoco Oil and married a Miss Alabama— Pat McDaniel from Clanton. They then settled in Gadsden and he bought an oil distributorship and became successful in business. He was a business Republican and became active in the State Chamber of Commerce. When the State Chamber Board went to Washington to visit the Congressional delegates, they were treated rudely by our Democratic delegates who were still voting their progressive New Deal, pro-union philosophy.

Martin left Washington and decided that Alabama at least needed a two-party system and that he would be the sacrificial lamb to take on the venerable Lister Hill as the Republican nominee for the U.S. Senate. Martin got the nomination in a convention and the David vs. Goliath race was on.

By late summer, the big-city papers could feel that Martin had some momentum. He was being perceived as the conservative and Hill as the liberal. Every Alabama courthouse was Democratic, all sheriffs, probate judges, all statewide elected officials. It was hard to imagine that the tradition of voting Democratic would change, but the winds of segregation were strong.

When the votes were counted in November 1962, Martin had pulled off the biggest upset in the nation. NBC's team of Huntley and Brinkley reported the phenomenon on the nightly news. Republican Eisenhower called Martin to congratulate him. However, things were happening in rural north Alabama similar to Chicago two years earlier. Martin had won by 6,000 votes, but three days later mysterious boxes appeared with just enough votes to give Hill the belated victory. The entire country and most Alabamians knew that Jim Martin had been counted out. Boxes came in from Walker and Fayette counties where he got zero votes.

Jim Martin would have been the first Republican Senator from the South in a century. Some people speculate that he would have been the vice-presidential candidate with Nixon in 1968. Regardless, he was the John the Baptist of the Southern Republican sweep of 1964 and is the father of the modern Republican Party in Alabama.

That 1962 Senate race was a precursor of what was to come.

The Goldwater Landslide

The so-called "Solid South" was Democratic more out of tradition and protocol than philosophy. Both national parties took the South for granted in national elections. The Democrats ignored us because we were automatically in the barn and the Republicans ignored us for the same reason, although philosophically Alabama white voters were more aligned with the Republican party and our members of Congress voted similarly to the Republicans. White Southerners were really Republicans but had a tradition of voting Democratic spawned by years of inherited distrust of the Radical Republican Reconstruction yoke lashed on their fathers and grandfathers.

Jim Martin was that quiet voice bold enough to stand up and say that the emperor had on no clothes. His 1962 journey was a harbinger of what was to come two years later when white Deep South voters took the plunge and came to Jesus.

In 1964, Alabama became a Republican state as far as national politics are concerned. The 1964 election was the turning point when the Deep South states of Alabama, Mississippi, Georgia, and South Carolina voted for Barry Goldwater and never looked back. It was the race issue that won them over. Goldwater and the Republican party captured the race issue and have never let go of it. For this reason, the South which was known as the "Solid South" for more than six decades because they were solidly Democratic are today known as the "Solid South" because they are solidly Republican. Presidential candidates ignore us during campaigns because it is a foregone conclusion that we will vote Republican, just as presidential candidates ignored us for the first 60 years of the 20th century because it was a foregone conclusion that we were going to vote Democratic.

From 1900 to 1964, Alabama voted for every Democratic presidential nominee except in 1948 when our electoral votes went to the third-party candidate Dixiecrat Strom Thurmond. Since that eventful 1964 Goldwater breakthrough, in the past 45 years there have been 12 Republican wins and one Democratic victory. So to say that 1964 was pivotal is an understatement.

George Wallace had ridden the race issue into the governor's office in 1962. It reached fever pitch in 1964. Democratic President Lyndon Johnson had passed sweeping civil rights legislation which white Southerners detested. The only non-Southern senator to oppose the civil rights legislation was Republican Senator Barry Goldwater of Arizona. When the Republican Party met at the old Cow Palace in San Francisco, they nominated Goldwater as their 1964 presidential candidate. Johnson annihilated him nationwide, but Goldwater won the South in a landslide. The South had been totally Democratic down the ballot from president to coroner for more than six decades. There was no Republican Party in Alabama to speak of. There were no elected Republican office holders. There was no Republican primary. The Republicans chose their token candidates in backroom conventions. Except for a few Lincoln Republicans in the hill country counties, it was hard getting a white Alabamian even to admit they were a Republican.

That all changed in 1964. Goldwater and the Republicans became identified with segregation and the white Southern voter fled the Democratic Party en masse. As the fall election of 1964 approached, the talk in the old country stores around Alabama was that a good many good old boys were going to vote straight Republican even if their daddies did turn over in their graves. Enterprising local bottling companies got into the debate and filled up the drink boxes in the country stores with colas labeled Johnson Juice and Gold Water. It was as effective a poll as any other, and come election day, there were a good many papas turning over in their graves all over the South. The entire South seemed to change parties on that day.

Alabamians not only voted for Barry Goldwater but also pulled the straight Republican lever out of anger toward Lyndon Johnson's civil rights agenda. Alabama's nine-member congressional delegation, with more than 100 years of seniority, was wiped out by straight-ticket Republican voting. We gained a new slate of Republican congressmen, one of whom was Jim Martin. If Lister Hill had been on the ballot that day, the trashing he would have received from Jim Martin would have been so bad they couldn't have found enough votes to steal the election.

First Monday

When you say "the First Monday" to an old political observer in Alabama, they get a smile on their face and remember how it used to be in politics.

First Monday is an event that has been happening in the northeast Alabama town of Scottsboro for over 100 years. It is a gigantic old-timey flea market. People come from all over Jackson and surrounding counties to trade. The official name of the event is the First Monday Trade Day. As you can guess, it was held on the first Monday of every month. It started around the turn of the century in the early 1900s. In the past 20 years it has been moved to Sunday, but from 1900 to 1990 the first Monday of every month was a must event for an aspiring gubernatorial candidate.

First Monday Trade Day started with the local court sessions. Court would be held the first Monday of every month in Jackson County, which nestles in the northern corner of the state in the foothills of the Appalachians and borders Tennessee and Georgia. In those days, it took so long to travel to Scottsboro by horse and wagon that they decided to couple Court Day with a Trade Day.

Big tents were set up and people traded everything. It was bigger than just a flea market, it was like a carnival. Musicians and fiddlers would play while the traders plied their wares—guns, knives, Indian artifacts, produce and vegetables, chickens, goats, pigs, cows, horses, mules, and even dogs. Around the knife trading area would sit whittlers who would gossip and whittle all day long. They would chew tobacco and cut cedar into a big pile of cedar curls. There was lots of tobacco chewing and cigar smoking.

Obviously First Monday Trade Days was a must-event for a serious statewide political aspirant, especially before the advent of television.

George Wallace knew the importance of going to First Monday Trade Days in Scottsboro. Most state politicians had it on their itinerary during an election year, but Wallace was a regular. He built quite a personal following in Jackson County by attending their flea market. He always carried the county overwhelmingly.

In fact, this county is said to be where Wallace won the 1970 governor's race over Albert Brewer. Jackson County in extreme north Alabama should have been a natural county for fellow north Alabamian Albert Brewer under the "friends and neighbors" voting habits of Alabamians, especially given that Wallace was from extreme south Alabama. It is a populous county with a lot of votes. In the first primary, Wallace and Brewer broke even in Jackson County. In the runoff, Wallace pulled out all the stops. Brewer had him on the ropes and his political obituary was about to be written. His campaign put out some of the most racist and vicious smear sheets in state history. Wallace's people dropped those pamphlets all over Sand Mountain. They dropped them hard at First Monday. When Wallace came to First Monday the day before the runoff, you could tell the pamphlets were working. He drew the biggest crowd ever seen on First Monday (Lurleen had drawn a big crowd in 1966, too). They registered tons of new voters all over Jackson County and Sand Mountain. Wallace went from tied in this and the surrounding counties to a landslide. He beat Brewer in his home area with the race issue and that's where he turned the campaign around. They knew it was the most fertile area. They worked it and it worked.

Big Jim knew the importance of First Monday the same as Wallace. He would bring his band, the Strawberry Pickers. He had his shuck broom and suds bucket as an analogy that he was going to sweep out the Capitol of those corrupt Big Mules and Black Belters. The folks from Sand Mountain at First Monday were receptive to this message.

It's said that the First Monday Trade Day in Scottsboro is the longest continuing flea market in the country.

Mule Day

Another event in north Alabama has also become a must-do political event over the last several decades. Mule Day has evolved into a mainstay political pilgrimage. This annual event in Winfield in Marion County is held on the fourth Saturday in September. The Chamber of Commerce in this northwest Alabama county got behind this event 35 years ago and it has really caught on with aspiring statewide politicos.

Mule Day has had its share of marquee political candidates. Some who have attended are George Wallace, Big Jim Folsom, Jim Folsom Jr., Bob Riley, Bill Baxley, and Roger Bedford, just to name a few.

Politicians are allowed and indeed encouraged to participate in the parade. The parade is the big event and it is big. They start the events on Friday night with a beauty pageant and play. They also have a large outdoor flea market with arts and crafts, a run/walk event, a Mule Day antique car show, and of course a mule-judging contest.

The events culminate on Saturday night with a Civil War-period ball.

Many locals in Marion County area love to tell stories about the politicians who attend their event.

The animosity in 1986 between Charlie Graddick and Bill Baxley was pronounced. Although Baxley says today that he and Graddick were simply political rivals, not enemies, most political insiders at the time felt there was a genuine deep disdain the two men had for each other that probably went back to their philosophies and their law school years. Whatever the source or how permanent it was, the folks in Winfield could perceive this bitterness. Baxley and Graddick, in their bitter 1986 battle for governor, were both at Mule Day at the exact same time. They refused to shake hands or even acknowledge each other. They simultaneously campaigned down opposite sides of the street.

On another occasion during the early years of Mule Day, George Wallace attended as the sitting governor. A local lady who was not so keen on Mule Day had gotten to town at about the same time the large parade was to start. She supposedly was stuck in traffic for over two hours waiting for the parade to end. She was so furious that she sped her car to the police station to complain. They gave her no sympathy. She spotted a host of state troopers. She approached them and started complaining profusely. She told them that she demanded to be able to go to Montgomery and see the governor about this horrendous nightmare of a traffic jam caused by Mule Day.

One of the troopers calmly told her, "Ma'am, if you'll wait a few minutes you can tell him right here. He's in the middle of that parade."

15

My Favorite Political Jokes

In closing (as preachers and politicans always say when they are getting near the end but aren't ready to stop talking), here are some of my favorite political jokes that I have shared with audiences over the years.

Legislator's Brain

A man was forgetting everything, so he went shopping for new brain tissue. The salesman showed him the first jar and said, "This is brain tissue of an engineer, $5,000 an ounce." The fellow was not satisfied so the salesman showed him the brain tissue of a lawyer. It was worth $10,000 an ounce. The fellow wasn't satisfied. The salesman showed him the brain tissue of a surgeon. It was worth $25,000 an ounce. The fellow still was not satisfied. In exasperation, the salesman said, "I'll show you my prize possession." He went back into a vault and brought back a box which he said was the brain tissue of a state legislator which was worth $100,000 an ounce. The fellow asked, "Why in the world the brain tissue of a state legislator be worth $100,000 an ounce?" The salesman replied, "First of all it has never been used and second of all you don't know how many we had to kill to get an ounce!!"

Preacher and Politician

The preacher and the politician were best friends. They happened to die on the same day. The preacher got to heaven first. St. Peter met him and took him to the south side of heaven and showed him his house—it was a shack. The politician arrived and St. Peter took him to the north side of heaven, completely in the opposite direction from his friend the preacher. As they progressed the houses started getting bigger and bigger and finally

St. Peter put the politician in a four-story mansion with a golf course and a swimming pool and servants. The politician told St. Peter, "I'll miss my friend the preacher but this will be fine."

Later, an angel questioned St. Peter, "Didn't you make a mistake by putting that great preacher in a little house and that politician in a mansion?" St. Peter said, "No, preachers are a dime a dozen up here, but it's been 50 years since we've had a politician."

Preacher's Son

An old country preacher had a teenage son, and it was time the boy should give some thought to choosing a profession. Like many youths, the boy didn't really know what he wanted to do, and he didn't seem too concerned about it. One day, while the boy was away at school, his father decided to try an experiment. He went into the boy's room and placed on his study table four objects: a Bible, a silver dollar, a bottle of whiskey, and a *Playboy* magazine.

"I'll just hide behind the door," the old preacher said to himself. "When he comes home from school today, I'll see which object he picks up. If it's the Bible, he's going to be a preacher like me, and what a blessing that would be. If he picks up the dollar, he's going to be a businessman, and that would be okay, too. But if he picks up the bottle, he's going to be a no-good drunken bum, and Lord, what a shame that would be. And worst of all if he picks up that magazine he's going to be a skirt-chasing womanizer."

The old man waited anxiously and soon heard his son's footsteps as he entered the house whistling and headed for his room. The boy tossed his books on the bed, and as he turned to leave the room he spotted the objects on the table. With curiosity in his eye, he walked over to inspect them.

Finally, he picked up the Bible and placed it under his arm. He picked up the silver dollar and dropped it into his pocket. He uncorked the bottle and took a big drink, while he admired the magazine's centerfold.

"Lord have mercy," the old preacher disgustedly whispered. "He's gonna run for Congress."

Water into Wine

There are different sects of Baptist—one division believes in using red wine in the sacrament rather than grape juice.

One day the deacon in charge of getting the wine could not go, so he asked the pastor to go for him. The pastor dutifully obliged and set out to get the wine for communion the next Sunday. He, of course, did not want to get it in the town he lived in, so he set out to the adjoining town. He picked the cheapest wine he could find and headed home. He decided to taste the wine to see if it was all right. It was. After a few more miles, he decided to try the wine again just to make sure. He tried it a couple of more times and his car started weaving. A state trooper pulled him over and the pastor said, "Good day, sir. You and I are in the same business of saving lives." The trooper looked over on the seat and said, "What is that in the bottle?" The pastor replied, "Why, that's water." The trooper said, "Let me smell that." The trooper smelled it a couple of times and said, "That smells like wine." The pastor replied, "Praise the Lord! He's done it again!"

Nun in New Orleans

A drunk street person gets on a bus in New Orleans. He reeks of sweat and alcohol. The only place for him to sit is by a nun all dressed in her finest. She glares at him. Finally, the drunk asks what she thinks causes arthritis? The nun lets him have it—arthritis is caused by sin, dark wicked sin of drinking, sex, all kinds of sin. After her deluge she says, "Why do you ask?" The drunk replies, "Oh, I just read in today's paper where the Pope's got arthritis."

Jonah and the Whale

A Baptist Sunday School teacher was teaching a lesson on Jonah and the whale. In the class was a sort of skeptic. He did not believe everything literally. So the Sunday School teacher began his lesson, "Jonah was swallowed up by this huge whale." The skeptic raised his hand and said, "You know a person couldn't be swallowed up by a whale." The Sunday School teacher replied, "That's the way it's written in the Bible and I believe that's the way it is." He continued, "After several days in the belly of the whale—"

The skeptic raised his hand again and asked, "You really believe that Jonah could live in the belly of a whale for several days?" The Sunday School teacher replied the same way in a tone of exasperation, "I believe what the Bible says. I believe what the Bible says is what it means."

Then the Sunday School teacher continued, "After several days in the belly of the whale the whale spit Jonah out on the shore." The skeptic raised his hand again and said, "Do you really believe that a fish swallowed Jonah, he lived in his belly several days, the whale spit him out, and Jonah was still well?" The Sunday School teacher gave the same reply, "The Bible says it, I believe it, and that's the way it is!"

Then the skeptic said, "Well, how do you know that's true?" The Sunday School teacher said, "When I get to heaven, I'm gonna ask Jonah if that's true!" The skeptic, thinking he had him tricked, asked the Sunday School teacher, "What if when you get to heaven Jonah isn't up there—he did not make it to heaven?" The Sunday School teacher replied, "Then you can ask him!!"

Old Joe and the Suit

Old Joe was a backsliding old bachelor who happened to live across the street from the First Baptist Church. It bothered the congregation that Old Joe would sit in his swing on his front porch and not attend church services. So one day the preacher came to see Old Joe and said, "Joe, we miss you in church, why don't you come down and go to church with us?"

Joe said, "Preacher, I just haven't got a suit to wear, and I don't have the money to buy one, and I would just feel out of place." So the preacher took him down to the men's store and bought him a nice suit of clothes. He said, "Now, Joe, you no longer have an excuse."

Joe said, "No, preacher, this is the nicest thing anybody's ever done for me. I promise I'll be in church Sunday." The next Sunday, the preacher looked out in the congregation and there was no Joe. After church, he walked by Joe's house and there was Old Joe sitting out in the swing with his new suit on, looking real spiffy.

The preacher said, "Joe, I'm confused. I thought if I got you a new set of clothes, you would come on to church." Joe replied, "Preacher, I've been to church." The preacher said, "I didn't see you!" Joe said, "Well, preacher, when I got up this morning and put on my new suit of clothes and hat you bought me, I looked so dignified and prosperous that I went on to the Episcopal Church!!"

Franklin Roosevelt

FDR, who was basically a shy person, was not comfortable with the many social and political meetings he had to attend. He was particularly dreading an upcoming reception and said to Eleanor that he sensed that people never truly listened to what he said to them. He told her that he was going to do something totally different that night.

He did—he greeted everyone who spoke to him with "I killed my grandmother today." Just like he said, they never ever commented other than to say that's fine Mr. President, you're doing a great job, Mr. President. You look well, Mr. President.

Finally, he greeted the Bolivian ambassador and gave him the same line, "I killed my grandmother today." The ambassador leaned over and said, "Mr. President, I'm sure she deserved it."

Baseball Fans

Tom and Ed were inseparable best friends and rabid baseball fans. They went to every game. They kept records and trivia about every major league team. One day they got to wondering if baseball was played in heaven. They made a pact that whichever one died first would come back and tell the other if baseball was played in heaven.

Well, Tom died and sure enough came back and woke Ed up one night and said, "I got good news and bad news. Good news, They got baseball in heaven; bad news, you're pitching Wednesday!"

The Disheartened Politician

"What happened?" a friend asked a disheartened politician who had just been walloped at the polls. "Well," said the loser, "I made the mistake of telling the voters I was a down-to-earth candidate and they decided to plow me under."

I Don't Know Any of Them

Two voters met on the town square in a Western town and began discussing the coming election. Said one: "I don't want to vote for any of the candidates. I don't know any of them." The second voter responded: "I don't know what to do, either. You see, I know all of them."

The County Judge Candidate

One night a candidate for county judge was called long distance by his manager, who said: "Bill, they're telling it down in this part of the county that you ain't drawed a sober breath since May 10 when you announced."

The candidate replied: "For God's sake, Bill, you didn't wake me up in the middle of the night to tell me that, did you? I can't pay any attention to such a statement. I'm too busy fighting false rumors!"

Index

A

Adams, Ralph 42, 43, 148
Aderholt, Robert 244
Alabama–Auburn Game 238
Alabama Constitution 3, 4, 7, 53, 157, 191, 246–247
Allen, Gerald 243
Allen, Harlan G. "Mutt" 190
Allen, Jim 43, 109, 144–146, 246
Allen, Jim, Jr. 43
Allen, Kelly Adams 43
Allen, Maryon 246
Andrews, George 26
Andrews, L. K. "Snag" 30
Armbruster, Margaret 222
Azar, Ed 28

B

Bachus, Spencer 152
Bankhead, John 137, 220
Barbour County 222–225
Barron, Lowell 187–190
Bassett, Gardner 64, 70, 167–172, 169, 173, 179, 198, 199, 200
Bass, Ray 51
Baxley, Bill 61, 79, 84, 87–89, 105–115, 183, 221, 232, 246, 256
Baxley, Keener 105, 106, 112
Baxley, Lema 105
Baxley, Lucy 97–98, 218, 226, 245
Beasley, Billy 51, 183
Beasley, Jere 51, 84, 108, 109, 144, 183, 202–203, 232
Beasley, Rebecca Parrish 51
Bedford, Maudie Darby 182
Bedford, Roger 178, 182–184, 221
Bentley, Diane Jones 99
Bentley, Robert xvii, 98–104, 208, 209, 217, 225, 228, 243
Bibb, William Wyatt 224
Biddle, Jack 187
Big Mules 4, 5, 7, 8, 10, 100, 108, 223, 225, 255
Black Belt 3, 7, 10, 15, 47, 107, 124, 144, 222, 223, 231, 233, 242, 247, 248, 249
Black, Hugo 228
Black, Marcel 155
Blount, Bill 221
Blount, Winton M. "Red" 195
"bogeymen" 225–226
Bonner, Jo 153, 243
Bonner, Judy 243
Bourbon Democrats 7, 223, 224
Boutwell, Albert 30, 221
Boykin, Frank 9, 26, 27
Boys State and Girls State 236–238
Brandon, William "Plain Bill" 214, 217
Brantley, Alex 198
Brassell, Tom 212
Brewer, Albert 70–83, 84, 107, 122, 211, 216, 228, 232, 255
Bridges, Edwin C. ix
Browder, Glen 188–189
Brown, Leonard 66
Bryant, Bear 39
Buck's Pocket 87, 226–227
Butler, Julian 221
Byrne, Bradley xvii, 99–102

C

Cabaniss, Bill 157
Campbell, Loy 188
Camp, Billy Joe 49
Carnley, J. A. 3
Carnley, Sarah 3
Carter, Jimmy xviii, 128, 146
Chamberlain, Bart, Jr. 43
Civil War xiii, xiv, xv, 124, 125, 173, 207,

209, 222, 223, 256
Clinton, Bill 158
Cobb, Bill 240
Coker, Tom 144, 145
Colley, Jere 238
Collins, Bob 188
Comer, Braxton Bragg 217, 219, 223
Confederacy xiii, xiv
Cook, Drexel 82
Cooper, Roland 243
Copper, Danny 240
Cosby, W. F. "Noopie" 49
Crawford, Fred 240
Curlee, Glen 125

D

Davis, Artur 99
DeGraffenreid, Ryan 22, 23, 39, 54, 66, 67, 245
DeGraffenreid, Ryan, Jr. 245
Denton, Jeremiah 92, 133–134, 146–149, 206
Dial, Gerald 187
Dickinson, Bill 149–151, 150, 221
Dixiecrats 36, 247–249, 250
Dixieland xiii, 76
Dixon, Frank 214, 217
Donaldson, Scott 244
Drake, Tom 48
Dumas, Larry 55
Dykes, Fred 117

E

Edwards, Jack 151, 220, 221
Elite Restaurant 27
Elliott, Carl 54, 69, 95, 142–144, 220
Ellis, Butch 210
Ellis, Handy 5, 7, 210
England, Chris 243
England, John 243
Espy, Joe 221
Everett, Terry 203

F

Faulkner, Jimmy 37
Fine, Joe 178, 182
Fite, Rankin 13, 179, 179–181, 182, 186, 211
Flowers, Ginny 118–263
Flowers, Richmond 54, 69, 143
Flowers, Walter 220
Folmar, Emory 47, 48
Folsom, Bama 93
Folsom, Jamelle 14, 93, 184, 185
Folsom, James E., Jr. 4, 19, 20, 39, 91–94, 93, 182, 216, 224, 228, 245
Folsom, James Elisha "Big Jim", Sr. xv, 3–24, 26, 35, 53, 66, 69, 92, 107, 143, 179, 186, 213, 214, 216, 218, 220, 223, 224, 225, 226, 228, 231, 255
Folsom, Marsha Guthrie 93
Ford, Craig 245
Ford, Joe 245
Fowler, Conrad "Bully" 210
Fowler, Conrad, Jr. 210
"friends and neighbors" politics xv, xvi, xvii, xviii, xix, 173, 199, 249, 255
Fuller, Albert 14

G

Gallion, McDonald 107, 110
"Get-Acquainted Race" 4, 22, 67, 214–215, 219
Gibson, Fred 33
Gilchrist, Bob 55, 69, 143
Givhan, Walter 211
Goat Hill xiv, 47, 116, 118, 119, 120, 121, 123, 178, 183, 212, 216
Goldwater, Barry 253
Goldwater landslide xv, xviii, 54, 87, 141, 143, 149, 151, 196, 252–254
Goodwyn, Joe 122
Graddick, Charlie 87–89, 113, 115, 256
Grant, George 149, 150
Graves, Bibb 3, 53, 214, 217
Gray, Fred 126
Great Depression 32, 139, 229, 230
Griffith, Parker 104
Groom, Winston 226

H

Hammett, Seth 46, 218
Harper, Oscar 41, 43, 51, 60, 61, 81
Hawkins, Jack 239
Hayman, John and Clara Ruth 156
Heart of Dixie xiii, xv, xix, 98, 99, 230
Heflin, "Cotton Tom" 154
Heflin, Elizabeth Anne 159
Heflin, Howell 142, 148, 154–165, 231
Heflin, Marvin 155
Henderson, Charles 217, 219
Hill, Elvin 209
Hilliard, Earl 205, 245
Hilliard, Earl, Jr. 245
Hill, Lister xi, 26, 69, 95, 131, 132, 135–137, 138, 144, 146, 147, 149, 154, 220, 221, 249, 251, 254
Hill, Mike 209, 210
Hobbie, Bill 20, 21
Hobbie, Walker 21
Holley, Jimmy 176, 177
Hooper, Perry, Jr. 196, 245
Hooper, Perry, Sr. 87, 195–196
Hornsby, Sonny 195
Horton, Bobby 240
Hubbert, Paul 47, 100, 116–123, 189
Huddleston, Jack 192
Hunt, Guy 87–91, 93, 115, 117, 214, 216, 220, 224, 228
Hunt, Helen 90–91

I

Ingram, Bob 71, 73, 190, 212
Inherited Names Help 244
Ivey, Garve, Sr. 143
Ivey, Kay 93

J

James, Fob 52, 61, 74, 84–86, 87, 88, 93, 100, 202, 214, 216, 220, 224, 228
James, Tim xvii, 99, 101, 102
Jaxon, Jay 240
Jelks, William 222
Jemison, Mike 62
Johnsey, Walter 232
Johns, Johnny 221
Johnson, Frank Minis, Sr. 125
Johnson, Frank M., Jr. 122, 124–129
Johnson, Lyndon xix, 54, 150, 253, 254
Johnson, Roy 47
Johnson, Ruth Jenkins 125
Jolly, Mary 143
Jones, Allen 151
Jones, Bob xvi, 139–141, 141
Jones, Don 221
Junkins, Bobby 141, 142

K

Kilby, Thomas 214, 217, 219
Kimbrell, Fuller 14, 182, 186–187
King, Martin Luther, Jr. 124, 126
Kolb, Reuben 107

L

labor unions 229–231, 251
Lamberth, Broughton 190
Lamb, Mary 10
Lee, A. C. "Coley" 234
Lee, Harper 233
Lee, McDowell 41, 144
Liuzzo, Viola 127
Livingston, Ed 30
Long, "Curly" 172
Long, Frank 43
Lunsford, Jimmy 85

M

Mabry, Henry 184
"The Machine" (at UA) 138, 183, 220–222
Main, Jim 29
Manley, Rick 47, 187
Mann, Floyd 26, 201
Martin, Jim 69, 195, 250–253
Martin, Pat McDaniel 251
Mathews, Pete 123, 184
McArthur, Mac 112, 114, 183
McCorquodale, Joe 47
McCorvey, Gesser T. 249–250
McDonald, Sid 86, 202, 232
McGinnis, Andy 240
McLendon, Bryant 30

McMillan, George 46
Merrill, Horace xvii
Merrill, John xvii, 244
Merrill, Pelham xvii
Metcalf, Neil 72
Miller, B. M. 217, 235, 243
Miller, U. L. 173
"Miss Mittie" 210–213
Mitchell, Wendell 146
Mobile xiii
Mondale, Walter 45
Monroeville 233–236
Montevallo Mafia 239
Moore, Roy 98, 100, 102, 196

N

New Deal 19, 95, 136, 137, 139, 141, 230, 248, 249, 250, 251

O

Obama, Barack xix
Oden, Emmett 192
O'Neal, Emmet 217

P

Parrish, Mrs. Bertie 51
Patterson, Albert 14, 25, 37
Patterson, John 16, 25–31, 35, 37, 54, 66, 69, 143, 201, 215, 216, 219, 228
Pemberton, John 172
Persons, Gordon 215, 216, 219
Poole, Bill 243
Poole, Joe 7
Poole, Phil 245
Poole, Victor 245
Preuitt, Jim 49, 50
Price, Ralph "Shorty" 240–242
prison road camps 13

R

Raby, Steve 158, 159
racism 46, 47, 59, 60, 66, 107, 108, 113, 122, 154, 185, 246, 249, 255
Rainer, Jack, Sr. 43
Rains, Albert 141–142, 220
Reconstruction xv, 7, 87, 133, 195, 222, 224, 225, 252
Reed, Greg 243
Reed, Joe 108, 122, 187
Reeves, Ben 167, 170, 173, 198, 199, 200
Riley, Bob 29, 96–98, 103, 216, 219, 226, 228
Rives, Richard T. 127
Roberts, E. L. 190
Robinson, John 140
Robison, Vaughn Hill 55

S

Scottsboro First Monday 254–255
segregation 54, 68, 72, 124, 126, 127, 248, 250, 251, 253
Selden, Armistead 144, 145
Sessions, Jeff 153
Sewell, Terri 244
Shehane, Miriam 205
Shelby County 208–210
Shelby, Richard 131, 132–135
Sherlock, Chris 4
Shorter, John Gill 222
Siegelman, Don 94–96, 96, 182, 184, 219, 221, 224, 228
Singleton, Bobby 243
"Small-Town Effect" 227–229
Smith, Charles "Mister", III 43
Smith, Jim xvi
Smith, Joe 55
Snodgrass, John 18, 19
Solomon, Jim Bob 82
Sparkman, John xi, xvi, 26, 58, 95, 131, 132, 136, 137–138, 139, 142, 146, 147, 154, 220, 249, 251
Sparks, Chauncey 3, 33, 34, 47, 214, 217, 223
Sparks, Ron 102, 103
Squatlow 110
Stanton, Elvin 49, 58, 63
Steagall, Henry 3, 19, 82
Stewart, Donald W. 92, 221, 246
Stout, David 188
Strange, Luther 92, 93
Strange, Todd 240

Strawberry Pickers 5, 6, 22, 255

T

Tennessee Valley xvi, 18, 70, 124, 137, 139, 141, 230, 248, 251
Terry Family Reunion 231
Thomas, Joab 227
Todd, A. W. 69, 143
Troy University 42
Turner, Alton 82
Turner, Dan 52
Turnham, Pete 174–176
Tuscaloosa County's Prominence 243
Tuskegee Institute 36
Tyson, John 55, 72

U

University of Alabama xi, xvii, 15, 28, 29, 33, 35, 42, 50, 54, 86, 93, 94, 95, 96, 99, 106, 109, 110, 121, 125, 132, 136, 137, 138, 150, 151, 152, 153, 182, 183, 201, 220, 221, 222, 227, 240, 243

V

Victims of Crime and Leniency 205

W

Waggoner, Jabo 185, 245
Waggoner, Marilyn 185
Walker, Deloss 85
Wallace, George 3, 22, 25, 32–64, 71–73, 87, 94, 100, 107, 108, 113, 122, 124, 127, 144, 172, 180, 183, 213, 214, 216, 217, 218, 221, 224, 225, 228, 249, 253, 255, 256
Wallace, George, Jr. 61, 203, 245
Wallace, G. O. 32
Wallace, Janie 64
Wallace, Lurleen Burns 34, 65–69, 143, 224, 228, 246
Watkins, Keith 135
Watson, Billy 43
Webb, Samuel 222
Wells, Tommy 221
white supremacy 223, 248, 250
Wilcox County Prominence 242
Wilder, Bob 82
Williams, Randall 65
Windham, Kathyrn Tucker 210
Winfield Mule Day 256–257
Wingo, Rich 243
Wiregrass xvi, 7, 19, 105, 107, 111, 112, 151, 213
Woods, Charles 69, 143
Wynette, Tammy 183

X

Xides, Ed 28
Xides, Pete 28

Y

Yellow Dog Democrat xv